Morris High School
and
THE CREATION OF THE NEW YORK CITY PUBLIC HIGH SCHOOL SYSTEM

Morris High School
and

THE CREATION OF THE NEW YORK CITY PUBLIC HIGH SCHOOL SYSTEM

Gary Hermalyn

THE BRONX COUNTY
HISTORICAL SOCIETY
THE BRONX, NEW YORK

For information, address
The Bronx County Historical Society
3309 Bainbridge Avenue
The Bronx, New York 10467

Library of Congress Cataloging-in-Publication Data

Hermalyn, Gary.
    Morris High School and the Creation of the New York City
    Public High School System / by Gary Hermalyn.
    Includes bibliographical references and index.
    ISBN 0-941980-31-6
    1. Morris High School–History.
    2. Public Schools–New York (N.Y.)–History.   I. Title.
    LD7501.N517H47   1994
    372.9747'275–dc20 93-22083
                                    CIP

Designer: Henry C. Meyer, Jr.

ISBN #0-941980-31-6

Dedication

To Samson and His Mother

CONTENTS

LIST OF ILLUSTRATIONS

LIST OF ILLUSTRATIONS

LIST OF TABLES

FOREWORD

The history of a school is also the story of a community and of the social issues that shape education. Looking at the origins of the Morris High School offers a view of New York City at the turn of the twentieth century and an understanding of a major educational reform movement.

The poverty stricken condition of an unprecedented number of immigrants to the city in the late 1800s spawned a variety of social reform movements. The power of education to transform individual lives and society emerged as the basic tenet of the reformers, prompted by innovative conceptions of education that were being developed in the United States and in Europe. A new vision replaced the rote memorization and drills that were standards of American education with lessons based on an understanding of the human mind and a focus on the social ends of education. With this went the view of education as a practice to be carried out by thoroughly knowledgeable professionals. The goal of schools was no longer to impart circumscribed sets of facts, but the correction of the conditions of students' lives.

The education reform movement also focused on the changing nature of New York City. The consolidation of the city pointed to the need for a centralized location of administration for the schools and for a more centralized approach within the schools.

The establishment of Morris High School embodied many of the goals of the reform movement. As one of the city's first public high schools, it represented a belief in the ability and necessity of public education to encompass all of a child's developing years. The majority of the initial staff of Morris High School was college educated, a rarity in those times and a testimony to the view of education as a professional and valued endeavor. The location of the school in The Bronx was a response to the growing population of the borough and a recognition of its incorporation into New York City.

As I list the underlying premises of the beginnings of New York City's high school system, I think of how close they are to our educational goals today. To read the full history of Morris High School in the following pages is not only to read of the past. This history offers an understanding of the emergence of much of the educational vision that guides us now. It reminds us of the successes and strengths of our public schools and it reaffirms their importance.

Jorge L. Batista
Regent, The University of
the State of New York

ACKNOWLEDGEMENTS

My warmest gratitude is extended to Professor Richard Streb to whom I shall always be indebted for his kindness, strength of spirit and gentlemanly comportment and to my editor, Dr. Elizabeth Beirne, whose endurance, practicality and extraordinary abilities led me through the dark maze.

I would also like to salute the staff of Morris High School: to former Principal Carmen Russo, and to former Assistant Principal Frank Melia, who, following the Morris tradition, were respectively appointed Executive Director of the New York City High Schools Division and Principal of Christopher Columbus High School during the editing of this work, and to the present Principal Lourdes Garcia; to Ms. Natalie LaScalzo of the Morris High School Landmarks Committee, and Ms. Shirley Holliday, the school's librarian. The material they saved, including the original student records and the Morris High Scrapbook were quite invaluable. More importantly, their appreciation for the history of their school not only saved the building from the wrecker's ball, but probably the school itself.

The staff of The Bronx County Historical Society, as always, was superb in their support. These fine people take great pride in their work and the recent results of scholarship emanating from The Society are evidence of their caring and professional attitude. There is simply no finer research facility in New York than that provided by The Society's Theodore Kazimiroff Research Library staff. My thanks to Education Programmer Daniel Eisenstein, former Librarian Myrna Sloam, former Education Outreach Officer Jay Filan, Education Assistant Ivette Arroyo, Associate Librarian Laura Tosi, Cataloger Mary Ilario, Secretary Kathleen Pacher, Senior Secretary Kay Gleeson, Curator Kathleen A. McAuley, Senior Bookkeeper Mildred Nestor, Senior Researcher Arthur Seifert, Records Historian John McNamara, Photographer Lisa Seifert, President Jacqueline Kutner and Past Presidents Raymond Crapo, Robert R. Hall, Ronald Schliessman, and Professor Lloyd Ultan, noted author, and historian of The Bronx County Historical Society.

Thanks also to: Ms. Maralyn Alpert, Mr. Ray Beckerman, Mrs. Gobba Beirne, Ms. Margaret Beirne, Mrs. Esther Beller, Hon. Jonathan Bingham, Mr. Floyd Blaisdell, Mr. Dan Blum, Mr. Michael Boyd, Mr. & Mrs. Frank and Rosa Campbell, Mr. Bob Castellenete, Mr. Ken Clanton, Mr. Dicky Chin, Mr. & Mrs. James and Eileen Conroy, Mr. Nicholas Di Brino, Ms. May Doherty, Mr. Pat Donahue, Mrs. Dorfman, Mr. Sol Elbaum, Mr. & Mrs. Bob and Nate Esnard, Mr. Moustafa Fawzy, Mrs. Donna Field, Mr. Walter Fitzgerald, Mr. Danny Fitzmaurice, Mr. Bob Fox, Dr. Peter Francis,

Hon. George Friedman, Mr. Jose Fuentes, Dr. Jim Gaw, Mr. Tom Gibson, Mr. Walter Griest, Mr. Bert Gumpert, Mrs. Lena Chednofsky Hermalyn, Mr. Max Hermalyn, Mr. Roy Hermalyn, Baron Samuel Gustaf Hermelin, Prof. Hazel Hertzberg, Dr. Brian Holt, Mr. Sid Horenstein, Mr. Ishmael Ishmael, Mr. G. Khan, Dr. Kaiser, Professor Flora Kaplan, Mr. and Mrs. Elias Karmon, Mr. Jan Kornhauser, Mr. Marc Lampell, Mr. Peter Lemmo, Dr. Cheryl Litchman, Dr. Edward Lukawski, Mr. Peter Magnani, Ms. Edith McGinnis, Mr. & Mrs. Hank and Bernadette Meyer, Mr. Elwood Moore, Dr. Maureen Moore, Mr. Anthony Morante, Mr. and Mrs. J. & J. Musto, Ms. Margaret O'Connor, Mr. Steve Ostrow, Mr. Alan Parisse, Mrs. Libby Parisse, Mr. Edward Perlmutter, Mr. Paul Petzoldt, Ms. Rebecca Podgor, Ms. Rose Politi, Brother Edward Quinn, Ms. Mary Russell, Rev. Abraham Salkowitz and Mrs. Ray Salkowitz, Dr. Norbert Sander, Dr. Steve Schwartz, Mr. Ben Shaine, Sir Ernest Shackleton, Mr. Bob Sinatra, Mr. Alan Slatky, Mr. Gary Sosenko, Mrs. Goldie Spector, Mr. Kurt Steiner, Mr. Hank Stroobants, Mr. Barry Telphy, Ms. Marci Thurston, Mr. Bryan Weis, Mr. and Mrs. Henry and Sheila Wetstein, Mr. U. Vincent Wilcox, and Mr. Noah Zingman. Their suggestions and wise counsel helped make the entire project come alive.

Finally, special recognition is extended to Dr. David Ment of Columbia University Teachers College Special Collections, Mrs. Nancy A. Taylor of the Maine Historical Society, Mrs. Mary M. Riley of Bates College. C.C.N.Y., Oberlin College, Evander Childs and Stuyvesant High Schools, Packer Collegiate Institute, Amherst College Archives, Scarborough (Maine) Historical Society, Mr. Brendan O.P.H. of the Bogmen Chair Company, Professor Roger Wines of Fordham University, Dr. Peter Derrick and Mr. Joel Podgor of the History of New York City Project, Mr. Joseph DeJesus, Superintendent of The Bronx High Schools, Mr. & Mrs. David and Tomoko Meth of Writers Productions and to my dear parents, Mr. Sol Montcalm Hermalyn and Mrs. Isabelle Lee Hermalyn.

I would also like to acknowledge my abiding appreciation for the turn of the century educational leaders whose splendid teachers and administrators made possible a public high school system that became a model for the entire country.

Gary Hermalyn

Morris High School

and

THE CREATION OF THE NEW YORK CITY PUBLIC HIGH SCHOOL SYSTEM

INTRODUCTION

In 1896, the School Reform Law provided for the reorganization of the New York City Board of Education and the creation of the first public high schools in the city. One of the first actions of the new board was to take advantage of this law and organize three public high schools. In September of 1897, the Boys' High School, later renamed DeWitt Clinton High School, and the Girls' High School, later renamed Wadleigh High School, were opened in Manhattan. The third school to open that year was in the North Side,[1] in what is now The Bronx. Originally it was named the Mixed High School as there were both male and female students, then Peter Cooper High School, and finally in 1902, Morris High School in honor of Gouverneur Morris, the penman of the United States Constitution.

This investigation into the development of the first high schools found that very little work has been done on their history. In addition, no analysis has ever been made to determine why Morris High School was placed in The Bronx, or if there was any significance in its being the only mixed, or coeducational, school of the three.[2]

The approach of this study is generally chronological. It opens with a brief historical background of the New York public school system between 1805 and 1896, including a discussion of the reform movement led by Nicholas Murray Butler. This is followed by an explanation of the changes in the New York City Board of Education between 1896 and 1904, and a summary of City Superintendent William Maxwell's contributions. The major portion of the book is devoted to the history of Morris High School from 1897, when it opened, to 1904, when its new building was dedicated.

This story of one of the original high schools is made possible because Morris High School remains in its original building[3] and its early records are preserved.[4] And yet it seems quite fitting that the history of the most influential of the three schools would be written. Its founding principal, Dr. Edward J. Goodwin, was considered by his peers to be among the first rank of educators. Dr. Goodwin helped to develop the New York City high schools, along with their curriculum, and trained a good portion of the next generation of New York City high school principals. In addition, the Morris High School building housed one of the finest education facilities in the country and was considered to be the master work of its architect, C.B.J. Snyder.[5]

NOTES

[1]The North Side or the Annexed District was the section of the city of New York east of the Harlem River and north of the East River that became the Borough of The Bronx in the 1898 consolidation of Greater New York. This consolidation enlarged the city by adding Queens, Brooklyn and Staten Island to Manhattan and The Bronx. The Borough of The Bronx was named after the Bronx River. Frederic Shonnard and W.W. Spooner, *History of Westchester County, New York* (New York: New York History Co., 1900); reprint edition (Harbor Hill Books, 1974), pp. 1, 2, 89, 625.

[2]Three published items on Morris High School include two articles and a dissertation. See: Irwin Stark, "Miss Twamley Would Have Liked This Article," *New York Times,* 7 January 1978; Marie Syrkin, "Morris High School, Class of '16," *New Republic* 3,590 (November, 1983): pp. 22-27; John V. Walsh, "Social and Economic Backgrounds of Morris High School Students," Ph.D. Dissertation, Fordham University, 1937.

[3]Wadleigh High School closed down on June 30, 1954. The building now houses Wadleigh Intermediate School. See New York City Board of Education Building Records Cards, Special Collections, Milbank Memorial Library, Teachers College, Columbia University, New York.

[4]DeWitt Clinton High School moved to a new building in The Bronx in 1929. Its original building became Haaren High School and remained in use as a school until 1980. In 1986 Rafael Vinoly Architects redesigned the building for John Jay College of Criminal Justice and added a six-story structure. The college began operating in the building in 1988. John Jay College entryway plaque to auditorium, viewed by author, January 17, 1992.

[5]See C.B.J. Snyder's plans for Morris High School on pages 100 & 101. G.W. Wharton, "High School Architecture in the City of New York," School Review 2 (June, 1903): pp. 474, 476.

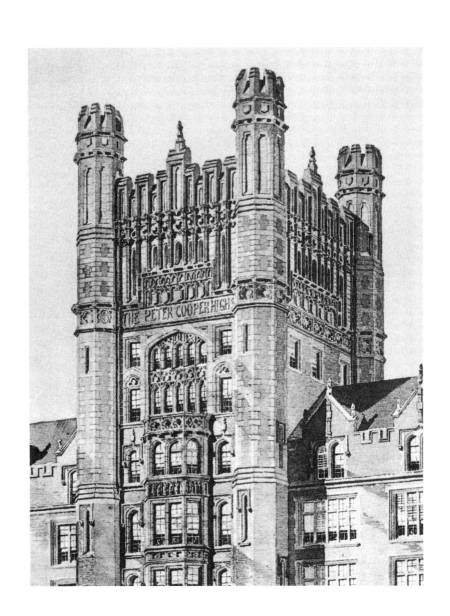

HISTORICAL

BACKGROUND

The New York City Public School System: 1805-1896

THE FIRST SCHOOLS in New York City arose informally, and usually in a religious context. By 1800, there were several kinds of education available; the church schools, the common pay schools run by independent schoolmasters and mistresses, and expensive private tutors.[1] As the population of the poor in the city rapidly increased, so did the crime rate and the other problems associated with poverty. A reform movement developed in response to these issues, which included in its aims improvement of educational opportunities.[2]

One result of this reform movement was the Free School Society,[3] incorporated in 1805, with DeWitt Clinton as its first president. The aim of the Society was to establish a free school system for poor children whose schooling was not being provided for by a religious group.[4] According to education historian Diane Ravitch, the Society followed the European two-track system of education, one for the rich, and one for the poor.[5] Other historians felt that the Free School Society's intention was only to augment the efforts of the churches.[6] In any case, a year after the Free School Society's formation, its first school was opened in an apartment in lower Manhattan, and its first school house was built in 1809.[7]

The teaching methods in these schools were based on the Lancasterian system of instruction devised primarily for elementary schools, by Englishman, John Lancaster. The method was to divide classes into groups of ten or fifteen pupils, with each group under the direction of a student monitor from a higher grade. A question and answer system was used in a fashion that required rote memorization and exact recitation. Although quite rigid, it was economical since one teacher could be employed for a school with up to five hundred children.[8]

A landmark event in the history of the New York City public schools occurred in 1820 when a controversy developed between the Free School Society and the Bethel Baptist Church. At this time the Society had four schools in operation with an average attendance of 2,023, and had been receiving public funding support for seven years. In 1820, the Bethel Baptist Church succeeded in securing funds from the city's common school fund. The Free School Society opposed the granting of funds to the Baptist Church on the grounds that a sectarian institution should not receive public funds for purposes of expanding religious schools. By 1825, the Society succeeded in having the common school funds denied not only to the Bethel Baptist Church but to all religious groups.[9] Ravitch maintains that: "With this step, the concept of a common school, as it was developing in New York City, was clearly transformed: the common school was to be not only free and open to all, but was to be devoid of religious sectarianism."[10]

Immediately after this victory, the Free School Society reorganized itself and changed its name to the Public School Society of New York. All of the Society's buildings and real estate were turned over to the city of New York, but remained under the Society's control. In addition, a provision was made to charge a moderate fee. This proviso also stated that: "Payment might be omitted. . . and that no child should be denied the benefits of education on the ground of inability to pay."[11]

In 1832, the Public School Society was again involved in a conflict. This time, it was with the Catholic Church. Ravitch refers to this as the first of New York City's "great school wars."[12] At this time, there was a significantly large and growing population of poor Irish immigrants in New York City. They were the first large Catholic group to arrive, and conflict developed between the "native" Protestants and the Irish Catholic immigrants who were blamed for the horrible conditions in which they lived.[13]

As early as the 1830s, however, the Irish emerged as a political force, and one that was soon to exert itself against the Public School Society. The Catholics were repelled by what they believed was a condescending attitude and inherent Protestantism of the Public School Society's schools. Very few Irish Catholic children were enrolled in the Society's schools. The Public School Society did not understand the relationship of Irish Catholics to Protestantism and viewed the lack of attendance in their schools as a result of ignorance. The two groups were widely divided, and so the Catholics decided to start their own schools. This was difficult, however, because of the shortage of Catholic teachers and the impoverished condition of the group.

In 1839, Bishop John Hughes, head of the the New York diocese, set out to remedy the situation, and petitioned the governor of New York to provide aid to the Catholics for their own schools. The Catholics claimed that their schools were open to all, and, as taxpayers, they had the right to send their children to schools of their own choice. The Public School Society

New York Free School No. 1 was opened in 1809 on Tryon Row, New York City.
The Bronx County Historical Society Research Library.

was characterized by the Catholics as a private, closed corporation that was free to carry out its own programs, which were slanted in a non-denominational Protestant way. Further, they contended that the Society did not respond to the needs of the city's population, particularly the Irish Catholics. More importantly, the Society did all of this without governmental control, despite the fact that it received public funds.[14]

By 1842, the Catholics were able to apply enough political pressure to push a bill through the state legislature that created a school system in New York City that was indeed "public." The new system followed the state common school system based on separate town boards. The city's Board of Education was set up with two elected commissioners from the city's seventeen political wards, similar to town education boards. Each ward elected its own trustees who generally ran the local school board.[15]

The school system that was created in 1842 was emphatically non-secretarian.[16] The Catholics, however, did not really win. While they won their battle to set up a non-denominational school system, they were unable to receive a share of the public money. Consequently, they decided to build a separate system of their own.[17]

The growth of the new public school system was slow during the first five years, but expanded rapidly thereafter. In 1852, the Public School Society disbanded and turned over its operations to the Board of Education. At that point, there were 23,273 pupils in average daily attendance in the city's schools, and 19,315 pupils attending the Public School Society's schools.[18]

According to nineteenth century historian Thomas Boese, the educational system had ". . . as many independent boards as there were wards in the city – a complex machinery of trustees, inspectors, and commissioners from all classes of society, and with powers and duties not so sharply defined as to prevent injurious disputes – with the central Board of Education virtually dependent upon the dictum of the local ones, with officers of every grade without experience, it would seem a wonder that the new system had not died at its very birth."[19]

Over the next decades, several changes were made in the Board's structure. In 1864, seven school districts were set up, each with several wards under it. In the early 1870s, further adjustments resulted in the Board of Education becoming much more of a city agency. The new system, which was created in 1873 and remained substantially the same until 1896, gave the mayor of New York the right to appoint the members of the Board of Education. The local boards had the power to ". . . appoint teachers, nominate principals to the Board of Education for approval, and subject to the general rules prescribed by that Board, provide books, fuel, and all other supplies, select and recommend school sites, and under the authority of the central board, secure proposals, award contracts, and audit and certify bills for the payment of the cost of repairs, etc. as provided by law."[20]

In 1874, New York City and the school system were greatly enlarged by the annexation of the region east of the Harlem River, and west of the Bronx River, now a section of The Bronx. Until that year the city of New York only comprised the island of Manhattan. Now the new area became the twenty-third and twenty-fourth wards. And with this addition, the number of primary and grammar schools in the New York school system totalled 115.[21]

The Secondary Schools

ALMOST ALL of the schools involved in the New York public school system to this point were grammar or primary schools. With few exceptions, the early secondary schools in New York City were private academies. Some of these academies, however, were quasi-public in the sense that they were recognized by The New York State Regents, conformed to state regulations, and sometimes even received state funds despite the fact that they charged pupils a fee.

The first New York secondary school began as a grammar school in 1763 in association with King's College (today, Columbia University). The City of Brooklyn's Erasmus Hall Academy was the first secondary school chartered by the Regents of the State of New York in 1787.[22] The first free public high school in the United States began in Boston, in 1821, with the English Classical School.[23]

An early attempt to operate a public high school came in 1825 when John Griscom and Daniel Barnes opened an incorporated male high school that was funded through public subscription. A year later, a female high school was opened. These schools followed the Lancasterian system, which was designed for elementary schools and did not adapt well to the teaching of higher subjects. As a result, these high schools were discontinued in 1831.[24]

In 1847, the state legislature authorized the New York City Board of Education to establish a free academy so that the pupils in the city's elementary schools could extend their education.[25] A building for the first academy was built on Lexington Avenue and Twenty-third Street and classes began in January of 1849. Students were admitted after taking entrance examinations and initially were required to be at least twelve years of age. Both the entrance requirements and the age limit, which was finally set at

The Free Academy, c. 1862, was located on 23rd Street
and the corner of Lexington Avenue. It was established in 1849.
In 1866, it was renamed the College of the City of New York.

The Bronx County Historical Society Research Library.

fourteen years, were gradually raised. The program of study was originally five years long. In 1853, the state Regents granted the Free Academy the right to bestow college degrees and to call itself the "Free College." Thus, in 1854, a full collegiate course of four years was introduced with a sub-freshman preparatory course of one year. The school formally became the City College of New York in 1866.[26]

The Free Academy was for boys only, but immediately upon its establishment a movement was begun to open a similar school for girls. It was not, however, until twenty years later that the Board of Education established such a school. In 1870, the Daily Female Normal and High School opened in a rented building on Broadway and Fourth Street. In the following year it became known as the Normal College (now Hunter College). The original course of study to train and educate teachers was three years, but was later expanded to four years.[27]

An outgrowth of the evening grammar schools, the first evening high school was introduced in 1866, in Grammar School 35 and was called the New York Evening High School. It initially had 7 teachers and 200

Daily Female Normal and High School was established by
the Board of Education in 1870 and became Normal College
(Hunter College) in 1871.

The Bronx County Historical Society Research Library.

students.[28] Then, in the late 1880s, three more evening high schools were
opened to accommodate students who worked. In addition, the Board of
Education ". . . set up a highly popular evening lecture series for working
men and women. In response to reform critics, the Board experimentally
introduced manual-training courses such as crafts and woodworking for
boys and sewing and cooking for girls. By 1890, almost 20,000 students
were pursuing a manual-training course of study."[29]

By 1895, there were four evening high schools in session in New York
City. According to the *Annual Report* of the Board of Education for the year
ending December 31, 1896, a significant shift in emphasis took place in the
course of study for these schools, and regulations were modified to make
the program more rigorous. As a result of the more demanding program,
many evening high school students left and one school was discontinued.
In 1895, 6,710 students registered in the evening high schools, with an
average attendance for each session of 1,804. The average age of the

students was between twenty and twenty-one years of age, with the oldest being sixty-two.[30]

The City of Brooklyn organized its first public day high schools in 1878. In that year, the Central Grammar School opened with six hundred students and a course of study that covered two grades above the sixth. It was not called a high school until 1884, but was usually referred to as the "Central School." By 1891, the Central School had become the Girls' High School and the Boys' High School, each with a separate site. The Boys' High School had three programs of study: a commercial course of two years, a scientific course of three years, and a language course of four years. The Girls' High School offered a commercial course of three years, and a language course of four years. Brooklyn also opened a Manual Training High School in 1894.[31] In 1895, Erasmus Hall Academy transferred its property to the Brooklyn Board of Education, and opened in September of 1896 as Erasmus Hall High School.[32]

In the future borough of Queens there were two high schools, one in Flushing, founded in 1875, and one in Long Island City, organized in 1889. High school departments were also located in grammar schools in Far Rockaway, Newtown Village, and Woodside. By the 1890s Staten Island had three high school departments located at Tottenville, Stapleton, and Port Richmond. These high school departments were apparently curriculum extensions within the grammar schools that accommodated students who desired further education.[33]

The Reform Movement
And
Nicholas Murray Butler

THE GREAT WAVES of immigration that began in the late 1870s and steadily grew brought new and more complex problems to New York, where many of these people settled. Before 1880, most of the immigrants were Irish and German, but after this time they came from Italy, Russia, and Eastern Europe.[34]

The immigrants settled in ghettos with their own people, where they could speak their languages and retain their cultures and religions. This phenomenon served to separate the immigrants, not only from other groups, but also from Americans who were predominately Anglo Saxon Protestants who were threatened by the sheer numbers of immigrants. In the eyes of many Americans ". . . these people, with their lower standards of living, their strange manners and customs, their tendency toward congregating in 'little Italys' and 'ghettos' in our larger cities, and their affiliation with the Roman Catholic, the Orthodox Christian, and the Hebrew faiths, seemed definitely inferior, and for the most part largely incapable of assimilating themselves to a proper appreciation of the traditional American ideals and the American way of life."[35]

Since the poor immigrants seemed unable to Americanize themselves, it was clear to some of the established Americans that they must be helped. There arose from the middle and upper-middle classes of college-educated Protestants individuals who sought to implement reforms in the hope of socializing and Americanizing the immigrant population of the city. Many went right into the ghettos and sought to work with the poor in settlement houses. After the 1890s, some of these reform groups were supported by wealthy business leaders such as John D. Rockefeller, Andrew Carnegie, J.P. Morgan and V. Everitt Macy.[36] These reformers ". . . were inspired by a sense of mission. Though they worked on a broad range of interrelated

9

problems, the common denominator for almost all of the social reformers was their belief in the importance of education. Education was the key to the future for individuals and for society as a whole. . . ."[37]

The reformers took many approaches to education. Grace Dodge, for example, was responsible for organizing a variety of educational efforts from the Kitchen Garden Association which taught household management, to the founding of the Industrial Education Association which promoted industrial education and manual training for the public schools."[38]

The leader of the reform movement for the New York City public schools was Nicholas Murray Butler. Like other reformers, Butler participated in national efforts, but his main mission, especially during the 1880s and 1890s, was the reform of New York City's woeful education system.[39]

Butler received his undergraduate and graduate education at Columbia University, where he was awarded a Ph.D. in 1884. Before embarking on his extraordinary career, he travelled and studied extensively in Europe.[40] He returned to America with the view that the field of education should be a science. In 1885, Butler took over the philosophy classes of his mentor, Professor Archibald Alexander at Columbia. In 1887 he became the president of the Industrial Education Association. Under his leadership this organization evolved into the New York College for the Training of Teachers which in 1891 became Teachers College. From 1901-1945 Butler was President of Columbia University, during which time he was also Vice Presidential candidate for the Republican Party in 1912, and a 1931 recipient of the Nobel Peace Prize.[41]

Although involved in educational reform on many levels from the kindergarten through the university, Butler was particularly concerned with the role of secondary education. On a national level, he was involved in the organizing of the National Education Association's [NEA] Committee of Ten on Secondary Education, and he helped establish the College Entrance Examination Board for the Middle States and Maryland. Butler was also a founder and editor of the influential *Educational Review*, which began publishing in 1891. It quickly became one of the leading educational journals.

It was in New York City, however, that Butler led the most devoted and demanding struggle for education. One of his first moves in this direction was to organize in 1894 the Public Education Society, which aimed to awaken "an apathetic public to the degradation of its schools."[42] This citizens' group was the forerunner of the Public Education Association.[43] Butler believed that reform in education must begin with the secondary schools and wrote in 1894: "The elementary school is helpless if the secondary school refuses to cooperate with it on raising the standard of scholarship and in improving the methods of instruction; and but few colleges are strong enough to demand of the secondary schools more and better work

Nicholas Murray Butler, President of Columbia University, c. 1920s.

Special Collections, Milbank Memorial Library,
Teachers College, Columbia University.

than the latter are now doing."[44]

In 1890, Butler proposed a course of study for high schools ". . . for the typical American secondary school is one in which nine elements are always represented: namely, the mother-tongue, geography and history, natural science, mathematics, Latin, Greek, French and German, drawing and constructive work (manual training), and physical training."[45] This program, Butler maintained, combined the elements of the English, French, and German systems of education. As the others also suggested, he wanted languages and mathematics to begin in the elementary school.[46]

In an 1893 *Harper's Weekly* article about the Committee of Ten on Secondary Education, Butler stressed the "crucial importance" of secondary education in the American system. He claimed that the need for "efficiency" in high school education was paramount for two reasons. First of all, most high school students did not go on to college, but rather went on "to take up the active pursuits of life, and to endeavor to earn their own living." Thus, the education of these students was vital to the "whole country." Secondly, any reform in education, according to Butler, "came from the high levels." He wrote: ". . . the elementary schools, the only place where the great mass of the population receive any systematic instruction, must be improved and uplifted, if at all, by forces emanating from the secondary schools."[47]

Butler was impressed by the huge number of students in the elementary schools revealed in the 1889-1890 figures of enrollment. He wrote: "Anything that can be done to raise the standard, improve the efficiency, and broaden the opportunities of the secondary schools reacts favorably upon this immense school population beneath them."[48] One of the main deficiencies, he felt, was that high school students ". . . usually received short courses of instruction on a large variety of subjects, and gaining power and substantial, thorough knowledge from none of them."[49]

It was Butler's conclusion that the "American secondary schools were far inferior to similar institutions in France and Germany," and further that the system was "defective in itself, and that it was operating to injure the progress of the elementary schools."[50] "Butler insisted on the importance of, and the need for, a good high school system. It was the NEA Committee of Ten's Report that was to become Butler's platform for his long campaign to establish a high school system in New York City."[51] Butler hailed the NEA report as ". . . the most important and systematic single document dealing with education that has yet appeared in this country. . . . It will mark an epoch in our educational development, and in time will be as celebrated in Europe as it is certain to be useful and stimulating in America."[52]

Butler emphasized the way in which the Committee of Ten focused on the role of secondary education: "They [secondary schools] are asked, first of all to cease the practice of teaching a subject – Latin or Algebra, for instance – differently for pupils who are going to college, for those who are going to scientific school, and for those who presumably are going to neither."[53] In an 1894 article, Butler offered an outline of the Committee of Ten's four sample programs, *i.e.* the classical, modern language, Latin-scientific, and English programs. All programs recommended four years of English and mathematics, two years of history, one year of geography, and two years of science, *i.e.* physics and chemistry. The language requirements varied for each program.[54]

The NEA Committee of Ten Report was controversial from the start. Published in 1893, [55] the committee's major critics felt that the report over-emphasized the ideal of a college preparatory program of studies for all students, and they particularly reacted to the "pre-occupation with 'literary high schools and academies.'" William Maxwell, superintendent of the Brooklyn schools, criticized the "excessive devotion to the classics."[56] The committee did take the position that all secondary school graduates should be considered qualified for admission to college, whether or not they intended to go on to school. The report, however, specifically avoided a track system as it was committed to a philosophy of equal education and opportunity for all.[57] The aim of the Committee of Ten was to fit secondary education into the "continuum from kindergarten to university." The discussion and criticism generated by the report helped refine and mold educational programs for many years to come.[58]

For example, the Committee of Ten Report by no means settled the question of the relationship between the high schools and the colleges. During Butler's tenure as president of the National Educational Association (1894-5) ". . . he encouraged the formation of a new committee to develop a practical plan on which schools and colleges could agree."[59]

In 1895, the NEA Committee on College Entrance Requirements was formed consisting of representatives from both high schools and colleges. In 1899, this committee published its conclusions,[60] one of which was that secondary schooling should be the rule regardless of the pupil's destination. The general program the Committee on College Entrance Requirements recommended was based on ". . . a set of constants or studies to be taken by all pupils without reference to courses of study, with the rest of the program for each pupil filled out by free electives."[61]

The constants proposed were four years of foreign languages, two years of mathematics, two years of English, one year of history, and one year of science. The combination of these constants and the electives allowed the student to determine the best course of study for an individual's needs. The idea behind this committee's flexible program was that it was "designed for life while at the same time being one that colleges would presumably accept."[62]

The report of the NEA Committee on College Entrance Requirements "did not arouse much interest."[63] Moreover, it did not settle the issue of the high school and college relationship, any more than the Committee of Ten's report did. Butler, following the lead of Harvard President Charles Eliot and with his support, advocated the setting up of a board on the issue.[64] As a result, the College Entrance Examination Board (CEEB) of the Middle States and Maryland was established in 1900.[65]

The purpose behind the CEEB was to establish uniform standards for admission to colleges. The first exams, prepared by committees that had both college and high school representation, were held in June, 1901. Although the CEEB was not without its critics, it did succeed in attracting many colleges. The board ". . . existed to prepare and to administer examinations on a uniform basis and to report scores for colleges to interpret in relation to their own specifications."[66]

Throughout the 1890s, the reformers struggled to define the place of the secondary school in the educational scheme. "Was it to be the 'people's college' or part of an articulated system extending through college?"[67] The Committee of Ten, the Committee on College Entrance Requirements, as well as the College Entrance Examination Board, tended to establish the secondary school as a step in the process from elementary school, to secondary school, and then to college. These reform efforts also provided uniform standards for the secondary schools.[68]

The issue remained, however, as to whether high schools, particularly public high schools, were to be college-oriented as the private secondary schools were.[69] The answer, particularly in New York City, was that this was not to be the case.

Educator and psychologist, G. Stanley Hall, like many of the reformers, was an advocate of the idea of high school as the "people's college." He wrote: "When the public high school really becomes, as it surely will, the people's college, permeated with the idea of fitting for life, which is a very different thing indeed from fitting for college, then secondary education will become truly democratic; it will have plenty of local color and fitting for colleges will become . . . a mere incident."[70]

Another educator of the time, Paul Hanus, of Harvard University and a member of the NEA Committee on College Entrance Requirements, claimed that the high school should "give training that prepares for the duties of good citizenship." This meant that both vocational and social training should be offered with a stress on historical perspective. Of particular concern to him was the education of ". . . that great majority of our editors and politicians who are without a college education . . . [a high school education] may help them value a wise conservatism and to recognize the comprehensiveness and the complexity of present-day political and economic problems and thus make them more intelligent and safer leaders of the people and may we not hope through the same instruction to increase the number of men and women in the community who also appreciate the magnitude and difficulty of present-day programs and decline to be taken in by plausible but fallacious solutions."[71]

Hanus argued for the intrinsic worth of secondary education, and believed it should not be thought of as a mere preparation for further education. He contended that high school must "afford equal opportunities to all pupils." In pursuance of these vocational and social aims, it was necessary for the high school to provide manual and commercial courses.[72]

Butler agreed: "It is not enough that our education should give pupils a knowledge of the civilization which surrounds them . . . it must also fit them to take hold of that civilization at some definite point and so to support themselves in it. That is, it must add efficiency to knowledge; and efficiency, in these days of highly organized and minutely differentiated societies, implies a great deal."[73]

For one thing, however, efficiency implied diversity of offerings at the high school level. Consequently, Butler strongly rejected the notion of a uniform course of study for all high school students. He claimed: "No generation of pupils can be made efficient by any uniform course of study. Such a course will produce efficiency in those to whom it is best adapted, the others must go to the wall."[74]

The educational reformers of the 1890s, therefore, believed that high schools had a great potential for enhancing society. The efficiency of secondary education was a common theme for all who advocated the development of public high schools. Part of the general argument for public high schools was that if the government was truly "of the people, by the people, and for the people," the welfare of society was dependent on the education of its citizens, and, thus education should not be left to chance. It was held that ". . . the public school system stands in precisely the same relation to the body politic as other great institutions established for the well-being and safety of society."[75]

The notion that public high schools were a social responsibility brought forth the issue of public funds for that education. There were those who were against such public support, as they felt it was enough for the government to assure that people could read and write. Advocates of public support usually argued that governmental backing strengthened the nation through the promotion of "freedom and wisdom of choice."[76]

Butler was an advocate of public support for high schools, and for higher education as well. On this issue he wrote: "The duly constituted authorities of any school district or other political unit may establish and maintain schools of the kind or grade for which the voters consent in regular form to bear the expense . . . . There is a wide-spread belief that elementary education under government control is a matter of right, but that secondary and higher education under government control are improper invasions of the domain of liberty. There is no ground in our public policy for this belief. The government has the same right to do for higher education that it has to do for elementary education."[77]

In Butler's view, tax-supported schools were "public in the fullest possible sense." They could not, therefore, be "maintained for the benefit of persons of any special class or condition."[78] Education, then, and particularly public high school education, was not only democratic, it promoted democracy. Thus, Butler felt: "If the school is to be the training-ground for citizenship, its products must be usefully and soundly equipped as well as disciplined and well informed . . . . Acting upon this conviction, the great modern democracies . . . are everywhere having a care that in education provision be made for the practical, or immediately useful."[79]

The
School Reform Law:
1896

I N THE INTRODUCTION to *Education in The United States,* a series of monographs prepared for the United States exhibition at the Paris Exposition in 1900, Nicholas Murray Butler wrote: "Spontaneity is the keynote of education in the United States. Its varied form, its uneven progress, its lack of symmetry, its practical effectiveness, are all due to the fact that it has sprung, unbidden and unforced, from the needs and the aspirations of the people. Local preference and individual initiative have been ruling forces. What men have wished for that they have done. They have not waited for state assistance or for state control."[80]

While there may be some question about whether the reform movement of the late nineteenth century sprang from "the people," it is clear that its success was largely due to the initiative of Nicholas Murray Butler. Butler and his fellow reformers did not wait for the government to act first; instead, they took the first steps themselves.

If, however, public funds were to be used to support the system they proposed, then governmental assistance and legislation were necessary and Butler was acutely aware of this. He and his colleagues began their campaign to legally reorganize the New York City public school system as early as 1889. At that time, the Public Education Association submitted a "memorial to the Board of Education," which was the initial step in the school reform movement. This group called for a city commission to study the problems of the schools.[81]

The reformers felt that the deplorable conditions of the schools, *i.e.,* the unprofessional teachers, the out-of-date curricula, the lack of proper facilities, etc., were the result of the decentralized ward-based system that had been in effect since the Board of Education was first organized in 1842. With the local boards in control of the management of the schools, chaos prevailed. Appointments to positions were based on political connections, rather than on experience and ability. In an 1895 editorial in *Harper's Weekly,* both the New York and the Brooklyn schools were called "notoriously deficient." The editors claimed that school

> . . . accommodations are inadequate and badly distributed, the sanitary conditions, except in a few of the newest buildings, are bad, no proper provision is made for play grounds and for physical exercise, and modern improvements in text books and methods of teaching are, as a rule, stoutly resisted. It is not often that defects such as these can be directly traced to administrative faults, but both in New York and Brooklyn this can be done. The superintendents have too little direct authority and power over the educational work, and a vicious system of ward trustees in New York and of local committees in Brooklyn provide a resting place for all sorts, political and personal, and effectually blocks all large plans for improvement initiated by the central body.[82]

In 1893, the mayor of New York City appointed a commission to study the problems of the school system. That commission's report supported the charge by Butler and his colleagues that reform was in order, but it did not go far enough in its recommendation for a centralized plan to suit the reformers. The 1894 change in the New York State Constitution made it necessary for any alterations in the city's school system to be approved by the state legislature, as well as by the mayor and the governor. This was an opening that gave the reformers a means of achieving their ends. Butler immediately put together a coalition to lobby the state legislature for a centralization plan. He also prepared the necessary proposals for the legislative approval. Yet, it took two years for various civic groups to mobilize support.[83]

The struggle for the School Reform Bill was a lengthy and nasty battle. On the reformers' side, the opposition was viewed as mean and unscrupulous, for whom "no lie was too preposterous and no slander too silly to be sedulously circulated."[84] Those who opposed the reform included commissioners and school principals. In an effort to rally teachers against the plan, they told the teachers that they would all be removed from office if the reformers got their way, and that public school teachers would have to wear uniforms. The teachers were also led to believe that appointments for new teachers under the reform board would favor graduates of private schools and colleges.[85] Some people tried to work both sides of the issue. One principal for example, who seemed to be an unrelenting opponent of reform, was bargaining to secure an assistant superintendent appointment in the reform administration.[86]

Butler and his colleagues attempted to get the necessary legislation through Albany in 1895. There was, however, a great deal of opposition, and the reformers were not able to counter it sufficiently. Teachers, principals, administrators, as well as the ward trustees lobbied against the bill,[87] as the reformers did not consult with any of these groups."[88] Many of the teachers rejected the centralized plan because they felt it would mean more supervisory authority over them. There were also indications that the ward trustees "commanded" the teachers to oppose the bill.[89] In any case the bill did not pass the state assembly in April of 1895.[90]

Butler and his fellow reformers were not daunted as they regrouped behind the newly formed Citizens' Committee of One Hundred on the Public School Reform. This group represented the cream of the city's professional and business leaders. In addition to Butler, then Dean of Columbia University, the Committee of One Hundred included Stephen Olin, John Pine, E. Ellery Anderson and John Clark, all Wall Street lawyers, Seth Low, a Brooklyn merchant and former mayor of Brooklyn, Abram Hewitt, a manufacturer and former mayor of New York City, E. L. Godkin, editor of the *Evening Post,* and bankers J. Kennedy Tod and Elihu Root.[91] In a newspaper article announcing the formation of the committee it was reported that:

> Professor Nicholas Murray Butler, of Columbia College, read a "platform" as a basis of procedure. This document recited the necessity for revision and adjustment of the pubic school system, administered, as it was, under a law which, while often amended, had not been revised or codified for nearly fifty years. The original law was framed when New-York lay below Fourteenth street and what was now the upper villages. The power was divided between the central Board of Education and twenty-four local or ward boards of trustees, and one board for each of the old wards of the city. "We therefore," the platform continues, "favor such revision of the existing school law as will centre both power and responsibility in the Board of Education, provide for the appointment, promotion and transfer of teachers by officials whose training and experience fit them for such duties: divorce the educational from the business administration of the schools, and remove the entire system from the influence of party or personal politics.[92]

Through the influence of its members, the Committee of One Hundred was quite successful in rallying support for centralization of the Board of Education. With the alliance of editors and publishers on the committee, Butler was able to gain control of the press, and he made good use of this power in gathering public support.[93] The opposition did not disappear, however. Teachers still resisted, held rallies, and circulated petitions against the new bill.[94]

In April of 1896, despite the teachers' protests, the necessary steps were achieved for the passage of the School Reform Law, and it was finally approved by the state legislature, Mayor William L. Strong,[95] and Governor Levi P. Morton. This law was a triumph for the reformers. It did away with the ward system and provided for a centralized board of education in the hands of professional educators. The editors of *Educational Review* summed up the achievement as follows:

> The gratifying conclusion of a long and weary contest is due primarily to the intelligence, public spirit, and determination of a group of men and women who have kept up the fight for years. . . . In Governor Morton, Mayor Strong, and the legislature of 1896, men were found willing to listen to argument on this school question, and independent enough to act promptly and decisively upon their convictions. The combination of these forces made victory possible. On July 1 the ward trustee system ceases to exist. It has for years sheltered incapacity, favoritism, political chicanery, and extravagance. It has effectually prevented any genuine supervision of the schools or any efficient organization and operation of the system as a whole. Where good schools are found in New York, they exist in spite of the trustee system; where bad schools are found, they are traceable directly to it.[96]

New York City Board Of Education: 1896-1904

UNDER THE REFORM LAW the school system was controlled by a powerful Board of Superintendents composed of professional educators, with a lay Board of Education that was responsible for the business side of the operation.[97] According to A. Emerson Palmer, Secretary to the Board of Education: "To the Board of Superintendents was instructed [*sic*] the practical management of the schools in general, only a veto power being vested in the Board of Education; on the theory that work of the character mentioned [nomination of principals and teachers] should be performed by experts trained in pedagogy and school methods, while the Board of Education should act, substantially, in the same capacity as the Board of Trustees of a college."[98]

The number of members on the Board of Education remained at twenty-one, and were appointed by the mayor. The city was to be divided into at least fifteen school districts, each with five inspectors appointed by the mayor. The Board of Supervisors was to be under the city superintendent with "as many assistant superintendents as the Board of Education may deem necessary."[99]

When Charles Bulkley Hubbell, a lawyer, was elected the president of the Board of Education, the reformers were in position to put their theories and ideas into practice.[100] One of the new board's first undertakings was to set up three public high schools for the city.[101]

The new board, however, did not have a chance to do much, as the city of New York was substantially changed within the next year. In 1897, the Greater New York Charter provided for the consolidation of the city of New York, then Manhattan and the North Side (The Bronx), with the City of Brooklyn, and the various towns in Queens and Staten Island. These five sections became boroughs of the enlarged city of New York, *i.e.* Manhattan,

The Bronx, Brooklyn, Queens, and Richmond, and each had a president elected by the voters of the borough. The overall city government was under a mayor, comptroller, and president of the Board of Aldermen, all of whom were elected on a city-wide basis. This group, along with the borough presidents, made up the Board of Estimate and Apportionment, "which was empowered to make policy for the city and to have authority over the city's finances."[102]

The new city charter, effective on January 1, 1898, required significant changes in the management of the schools. The newly organized centralized school board that had been created as a result of the 1896 School Reform Law had to be reconciled with the school systems in the freshly acquired boroughs. As a result, centralized control was diffused and the boroughs were allowed to maintain much of their power over local schools,[103] including control over what was being taught.[104]

In 1898, when the city of Greater New York was incorporated, there were 240 primary and grammar schools and three high schools in Manhattan and The Bronx. Brooklyn had 114 primary and grammar schools and four high schools. The situation in Queens and Richmond was different. The area of Queens had been several towns, and each town had its own school system. There were a total of fifty-six grammar schools, two high schools and six high school departments in various grammar schools. In Richmond there were twenty-nine school districts, and each had its own school, eleven of which were ungraded. Richmond also had three high school departments in different schools.[105]

Although the city was divided into five boroughs, the charter provided for only four school boards by placing Manhattan and The Bronx under one board. The Board of Education of the old city of New York (Manhattan and The Bronx) became the School Board for the Boroughs of Manhattan and The Bronx. John Jasper, who had been city superintendent and chairman of the Board of School Superintendents, became the borough superintendent of the schools for Manhattan and The Bronx after February 1, 1898.[106]

Each school board was given almost complete control over the schools in its borough. The central board's power was minimal, especially compared to what the reformers had envisioned. The Board of Education for the city of Brooklyn became the school board for that Borough. The members of the pre-Greater New York boards for the Boroughs of Manhattan and The Bronx and of Brooklyn were permitted to finish their terms of office, but subsequent members were to be appointed by the mayor for three-year terms. The mayor appointed nine members for each of the Queens and Richmond school boards.[107] Each borough board was under a borough superintendent with at least two associate borough superintendents. In each borough there was also a borough board of superintendents

Charles Bulkley Hubbell,
President of the
New York City Board of Education in 1896.

The Bronx County Historical Society Research Library.

composed of the borough superintendent and the associate borough superintendents.[108]

For the city as a whole, a centralized board of nineteen members was created, made up of representatives from the four borough school boards, with eleven members from Manhattan and The Bronx including the president of the board, and six members from Brooklyn including their president, and one member each from Queens and Richmond who were the presidents of those boards. The charter provided that the Board of Education could appoint a city superintendent of schools, a superintendent of school buildings, a superintendent of school supplies, as well as an auditor, a chief clerk, and other officers.[109]

Generally, the central board was responsible for financial and physical matters, but it also established some minimum qualifications for teachers. The city superintendent had limited powers, which included nominating members to the Board of Examiners from a list prepared by the Municipal Service Commission. The semi-autonomous Board of Examiners reviewed applications for school jobs. In addition, the city superintendent presided over all of the meetings held by the Board of Examiners. He also reported on the conditions of the schools, but had no real authority to remedy defects.[110]

Despite the limited powers of the city superintendent under the borough board system, it was considered an important office, and the reformers were anxious to get the right person into the position. The first person offered the superintendency was Andrew Draper, the president of the University of Illinois, who was later to become the New York State Commissioner of Education. Draper declined, and withdrew his name in favor of William Maxwell, the city superintendent of the Brooklyn educational system. Maxwell was elected city superintendent in March of 1898. In the following month an editorial in *Educational Review* remarked: "This act [the election of Maxwell] may fairly be said to mark the victorious end of the long and weary fight to redeem the schools of the metropolis from politics, sloth, and low ideas that was begun in 1885. A small group of men and women has never wavered in the contest since the day it began. Most of those who are in enjoyment of the fruits of victory are late comers in the army. They are not familiar with the history of the struggle. They seem sometimes not to be aware of its desperate epoch-making character."[111] William Maxwell had been involved with the educational reform struggle for a long time, and *Educational Review* editor, Nicholas Murray Butler, was delighted with Maxwell's appointment.

All was not to go smoothly, however, during Maxwell's first years in office. The problems that arose were a direct result of the distribution of powers between the borough boards and the central board. For example, the city superintendent issued licenses for teachers and recommended the minimum requirements for the licenses, but the borough boards decided which kinds or grades of licenses were to be used. Consequently, the power of the city superintendent and his Board of Examiners was limited. "As licenses were granted by the Board of Examiners and appointments made by the Borough School Boards, a complete separation was made between the examining power and the appointing power."[112]

To add to the problem, the borough boards did not have to appoint teachers from the eligible lists drawn up by the Board of Examiners in any order. As long as a person was on the list, he or she could be appointed by the borough board at any time. The borough boards also appointed all the principals, and the principals had a say in all propositions that affected their schools.[113] The local schools and the borough boards, therefore, were very powerful. This system allowed for political patronage that resulted in the appointment of poorly qualified teachers.[114]

In addition to the problems of qualifications for teachers and the methods of appointment of teachers, there was no set salary schedule. Under the 1897 charter the salaries of teachers were at the discretion of the borough boards. Although the criteria for salaries and increases was supposed to be based on merit, grade taught, and experience, this was not enforceable in the borough boards. There was an attempt to change this situation in 1899 with the Ahearn Law (Chapter 417 of the Laws of the State of New York), which provided for formal regulation of the salaries of teachers in New York City. The Ahearn Law set up a fixed salary schedule for teachers and principals, and made salaries conditional on the approval of the borough board of superintendents.[115] The law, however, created more problems than it solved, since the Board of Estimate did not supply the necessary funds for the increased salaries called for by the law. The teachers became agitated further because while a few teachers did receive increases some were decreased in pay, and others remained at the same level.[116]

Finally, in 1900, a new law, called the Davis Law (Chapter 751 of the Laws of the State of New York), was passed superseding the Ahearn Law. This new law fixed the salaries for all the teaching and supervisory staff in all the boroughs and provided for twelve equal installments over a year. Further, it established a plan for equitably distributing the money throughout the boroughs, and insured that the necessary funds would be paid to the boards from the Board of Estimate through the "four-mill tax." On every dollar of assessed valuation of the real and personal estate in New York City, funds would go into a general school fund to pay the salaries of the city's educational personnel. The new salary schedules were put into effect shortly after the bill was signed in May of 1900.[117.]

Despite the legislation that helped remedy one aspect of the Board of Education's problems, the rift between the different segments of the board was growing. The situation was chaotic.[118] The borough boards were clamoring for money for teacher salaries and increases. Mayor Robert Van Wyck even slashed the school budget in 1900 and ". . . then wrote every Board member in every borough that board members would be personally liable if they could not stay within the appropriation allocated them by the Board of Estimate and Apportionment."[119]

City Superintendent Maxwell "was publically at odds with the central board and some of the borough boards." His call for a city-wide teachers examination was ignored by them. The central board even refused to print his first *Annual Report* because it was "offensive to school officials."[120]

The City Club, a prestigious group of New York business leaders, came to Maxwell's support and considered legal action against the Board of Education for "suppressing a public document."[121] The superintendent's first *Annual Report* was finally allowed to be published with the approval of the Board of Education, which acknowledged that the city superintendent had the right to express his opinions and to put his criticisms and recommendations in his report that "he deemed to be in the interest of the schools." The board, nevertheless, asked Maxwell to substantiate each of the charges he made that affected "the honor and integrity of members of the School Board of the Borough of Brooklyn."[122]

In that report Maxwell claimed: "A more serious weakness, though one not inherent, in the system as such, is the lack of harmonious cooperation of the several boroughs with one another, as in the matter of regulation salaries under the Ahearn Law; and of the authorities of one or the other borough with the central authorities, as seen in the deplorable lawsuit between the School Board of Brooklyn and the Board of Education and in certain workings at cross-purposes with regard to the existing minimum requirements for licenses, particularly high school licenses."[123]

John Jasper, the borough superintendent for Manhattan and The Bronx and an outspoken adversary of Maxwell's, wanted to further diminish the power of the central board and that of the city superintendent, if not actually abolish it. The feud became full-blown early in 1901 when Jasper responded in the newspapers to Maxwell's criticism in his second *Annual Report* of the manner in which English and manual training were taught in the schools.[124]

In this turbulent climate, Butler and his colleagues were actively engaged in an attempt to abolish the borough boards and centralize all of the power for the schools in the board of superintendents headed by Maxwell.[125] When Governor Theodore Roosevelt, in 1900, appointed a Charter Revision Commission to revise the 1897 charter,[126] the educational section of the charter's revision was assigned to the education reformers.[127] The new charter that became law in April of 1901 embodied their proposals for the New York City educational system.

The 1901 revised charter effectively abolished the four borough school boards. In their place was one Board of Education consisting of forty-six members appointed by the mayor. Twenty-two members of the board were from Manhattan, fourteen were from Brooklyn; there were four each from the boroughs of The Bronx and Queens, and two from Staten Island.[128] Because of the large size of the board, an executive committee of fifteen was created. It had members from each borough who were charged with the "care, government and management" of the school system.[129]

The most significant feature of the new centralized organization was the authority given to the city superintendent who became ". . . the real, responsible, professional head of the school system, and, in many respects, the most important agency in its development."[130]

The city superintendent presided over the Board of Superintendents which consisted of eight associate city superintendents. This board's extensive powers included: "The practical initiative in all matters purely educational. . . . It was authorized to recommend to the Board of Education grades and kinds of licenses, and the qualifications therefore; to establish, subject to the approval of the Board of Education, rules for the graduation, promotion, and transfer of pupils; to recommend textbooks, apparatus, and other scholastic supplies; to recommend courses of study; to prescribe regulations relative to methods of teaching, and make syllabuses of topics in the various subjects taught; and to nominate to the Board of Education persons to fill vacancies in the teaching force."[131]

The city superintendent continued as the chairman of the Board of Examiners. In addition, he was a non-voting member of the Board of Education, and he virtually coordinated the entire system.[132]

Although the reorganization seemed to be a complete break with the borough system, there were some compromises. For example, the previous borough and associate borough superintendents were made either associate city or district superintendents. In addition, all local boards were represented in the Board of Education by one member. The local boards were, therefore, integrated into the new system in a compromise effort. This was a means of acknowledging the areas that were newly a part of the city of Greater New York.[133]

Maxwell was very optimistic about the new organizational structure. He discussed the new charter before a meeting of the Public Education Association in November of 1901. At that meeting Maxwell made the point that: "The new charter will do much to lift the schools out of politics, but the schools will never be entirely free from politics until the teachers themselves are imbued with a professional spirit that shall absolutely forbid the use of political influence or any other influence than that of merit to secure appointment and promotion."[134]

The stage was now set for a strong professional administrator to organize and establish the New York City Board of Education into one of the finest systems in the country.

City Superintendent
William Maxwell

WILLIAM MAXWELL, unlike Nicholas Murray Butler and many of the other reform leaders, rose to his position as city superintendent through practical experience in the Brooklyn educational system. Until his retirement in 1918, Maxwell had a profound effect on the city's schools and his leadership helped shape Morris High School.

Maxwell was born in Ireland and attended Queen's College in Galway graduating in 1872.[135] He pursued post-graduate studies in philosophy and political science in Ireland, and was awarded a master of arts degree in 1874. Although these were the last of his formal student days ". . . his scholarly habits, and his extensive reading, study, and writing contributed as much as his distinguished public career toward winning the honorary degrees of philosophy conferred upon him by St. Lawrence University in 1890 and the doctor of laws granted by Columbia University in 1901."[136] The city superintendent was, therefore, referred to as "Dr. Maxwell," and although he did not have an earned doctorate, he was a scholar.[137]

Despite his academic background and two years of teaching experience in the Royal Academical Institution in Belfast, Maxwell could not secure a teaching position when he arrived in New York in 1874. Instead, he became a reporter and rose to the position of managing editor of the *Brooklyn Times*. While still with the newspaper, he became a part-time teacher and lecturer in Brooklyn's evening high schools. In 1882, he was elected associate superintendent of the Brooklyn Board of Education, and served in the capacity for five years, during which time he devoted himself ". . . to teaching, examining, and supervising classes in the elementary schools. The chief aim of his service was to substitute for rote and memoriter methods of teaching the modern scientific systems of instruction, an aim which he was markedly successful in attaining."[138]

William Maxwell, City Superintendent of
the New York City Board of Education, c. 1910.

*Special Collections, Milbank Memorial Library,
Teachers College, Columbia University.*

Upon his election in 1887 to the superintendent's position in Brooklyn, Maxwell did a thorough study of the system in order to determine how he could best improve it. Maxwell's program in Brooklyn was quite comprehensive and successful. He sought to modernize, professionalize, and standardize practices, much in the same vein as he was to do later on a larger scale in the New York City system. An innovative leader, Maxwell incorporated kindergartens into the elementary schools. Overall, he strove to remove the wide discrepancies in the quality of schools and to bring all the schools up to a standard of excellence.[139]

In Brooklyn, Maxwell was responsible for establishing a system of secondary education. At the beginning of his Brooklyn tenure, the Central Grammar School was a quasi-high school that offered two and three year courses beyond the elementary school. Under Maxwell, the Girls' and Boys' High Schools were established as an outgrowth of the Central School, Erasmus Hall was absorbed into the Brooklyn public school system[140] and a Manual Training High School was created while the seeds were sown for a new commercial high school as well.

With these successes, it is not at all unusual to discover that in 1893, Maxwell joined the other editors of *Educational Review* in decrying the lack of a high school in the "largest and richest city in the country [New York City]."[141] Later on, as Superintendent of New York City, he was responsible for the city's new high schools and their buildings, as well as the enhanced programs which were needed to meet the explosive increase in secondary school students.

A brief review of Maxwell's professional memberships and activities revealed his wide interest and influence in educational reform at the turn of the century. As an advocate of secondary schools, he served in the conference on English for the NEA Committee of Ten. He was chairman of the Committee of Fifteen appointed by the National Department of Superintendents, which was responsible for the influential reports concerning the organization of city school systems, the correlation of studies, and the training of teachers. Maxwell served on the committee on English of the Association of Colleges and High Schools for the Middle States and Maryland, and was chairman of the Committee on Instruction in Municipal Government in American Institutions. In addition, he helped Nicholas Murray Butler found the *Educational Review,* and served as an associate editor for the journal.[142]

Maxwell waged a tireless campaign to improve the professionalism of teachers. He introduced the resolution that resulted in the 1895 law which required all New York State teachers to be ". . . graduates of a recognized high school and also of a school for the professional training of teachers, or from institutions of equal or higher rank offering similar instruction."[143]

During his tenure as city superintendent under the New York City borough board system, Maxwell attempted to raise the city's requirements for teachers' licenses. He also advocated the practice of teachers taking courses at colleges or universities to upgrade their licenses. He published the college professors' reports in his *Annual Report,* perhaps to encourage more teachers to take courses. Most of the reports on the teachers' training work were fairly routine, but some were negative and pointed out the specific problems with the teachers, particularly their lack of a broad education. For example, Professor Samuel Weir of New York University claimed: "One of the chief deficiencies which we find among the students [teachers] is the lack of the power of logical discrimination and the inability to do connected thinking. They seem to remember facts easily enough but the relations and the significance of the facts are more difficult for them to master. . . . Many students are not able to distinguish between a glib tongue and a ready and accurate judgement."[144]

Professor Joseph H. McMahon, of the Cathedral Library University Extension Center, reported that: "Teachers of any ability are very quick to avail themselves of methods, but my experience of them has shown that they are almost entirely wanting in general knowledge which is the basis for the truest and best teaching. Their technical training has to a large extent made their minds rigid instead of flexible and their lack of knowledge of the great questions of the intellectual world renders them apt to be narrow."[145]

Maxwell, however, stressed the positive responses and praised the teachers as a whole. In his first *Annual Report* as city superintendent he wrote: "Many teachers entered on courses of study with enthusiasm from the start. Many teachers, who began their studies in a reluctant if not sullen mood, in a short time became zealous and enthusiastic students. Hundreds of such instances have been brought to my attention. It is well within the mark to say that never in the educational history of this country was there so earnest an effort made on the part of a great body of public school teachers toward self-improvement as in the City of New York during the school year 1898-99."[146]

Clearly, Superintendent Maxwell was deeply concerned with the status and development of the teaching profession. His words, written in 1903, have a familiar ring to them: "How are we to account for this strange anomaly – that teachers should be called upon to do the work which is most needed to preserve the republic and yet receive so little recognition, either financially or socially at the hands of the people whom they serve?"[147]

After dismissing several popular explanations for this phenomenon, Maxwell offered his own interpretation of the issue: "Still less have they [teachers] realized that the teacher's calling requires the most thoro *[sic]* scholastic and professional preparation. The prevalent feeling, to our shame be it spoken, has been that anyone who knew the rudiments and could keep ahead of his pupils was good enough to teach in an elementary school."[148] Nevertheless, Maxwell persevered and actively worked to insure teacher's rights and fair salary schedules. He lobbied in Albany for the Davis Law, ". . . which guaranteed every teacher in New York City a living wage and a steady annual increment up to a comfortable income."[149]

When Maxwell appeared before Governor Theodore Roosevelt to support the Davis Law he was in direct opposition to the New York City Corporation Counsel representative and the president of the Board of Education, as well as some of its leading members.[150]

After the passage of the Davis Law, Maxwell immediately began using the salary schedules to help raise the standards of the teaching profession. It was reported that: "He stood with a club at every gate feeding to higher salaries, and has beaten back friends and foes alike who are not ready to show the equipment demanded [for a higher salary]."[151]

Maxwell was adamant about protecting the schools and the teachers from politics. Thus, he was an ardent supporter of the "four-mill" provision of the Davis Law for it assured that the educational system would be run without being subject to the vicissitudes of the economy or of politicians. In a similar vein, Maxwell made sure that the 1901 revised charter required that almost every position in the New York City public schools was subject to civil service methods.[152]

After the 1901 charter went into effect, Maxwell instituted new and even more rigorous standards for teachers' licenses. The new licenses required more scholastic training and additional study of the science of teaching "especially the application of psychology and logic to instruction." Promotions and salary increases were obtainable "only after specialized study on the part of successful teachers." "Eligible lists" were developed according to the new standards, and were enforced.[153]

Maxwell not only insisted on professionalism in his teachers, but he also felt that teachers should have a voice in forming the school curriculum and in determining teaching methods. He was proud of the success of the standardized curriculum he instituted in 1902 and attributed much of its success to the input of teachers. In 1904 Maxwell described how the curriculum was developed after the abolition of the borough boards and the institution of the new centralized administration:

> It became necessary to make a course of study that would cover the whole city and reconcile the differences in the various borough courses. This was a very difficult piece of work, one that required great care and delicacy, on account of conflicting plans and ideals. We finally succeeded in getting it done, and done with surprisingly little friction. I attribute that fact to my calling into counsel a very large number of principals and teachers in each of the boroughs, and assigning them to various committees charged with particular pieces of work. The result was that the teachers and the principals

of the schools felt, when the new course of study was promulgated, that it was in a very real sense their own course, and that it concerned them to make that course a success. They are making much more of an effort for the success of that curriculum than if it had been an equally good curriculum imposed upon them from the outside.[154]

While Maxwell's standardized curriculum was successful, it was not without its critics. A 1904 *New York Times* article reported on an investigation into the "entire system of the Board of Education." The investigators, who were appointed by the city's comptroller, said that the "purpose of education" was being lost because teachers and students were called upon to do too many things.[155] Later that year, another article claimed that the school courses were "too complex," and called for doing away with "special musical and physical training," and asked for a "chance for the three R's."[156] Despite such criticism, William Maxwell's standardized curriculum for the public schools of the city of New York remained in force while he was city superintendent.

Universal education, Maxwell believed, was necessary for an organized and harmonious society. In a speech delivered at the University of Chicago in December of 1902, he said: "Among the chief objects of organized society are, first, the development of the best powers – intellectual, moral, and physical – of the individual; and second, equality of opportunity in the pursuit of whatever makes life worth living. Universal education is the one essential condition under which these objects may be realized. Without universal education there cannot be universal individual development. Without universal education there cannot be equality of opportunity for all."[157]

Maxwell's standardized curriculum was meant to fulfill these objectives. Universal education, in his view, was to create a full-rounded individual, no matter what their vocation in life. He was particularly sensitive to the aesthetic aspect of education, as he felt that "school exercises should be so conducted as to produce a love for all things beautiful and good." This end would be accomplished through the various subjects, but especially drawing and reading. According to Maxwell, through drawing the pupil learned about both art and nature. Reading was essential, not just for its everyday practical application, but because: "The school work that does not lead to a love of good literature, and particularly poetry, comes perilously near the nature of a crime."[158]

For Maxwell there were "three great departments of education," the physical, the intellectual, and the moral. The public schools had to keep all three of these departments "constantly in view." The mission of the public school, in Maxwell's view, was ". . . closely related to all forms of social work. . . . Teachers must become conscious of the commanding importance of the school as a social factor influencing every form of humane endeavor, reflecting its spirit and aims in the life and conduct of the people, and, in turn, drawing inspiration and help from every department of the world's activity."[159]

One aspect of this "social work" function was to make the schools available to the community when they were not in use for schooling. Maxwell suggested that branch libraries and reading rooms be set up in the central public schools. During the evening, the schools were to be opened for self-improvement courses. His philosophy in this regard was that: "The public school best serves its neighborhood when it is made the center from which all organized civilizing and elevating influences, except, of course, those that are the peculiar province of the church, shall radiate."[160]

Maxwell was anxious to get the parents involved in the education of their children. He encouraged parents associations to be formed. He believed: "Such societies, if they are guided by wisdom, may do much to improve the condition of the public schools, and especially to establish those close relations between parent and teacher that are essential to the proper training of the child. Such societies may lead careless parents to see how deep a concern they have in the education of their children. They will bring home to the minds of many who do not now see it the usefulness of art education, of manual training and, of physical culture."[161] Maxwell also saw that these parents' groups could play a role in maintaining the quality of the school by seeing that plants and shrubs were planted, pictures hung on the walls, and artifacts and natural phenomena provided for the school collections.[162]

Two of Maxwell's most dedicated campaigns were conducted to secure effective legislation – against child labor, and for compulsory education. He was a member of the Child Labor Committee, which successfully proposed the Newsboy and Street-Trades Law preventing young children from working during school hours and at night in those trades. He helped draft and lobbied to secure the passage of the Compulsory Education Law, which made it mandatory to attend school until fourteen years of age. It also required attendance in evening school for children between fourteen and sixteen who did not have the rudiments of a grammar school education.[163] There were severe penalties for employers who violated the Compulsory Education Law, and Maxwell secured extra funds for attendance officers who were charged with the responsibility of enforcing the law.[164]

During his long tenure in the New York City public school system William Maxwell strove to make it the best in the world, and many felt he succeeded. On the occasion of the Superintendent's retirement, Arthur Somers, President of the Board of Education, in his address to the Board in January of 1918, praised Maxwell: "His remarkable genius for administration made possible the centralization and reorganization of the public school system in 1902 . . . . He is responsible for the development of secondary education in the City, for improved methods of training teachers, [and] for better school buildings. . ."[165]

NOTES

[1]Carl F. Kaestle, *The Evolution of An Urban School System: New York City, 1750-1850* (Cambridge: Harvard University Press, 1973), pp. 1-74.

[2]*Ibid.*, pp. 75-76.

[3]For a history of the Free School Society from a nineteenth century perspective, see William O. Bourne, *History of The Public School Society of the City of New York* (New York: G.P. Putnam's Sons, 1873).

[4]A. Emerson Palmer, *The New York Public School: Being a History of Free Education in the City of New York* (New York: Macmillan Co., 1905), pp. 10-12.

[5]Diane Ravitch, *The Great School Wars: New York City, 1805-1973: A History of the Public Schools as Battlefield of Social Change* (New York: Basic Books, 1974), p. 11.

[6]Kaestle, p. 81.

[7]Palmer, pp. 24, 34.

[8]For a discussion of the Lancasterian teaching methods see Ravitch, pp. 12-19.

[9]Palmer, pp. 47-62.

[10]Ravitch, p. 21.

[11]Palmer, p. 63.

[12]Ravitch, p. xiv.

[13]*Ibid.*, pp. 27-29.

[14]*Ibid.*, pp. 46-66.

[15]*Ibid.*, pp. 33, 76, 83.

[16]According to Glazer and Moynihan, New York was "the first of the original thirteen states to prohibit the teaching of religion in public schools." Nathan Glazer and Daniel Patrick Moynihan, *Beyond the Melting Pot: The Negroes, Puerto Ricans, Jews, Italians, and Irish of New York City* (Cambridge: MIT Press, 1963), p. 237.

[17]Ravitch, p. xiv.

[18]Thomas Boese, *Public Education in the City of New York: Its History, Condition, and Statistics* (New York: Harper and Bros., 1869), p. 74.

[19]*Ibid.*, pp. 68-69.

[20]Palmer, p. 165.

[21]*Ibid.*, p. 166.

[22]New York City Board of Education, Committee on Research, *Materials Suggested for Use in High Schools in Observance of the 100th Anniversary of the Board of Education, 1942,* Duane Library, Fordham University, Bronx, New York, pp. 1, 14-15.

[23]Richard and Joanne Wynn, *American Education,* Ninth Edition (New York: Harper and Row, 1988), p. 201.

[24]New York City Board of Education, *Materials Suggested for Use in High Schools,* p. 2.

[25]Chapter 206 of the NYS Laws in 1847 provided funding to establish a free academy from the Literature Fund, a state body which appropriated money to academic and other private schools. Florence Margaret Neumann, "Access to Free Public Higher Education in New York City," Ph.D. Dissertation, City University of New York,1984, pp. 36-37.

[26]In 1899 the sub-freshman course was expanded to a three-year program with high school status. In 1919, the State Legislature gave it legal recognition and it became known as Townsend Harris High School. New York City Board of Education, *Materials Suggested for Use in High Schools,* p. 23.

[27]Palmer, pp. 327, 328. By 1902 a seven year course was established. In 1903 The Normal College High School was made a regular high school though it remained a part of Normal College. Dr. Thomas Hunter, for whom Hunter College is named, was the first principal of the New York Evening School and the first president of Normal College. New York City Board of Education. *Materials Suggested for Use in High Schools,* pp. 3-4.

[28]Palmer, p. 158. New York City Department of Education, *Annual Reports of the City Superintendent of Schools,* Special Collections, Milbank Memorial Library, Teachers College, Columbia University, New York, p. 12.

[29]Ravitch, p. 113.

[30]New York City Board of Education, *Fifty-fifth Annual Report,* Year Ending December 31, 1896, Special Collections, Milbank Memorial Library, Teachers College, Columbia University, New York, p. 149.

[31]New York City Board of Education, *Materials Suggested for Use in High Schools,* p. 22.

[32]*Ibid.* In 1887, The Collegiate School, New York City's oldest school, began a secondary program ". . . to prepare boys for entrance to college." Jean Parker Waterbury, *A History of the Collegiate School: 1638-1963,* (New York: Clarkson Potter, Inc., 1965), p. 109.

[33]New York City Board of Education, *Materials Suggested for Use in High Schools,* p. 23.

[34]Thomas Kessner, *The Golden Door: Italian and Jewish Mobility in New York City, 1880-1915* (New York: Oxford University Press, 1977), pp. 5-6.

[35]Edward George Hartmann, *The Movement to Americanize the Immigrant* (New York: Columbia University Press, 1948), p. 17.

[36]For a study of the backgrounds and aspirations of these reformers see John Joseph Carey, "Progressives and the Immigrant, 1885-1915," Ph.D. Dissertation, University of Connecticut, 1968.

[37]Ravitch, p. 110.

[38]Richard Whittemore, *Nicholas Murray Butler and Public Education 1862-1911* (New York: Teachers College Press, 1970), pp. 34-35.

[39]For a biography of Butler, see Whittemore, and Nicholas Murray Butler, *Across the Busy Years: Recollections and Reflections* (New York: Charles Scribner's Sons, 1935).

[40]Whittemore, pp. 16-27.

[41]Lawrence A. Cremin, *The Transformation of the School* (New York: Alfred A. Knopf, 1969), pp. 170-171. Mark Hoffman, editor, *The World Almanac* (New York: Pharos Books, 1993), pp. 310, 341, 470.

[42]Whittemore, p. 65.

[43]For background on the Public Education Association see M.G. Van Rensselaer, "The Public Education Association of New York," *Educational Review* 16 (October, 1898): pp. 209-219. Sol Cohen, *Progressives and Urban School Reform: The Public Education Association of New York, 1895-1954* (New York: Teachers College, Columbia University, 1964).

[44]Nicholas Murray Butler, "Reform of Secondary Education in the United States," *Atlantic Monthly,* 1894, reprint, *Meaning of Education and Other Essays and Addresses* (New York: Charles Scribner's Sons, 1905), pp. 187-226.

[45]Nicholas Murray Butler, "The Function of the Secondary School," Address before the Schoolmasters' Association of New York and Vicinity, March 8, 1890, *Meaning of Education and Other Essays,* pp. 151-183.

[46]*Ibid.,* p. 163.

[47]Nicholas Murray Butler, "The Reform of High-School Education," *Harper's Weekly* 38 (January 13, 1894), p. 42.

[48]*Ibid.*

[49]*Ibid.*

[50]*Ibid.*

[51]Whittemore, p. 83.

[52]Butler, "Reform of High School Education," p. 42.

[53]*Ibid.*

[54]*Ibid.*

[55]United States Bureau of Education, *Report of the Committee on Secondary School Studies Appointed at the Meeting of the National Educational Association, July 9, 1892.* (Washington, D.C.: U.S. Government Printing Office, 1893), Special Collections, Milbank Memorial Library, Teachers College, Columbia University, New York.

[56]Edward A. Krug, *The Shaping of the American High School, 1880-1920* (Madison: University of Wisconsin Press, 1969), pp. 69, 74-75.

[57]Whittemore, pp. 83-84, 87.

[58]*Ibid.*, p. 88.

[59]*Ibid.*, p. 89.

[60]National Education Association, *Report of the Committee on College Entrance Requirements* (Washington, D.C.: NEA, 1899).

[61]Krug, *The Shaping of the American High School*, pp. 141-142.

[62]*Ibid.*

[63]*Ibid.*, p. 146.

[64]Whittemore, pp. 90-95.

[65]Krug, *The Shaping of the American High School*, pp. 146-168.

[66]*Ibid.*, p. 150.

[67]Whittemore, p. 78.

[68]*Ibid.*, p. 96.

[69]*Ibid.*, p. 97

[70]G. Stanley Hall, "Adolescents and the High School English, Latin, and Algebra," *Pedagogical Seminary* 9 (March, 1902): 104.

[71]Paul H. Hanus, "What Should the Modern Secondary School Accomplish?" *School Review* 7 (September, 1897): 434-435.

[72]Paul H. Hanus, "What Should the Modern Secondary School Accomplish?" *School Review* 5 (June, 1897): 396-399.

[73]Nicholas Murray Butler, "The Scope and Function of Secondary Education," Address before the University High School Conference at Champaign, Illinois, May 19, 1898, *Meaning of Education Contributions to a Philosophy of Education* (New York: Charles Scribner's Sons, 1915), p. 221.

[74]*Ibid.*

[75]George Stuart, "The Raison D'Etre of the Public High School," *Education* 8 (January, 1888): 285-286.

[76]Frank A. Hill. "How Far the Public High School Is a Just Charge Upon the Public Treasury," *School Review* 6 (December, 1898): 750.

[77]Nicholas Murray Butler, "Some Fundamental Principles of American Education," Address before the Convocation of the University of the State of New York, Albany, June 30, 1902, *Meaning of Education Contributions to a Philosophy of Education,* p. 333.

[78]*Ibid.*, p. 341.

[79]Nicholas Murray Butler, "What Knowledge is of Most Worth?" Presidential Address before the National Educational Association in Denver, Colorado, July 9, 1895, *Meaning of Education and Other Essays,* pp. 59-60.

[80]Nicholas Murray Butler, editor, *Education in the United States* (Albany: J.B. Lyon Co., 1900, reprint ed. New York: Arno Press and the New York Times, 1969), p. ix.

[81]David Conrad Hammack, "Participation in Major Decisions in New York City, 1890-1900: The Creation of Greater New York and the Centralization of the Public School System," Ph.D. Dissertation, Columbia University, 1973, p. 319.

[82]Editorial, "Public School Reform in New York and Brooklyn," *Harper's Weekly* 29 (February 9, 1895): 123.

[83]Hammack, "Participation in Major Decisions in New York City, 1890-1900," pp. 320-339.

[84]Editorial, *Educational Review,* 11 (May, 1896): 512.

[85]*Ibid.*

[86]*Ibid.*

[87]"New York Bills on Trial," *New York Times*, 13 February 1895, p.1.

[88]Hammack, "Participation in Major Decisions in New York City, 1890-1900," p. 339.

[89]"Teachers Under Orders," *New York Times,* 24 April 1895, p.6.

[90]Hammack, "Participation in Major Decisions in New York City, 1890-1900," pp. 339-340.

[91]*Ibid.*, pp. 316-317.

[92]"For School Reform," *New York Daily Tribune,* 7 February 1896, p.3.

[93]Hammack, "Participation in Major Decisions in New York City, 1890-1900," pp. 347-350.

[94]"The Teachers Protest," *New York Daily Tribune,* 27 March 1896, p.6. "How They Oppose the Bill," *New York Daily Tribune,* 9 April 1896, p.1.

[95]The Strong Administration, which represented an overthrow of the Tammany political machine, was supportive of educational reform. See George Francis Knerr, "The Mayoral Administration of William L. Strong, New York City: 1895-1897," Ph.D. Dissertation, New York University, 1957.

[96]Editorial, *Educational Review* 11 (May, 1896): 513.

[97]For a detailed study of the changes in the Board of Education during the period 1896-1904 see Marshall C. Spatz, "New York City Public Schools and the Emergence of Bureaucracy, 1868-1917," Ph.D. Dissertation, University of Chicago, 1975.

[98]Palmer, p. 188.

[99]*Ibid.*

[100]*Ibid.*, p. 354.

[101]Ravitch, p. 163.

[102]David M. Ellis, *et al., The History of New York State* (Ithaca: Cornell University Press, 1967), p. 379.

[103]The control extended to even allowing racially segregated schools in Jamaica, Queens, although they were banned elsewhere in the city. See Spatz, p. 290. The city charter made a point of authorizing the Boards of Education to teach English to foreign-born students. New York City Department of Education, *Annual Reports of the City Superintendent of Schools*, p. 12.

[104]Palmer, p. 272.

[105]*Ibid.*, pp. 284-285.

[106]New York City Board of Education, *Journal of the School Board for the Boroughs of Manhattan and The Bronx*, 1898, Special Collections, Milbank Memorial Library, Teachers College, Columbia University, New York, p. 245.

[107]Palmer, p. 272.

[108]*Ibid.*, p. 273.

[109]*Ibid.*

[110]Edward C. Elliott, "The New York School System of General Supervision and Board of Examiners," *Public Education Association of the City of New York*, No. 18 (October, 1913), p. 2.

[111]Editorial, *Educational Review* 15 (April, 1898): 414-415.

[112]Palmer, p. 274.

[113]*Ibid.*, p. 275.

[114]Selma C. Berrol, "William Henry Maxwell and A New Educational New York," *History of Education Quarterly*, Summer, 1968, p. 217.

[115]Palmer, pp. 276-279.

[116]New York City Department of Education, *Annual Reports of the City Superintendent*, pp. 59-66.

[117]The Davis Law salary provisions were incorporated into the Revised Charter of 1901. Palmer, pp. 280-281.

[118]Ravitch, p. 165.

[119]*Ibid.*, p. 165.

[120]*Ibid.*, p. 166.

[121]"City Club Aids Maxwell," *New York Times*, 24 January 1899, p. 6.

[122]New York City Department of Education, *Annual Reports of the City Superintendent*, p. 1.

[123]*Ibid.*, pp. 155-156.

[124]"Jasper After Maxwell," *New York Times*, 30 January 1901, p. 7. "Superintendent Jasper Answers Mr. Maxwell," *New York Times*, 18 April 1901, p. 1.

[125]Spatz, pp. 198-199.

[126]Butler reported that Governor Roosevelt had asked him to chair the Charter Revision Commission, but he felt that not enough people were willing to work for a revised charter. Butler, *Across the Busy Years*, pp. 369-370.

[127]Ravitch, p. 166.

[128]This was a gain for The Bronx because on the borough board there were apparently only two Bronx residents represented, Thomas W. Timpson, and Alfred H. Morris. Morris was also the only Bronx resident on the Board of Education for 1900 and 1901. New York City Department of Education, *Annual Report*, 1900, Special Collections, Milbank Memorial Library, Teachers College, Columbia University, New York, pp. 186-194; New York City Department of Education, *Annual Report*, 1901, p. 204.

[129]Edward Elliott, p. 3.

[130]*Ibid.*

[131]*Ibid.*

[132]Spatz, pp. 301-302.

[133]In the next decade this compromise was criticized. See Edward Elliott, pp. 1-16. See also Charles W. Eliot, "The Board of Education and the Professional Staff," *Public Education Association of the City of New York,* No. 22 (February, 1914), pp. 1-15.

[134]"Possibilities of New Educational Charter," *New York Times,* 23 November 1901, p. 1.

[135]For a biography on Maxwell see Samuel P. Abelow, *Dr. William H. Maxwell: The First Superintendent of Schools in the City of New York* (New York: Sheba Publishing, 1934). See also John Vincent Mooney, Jr. "William H. Maxwell and the Public Schools of New York City," Ed.D. Dissertation, Fordham University, 1981.

[136]Editorial, "City Superintendent Maxwell of New York," *Educational Review* 27 (January, 1904): 5.

[137]Most American doctorates of this period were honorary. The formal graduate education for the doctorate began as recently as 1876 at Johns Hopkins University. By 1890 only about 125 doctorates had been conferred, and by 1900 about 250. See Bernard Berelson, *Graduate Education in the United States* (New York: McGraw-Hill, 1960), pp. 6-14.

[138]Editorial, "City Superintendent Maxwell," p. 5.

[139]*Ibid.*

[140]*Ibid.*

[141]Editorial, *Educational Review* 6 (June, 1893), p. 98

[142]*Ibid.,* pp. 16-17.

[143]Editorial, "City Superintendent Maxwell," pp. 16-17. During this period teacher requirements varied widely from state to state. Most states did not differentiate between a high school and an elementary school teacher. California and New York were among the few exceptions. California had the highest qualifications for high school teachers in the country, and required a diploma from a university or college with special courses in education. New York State required certification, which could be from a training school, normal school, college or university, or from the state itself. See Frederick E. Bolton, "The Preparation of High School Teachers: What They Do Secure and What They Should Secure." *School Review* 15 (February, 1907): 100-104.

[144]New York City Department of Education, *Annual Reports of the City Superintendent,* 1898-99, p. 71.

[145]*Ibid.,* p. 72.

[146]*Ibid.,* p. 59.

[147]William H. Maxwell, "The American Teacher," *Educational Review* 25 (February, 1903): 152.

[148]*Ibid.,* p. 155.

[149]Editorial, "City Superintendent Maxwell," p. 10.

[150]*Ibid.,* pp. 10-11.

[151]*Ibid.,* p. 11.

[152]*Ibid.,* pp. 11-12.

[153]*Ibid.,* pp. 12-13.

[154]William H. Maxwell, "The Teacher's Compensations," *Educational Review* 27 (May, 1904): 472.

[155]"Grout Men Condemn City School Course," *New York Times,* 26 January 1904, p. 3.

[156]"Expert Calls School Courses Too Complex," *New York Times,* 13 June 1904, p. 6.

[157]Maxwell, "The American Teacher," p. 146.

[158]William H. Maxwell, *A Quarter Century of Public School Development* (New York: American Book Co., 1912), p. 9.

[159]*Ibid.,* pp. 3-4.

[160]*Ibid.,* p. 2.

[161]*Ibid.,* pp. 3-4.

[162]*Ibid.*

[163]New York State Legislature, *Compulsory Education Law,* Chapter 671 laws of 1894, as amended by Chapter 988 laws of 1895, Chapter 606 laws of 1896, and Chapter 459 laws of 1903: *Newsboy Law,* Chapter 151 laws of 1903.

[164]For a discussion of the compulsory education and child labor laws and their effect on high school attendance see Moses Stambler, "The Effect of Compulsory Education and Child Labor Laws on High School Attendance in New York City: 1898-1917," *History of Education Quarterly,* Summer, 1968, pp. 189-213. See also Editorial, "City Superintendent Maxwell," p. 16.

[165]*The Election of William H. Maxwell As City Superintendent of Schools Emeritus* (New York: Boys Vocational High School, 1918) p. 13.

THE CREATION OF

MORRIS HIGH SCHOOL

The Mixed High School
In
The Bronx

THE 1896 SCHOOL REFORM LAW, in addition to providing for a centralized Board of Education for New York City, gave that Board the right to create high schools. The law stated:

> Said board shall have power to provide and maintain one or more high schools, as said board may, from time to time, determine; and all provisions of law relating to the acquiring of sites, the erection or hiring of buildings, and the furnishing and repairing thereof, for grammar, primary or evening schools shall be held to apply equally and to the same effect to said high schools. The said high schools shall be so organized as to provide the benefit of further education to pupils, both male and female, who shall have finished the grammar school course, and to other residents of school age equally prepared.[1]

The Board was given the power to make rules and regulations to govern the high schools, to appoint principals and teachers, and generally to manage and set educational policy for the schools.[2]

Eight months after the School Reform Law was passed in April of 1896, Charles Bulkley Hubble, president of the new Board of Education announced that:

> For the first time in the history of New York, the benefits of secondary education are about to be offered to the youth of this city, the establishment of high schools having already been provided for in an appropriation of two and one-half millions of dollars by act of the legislature passed at its last session. It is confidently expected that three model high schools will be opened in the autumn in various parts of the city in buildings altered for the purpose. . . . It is believed by those most competent to judge, that the establishment of this grade of instruction will have a most beneficial effect both upon the academic grade above it as well as upon all grades below.[3]

The decision to organize the high schools came about after several conferences of the Board of Education, including one with the presidents of the City College and the Normal College, and faculty members from the City College. The colleges were involved because they operated quasi-high schools at the time, which absorbed a small number of students directly from grammar schools.[4] The result of the conferences was the adoption of a proposal to establish three high schools, "one for boys and one for girls and the third at present undetermined to be opened at the beginning of the school year, September, 1897.[5]

The Board's special Committee on High Schools proposed that the high schools be organized in three departments, "in part distinct and in part running on parallel lines." There would be a classical course designed to fit students for the colleges, a scientific or English course in which one or more of the modern languages besides English was to be taught, and a commercial course which was to be competitive with the "best and most advanced schools of this kind." The committee also contemplated the addition of a high school devoted to the mechanical arts as a second step in the plan.[6]

On November 18, 1896, the Committee on High Schools requested, and was given approval for, an appropriation of $75,000 for 1897 in order to set up and operate the three schools.[7] One of the schools was in the area soon to be named The Bronx. At the March 3, 1897, meeting of the New York City Board of Education, the members resolved by unanimous consent that: "Grammar School No. 62 (old) [in the North Side at 157th Street and Third Avenue] be appropriated for the use of a High School for Boys and Girls . . . in order to prepare it for the occupation of such High School in September next."[8]

The placement of one of the city's first high schools in The Bronx was a logical choice.[9] For more than twenty-five years, The Bronx was viewed as the northern frontier toward which the ever-growing metropolis was expanding. The Board of Education called for a high school in the area as early as 1894. The *Board of Education Journal* for that year reported:

> Whereas, The great demand on the part of the citizens of New York for a higher education for their sons and daughters, as evidenced by the overcrowded condition of the College of the City of New York and the Normal College, and the hundreds of applicants annually who are unable to gain admission to these institutions, renders some action on the part of the Board of Education a necessity; therefore be it *Resolved,* that the feasibility of establishing at least two High Schools for the relief of the institutions named, and for the accommodation of the people living in the northern part of the city, one in the district north of the Harlem River and the other in Harlem, on the west side, be referred to the appropriate Committees on course of Study and Legislation.[10]

The fact that it was a mixed school for both girls and boys, and that it was placed in The Bronx, was consistent with the practices in other cities at the time. In a 1908 Columbia University masters thesis, Archibald Bain reported that, as in Boston, New York's separate gender schools were developed in the older parts of the city while the coeducational schools were put in the newer residential sections.[11]

Coeducation in secondary schools was a relatively new phenomenon. In fact, rigid separation of girls and boys was maintained in many of the public grammar schools in New York City during the nineteenth century, following the tradition established by the Public School Society.[12] The early private academies in the city were usually segregated by gender, and the Free Academy was as well.[13]

Interestingly, the public school systems in some cities, such as in Philadelphia, Baltimore, and New Orleans, were "distinctly anti-coeducational." However, the trend was growing towards more coeducational high schools in the United States: by the school year 1904-5, 44,896 pupils were attending single gender public high schools while 634,806 pupils attended coeducational high schools. During the same period, the majority of New York City public high school pupils were still in single-gender schools. Such schools had 17,509 pupils, compared to 12,184 in coeducation schools.[14]

William Harris, United States Commissioner of Education, in 1908 stated that: "Co-education of the sexes is preferred because it is *natural*, following the ordinary structure of the family and the society; *customary*, being in harmony with the habits and sentiments of everyday life, and with the laws of the State; *impartial*, affording one sex the same opportunities and culture that the other enjoys; *economical*, using the school funds to the best advantage; *convenient*, both for superintendent and teachers, in assigning, grading, teaching and discipline; *beneficial*, to the minds, morals, habits and development of the pupils."[15]

The coeducational nature of the Mixed High School represented another innovative step in the New York City school system.

Portrait of Gouverneur Morris
Penman of the United States Constitution.
c. 1790s.

The Bronx County Historical Society Research Library.

Naming
The School

THE CITY of New York's Board of Education decided to name its academic high schools after individuals, thus differentiating them from the commercial and manual training high schools.[16] At a meeting held on January 9, 1900, the secretary of the School Board for the Boroughs of Manhattan and The Bronx reported that Girls' High School was to be named Wadleigh, the Boys' High School, DeWitt Clinton,[17] and the Mixed High School, Peter Cooper.[18] The Regents of the University of the State of New York approved the name changes on January 1, 1901.[19]

The Mixed High School was thus originally named for Peter Cooper (1791-1883), the inventor of the steam locomotive, a manufacturer and entrepreneur who made most of his fortune in the ironworks concern of Cooper and Hewitt. Cooper was a civic leader who was credited with helping establish New York City's fire and police departments, the Croton water system and the public schools. He was a philanthropist as well and created the Cooper Union for the Advancement of Science and Art in 1859. This institution to this day provides tuition-free education.[20] When Cooper died in 1883: "The whole city went into mourning. Public and private bodies passed resolutions of respect and sorrow and on the day of the funeral many places of business were closed."[21]

Despite Peter Cooper's reputation, the people of The Bronx were unhappy with the fact that their new high school was not named after someone from the area. The Committee on High Schools reported on April 16, 1902: ". . . it has received an appeal from the citizens of The Bronx, through the organized bodies of that Borough, to change the name of the Peter Cooper High School to that of Morris High School . . . . Your committee gave a hearing to the residents of the Borough of The Bronx and after carefully weighing the arguments set forth by them, is of the

47

opinion that the appeal should be granted."[22] The petition was then approved by the Board of Education.[23] Morris High School was thus named after Gouverneur Morris of the prominent Morris family whose estate had covered the area called Morrisania in which the high school was built.[24]

The man in whose honor the new school was named was born in 1752. He was destined to play a major role in the affairs of New York City and the country during the revolutionary period and the early years of the republic. He attended Columbia College and went on to become a lawyer. Despite the fact that his mother was a staunch Loyalist, early in his career he "espoused the cause of the anti-government party." However, it was not until the introduction of the Declaration of Independence at the Continental Congress that he took a strong position in support of radical doctrines. At the Provincial Congress of 1775 and 1776, Morris was a delegate from Westchester County, of which The Bronx was then a part. His abilities attracted attention, and subsequently his services were "constantly employed in behalf of the nation."[25] As a member of the Federal Constitutional Convention of 1787, Morris was a strong advocate for the abolition of slavery, a powerful central government, and a president elected for life. He wrote the final draft that was submitted to the states for ratification, and thus became known as the penman of the constitution. Morris was the United States Minister to France at the time of the Directory and throughout the entire Reign of Terror. He also served as a United States Senator from New York State between 1799 and 1803. In addition, Morris was credited with being the first person to suggest an artificial waterway to connect New York harbor with the Great Lakes, and was subsequently appointed first chairman of the Erie Canal Commission. He was also involved in the laying out of the grid system for the streets of New York City.[26]

In his person, Gouverneur Morris so resembled George Washington that Jean-Antoine Houdon, the sculptor, used him as a model for Washington's figure. In New York's City Hall today there is a bronze statue of George Washington in the foyer: actually it is of Washington's head and Morris' body.[27] When Morris died in 1816, one of the most notable figures of a great generation passed on.

To solidify Morris High School's ties with Gouverneur Morris and with The Bronx, the Municipal Art Society commissioned two murals for the school.[28] One portrays Gouverneur Morris at the Constitutional Convention of 1787. The other, set in the homestead of Jonas Bronck, the first European to settle the area, depicts the treaty of peace between the Dutch settlers and the Indians in 1642.[29] The murals are still found in the school's auditorium.

The Bronx
At The
Turn Of The Century

AT THE OPENING of the twentieth century, The Bronx was coming
of age. Along with a huge population boom, the new borough
witnessed the electrification of its streetlights and homes, the
arrival of indoor plumbing and the appearance of public telephones in
stores. In transportation, trolleys and subways began to replace the horse-
drawn carriage, the Harlem River Ship Canal was opened and the Grand
Concourse was on the drawing board. The Bronx was blossoming.[30]

The Bronx, in the nineteenth century, had been an amalgam of four
small towns and sections of other towns that had been part of Westchester
County. Physically and politically, the future borough was separated from
Manhattan Island by the Harlem River and Spuyten Duyvil Creek. Yet, even
before sections of The Bronx officially became part of New York City, there
were plans to expand the city northward into that mainland area. For
example, in 1868, the numbering of Manhattan crosstown streets was
extended into the township of Morrisania in the southwestern section of
The Bronx. Then in 1869, the New York City Parks Department was given
authority over the Harlem River bridges and their approach streets,
extending the city's direct jurisdiction to the mainland.[31]

A desire to have new and more efficient municipal services[32] created a
movement by the people living west of the Bronx River (encompassing the
towns of Morrisania, West Farms, and Kingsbridge) to push for annexation
with the city of New York. Approved in 1874, the newly annexed area
became the twenty-third and twenty-fourth wards of the city of New York,
and the schools in this territory were made part of a new school district
under the control of the city's Board of Education.[33] On February 1, 1888,
New York City Mayor Abram S. Hewitt, in his *Message on the Harbor, the Docks,
the Streets, Rapid Transit, the Annexed District and the Tenement Houses*, stated,

Union Railway West Farms Trolley, c.1895.
The motorman, conductor, and assistant conductor are ready for a short shuttle run.
The Bronx County Historical Society Research Library.

"Our rate of taxation depends upon the growth of the unoccupied portion of the city, particularly north of the Harlem River."[34]

By the 1890s, The Bronx had an impressive park and parkway system composed of vast acreage that was planned by ". . . men who fought to preserve this land from subsequent tides of urbanization."[35] It was in 1884, that the state legislature approved the purchase of various parklands in the southern section of Westchester County that had been or were being considered for annexation to the city of New York. This move was largely a result of the success of Central Park, which provided a great impetus for the open space movement.[36] The new parks comprised over 3,757 acres and involved, in some cases, land that was not yet part of the city. Pelham Bay Park, for example, was in the towns of Pelham and Westchester, yet was purchased in 1888, seven years before those areas officially became part of New York.[37]

During the early 1890s the Greater New York Commission, led by Andrew H. Green, formulated a plan to have the larger city embrace all New York State territory bordering New York harbor including Staten Island. The boundaries would run along the existing northern boundary of the Annexed District straight across lower Westchester County to Pelham Bay. From there, the line would run across Long Island Sound to Little Neck on Long Island and directly south to the Atlantic Ocean.[38]

Initially, real estate interests in upper Manhattan, the Annexed District, and Brooklyn feared that so large a city would slight their particular sections. Party officials were reluctant to face the factional voting bloc hazards of such big districts, and upstate politicians were afraid of the power of an enormous new metropolis.[39] Resistance to consolidation was eventually broken down, especially in the city of Brooklyn, because it was clear that the new and enlarged city would offer an expanded tax base, create new public works, such as another East River bridge, and would allow a linkup into the city's fresh water supply system.[40]

On November 6, 1894, a non-binding referendum for consolidation was passed by voters in New York City and its outlying areas. The results in New York City, including the Annexed District west of the Bronx River, and the affected areas of Westchester County were:

New York	96,938 for	59,959 against
Mount Vernon	873 for	1,603 against
Eastchester	374 for	260 against
Westchester	620 for	621 against
Pelham Village	251 for	153 against

Brooklyn, Queens, and Richmond approved the referendum.[41]

Third Avenue El south of 160th Street, c. 1910.

The Bronx County Historical Society Research Library.

Tinton Avenue at 163rd Street, March 16, 1909.
The avenue's name originates from *Tintern,*
the original country seat of the Morris family in Wales.

The Bronx County Historical Society Research Library.

As Brooklyn's margin of victory was only 227 votes, there were great efforts put forth to stop consolidation. The New York State Legislature, with Brooklyn opponents leading the way, defeated the 1895 consolidation bill that was presented on the basis of the approved referendum.[42] All that was salvaged in 1895 was a separate annexation bill, signed by New York Governor Levi P. Morton on June 6, 1895, that brought into the city of New York the land east of the Bronx River to Long Island Sound.[43] While the township of Westchester voted to stay out, it was only by one vote so the tally was ignored and the township was annexed to New York City.[44]

From 1890 until consolidation of the city in 1898, the Department of Street Improvements of the Twenty-third and Twenty-fourth Wards had been in charge of building and maintaining the sewers, and the grading and paving of the highways, streets, avenues, and roads in the portion of the city on the mainland.[45] After years of neglect, the area west of the Bronx River was now well-served. This gave great impetus to the people of the towns and villages east of the river to join the city of New York.[46]

Thus the territory east of the Bronx River was brought into the city in a separate legislative act in 1895 and not as part of the Consolidation Act for Greater New York. This annexation, however, was an important step toward the completion of the whole plan of Greater New York.

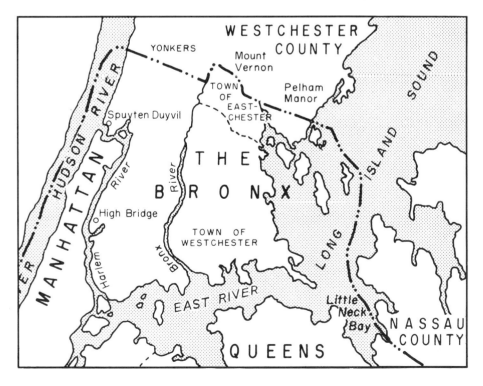

The Bronx in 1895.

The Bronx County Historical Society Research Library.

The events that led up to the 1895 annexation remain cloudy and confused. Much more research is needed in order to understand the convoluted politics of the towns and villages involved. The village of Williamsbridge, for example, had built an elaborate and expensive sewer project without an outlet. It was desperate to hook up to the Annexed District's main sewer line. Nonetheless, this village joined in a legal suit challenging the constitutionality of the annexation law. It seems the village and town governments had provided the basic foundation for growth, but now people realized it was advantageous to join the great city to the south and west.[47] In addition, the inability of the Westchester County sheriff to stop the problem of flourishing gambling halls and saloons prompted Senator William H. Robertson to introduce a bill in the New York State Senate to have New York City annex the area east of the Bronx River.[48]

The annexation of the southern part of Westchester County, which more than doubled the territory of the Annexed District, was authorized by Chapter 934 of the Laws of 1895. It stated that:

> All that territory comprised within the limits of the towns of Westchester, Eastchester, and Pelham which has not been annexed to the city and county of New York at the time of the passage of this act, which lies southerly of a straight line drawn from the point where the northerly line of the city of New York meets the center line of the Bronx River, to the middle of the channel between Hunter's and Glen Islands, in Long Island Sound, and all that territory lying within the incorporated limits of the village of Wakefield, which lies northerly of said line, with the inhabitants and estates therein, is hereby set off from the county of Westchester and annexed to, merged in, and made part of the city and county of New York.[49]

Looking east on 163rd Street at Jackson Avenue, March 4, 1908.
The Bronx County Historical Society Research Library.

It is of no small importance, however, that even after the annexation and the consolidation, Mount Vernon and Yonkers were considered the next logical choices to join New York City as additions to The Bronx.[50]

The annexation added 17,000 inhabitants, $20,000,000 of taxable property and $700,000 of indebtedness. The schoolhouses and other town property, however, were worth $400,000, so that $300,000 was all it cost the city for the whole territory. "That is a good investment," according to a June 8, 1895 article in the *New York Tribune* which continued:

> Although the full scheme of metropolitan consolidation is not yet realized, New-York has this week been made greater in area and population than it was. On Thursday, the Governor [Levi P. Morton] signed the bill annexing to this city a portion of Westchester County including Pelham Bay Park . . .
>
> [This area] will all form a part of the Twenty-fourth ward. This territory was, it will be remembered, to have been annexed to New-York along with the trans-Harlem district in 1873, but was kept out by the action of some of its residents. It has now been brought in largely through the efforts of Representative Fairchild, Assemblyman Stewart and the Rev. F.M. Clendenin.
>
> The advantages of New-York City secured by this annexation are numerous and important. The new territory has many miles of deep water front, sheltered from storms and unhampered by bridges. It brings within the City's jurisdiction the whole park system.
>
> [In addition] West Chester, long notorious as the worst-governed town in the State, can no longer have one gin mill for every eight people. Nor is it probable that the vile den known as the 'Little Monte Carlo' will be permitted by the New-York Police to flourish as it did under the lax rule of Westchester County officials.[51]

In the annexation bill, the new territory east of the Bronx River was to have a topographical survey showing the existing layouts, the elevations above high water, the position and extent of all the roads, streets, avenues, and lanes, division lines and boundaries of properties, and all buildings, creeks, brooks, and visible rock surfaces, etc. The work was planned to take about three years to complete at a cost of $150,000. This survey was to be the basis of all future work, and, immediately after its completion, the street layout of the new section would commence.[52]

The most important street improvement already proposed for the twenty-third and twenty-fourth wards was the Grand Boulevard and Concourse for which $10,000 was appropriated for a survey. "The Commissioner of Street Improvements . . . was authorized, by Chapter 130 of the Laws of 1895, to lay out and establish this roadway together with not more than fifteen (15) roads running transversely under said Grand Boulevard and Concourse. Commencing at a point on East One Hundred and Sixty-first Street, and Mott Avenue, running in a northerly direction, to Mosholu Parkway, intersecting its south side about two hundred and fifty feet east of Jerome Avenue."[53]

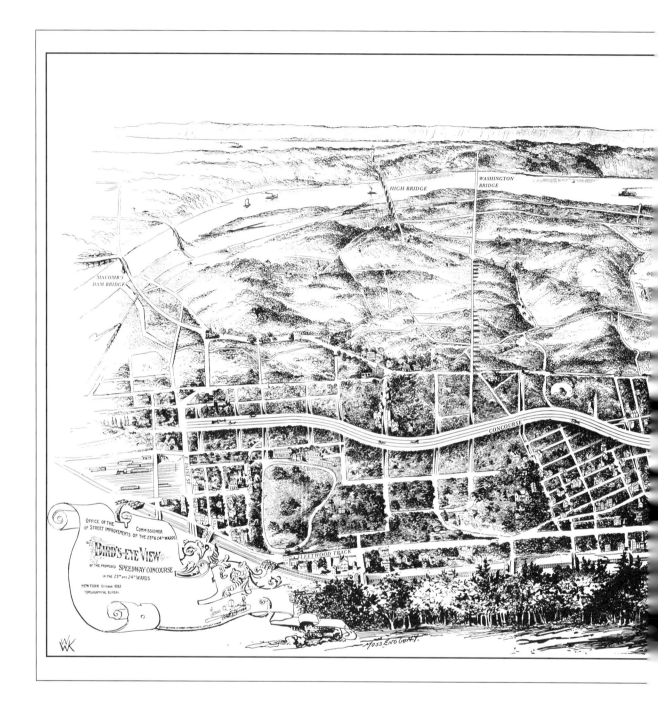

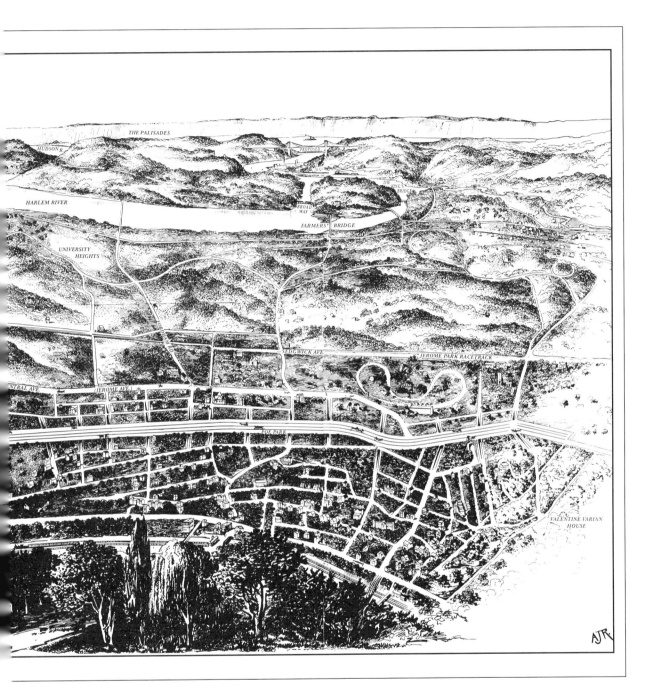

Drawing of the proposed Grand Boulevard and Concourse,
c. 1892.

The Bronx County Historical Society Research Library.

The defeat of the full consolidation of New York proved to be only a temporary setback. Soon after the annexation bill the political forces of Tammany led by Boss Richard Croker and the state Republicans led by Boss Thomas Platt worked out the difficult problems. The Lexow Bill, named for State Senator Clarence Lexow, asked the legislature to create a charter commission and to establish Greater New York. The bill was passed and then signed into law by Governor Morton on May 11, 1896.[54]

On January 1, 1898, the city of Greater New York was created when Brooklyn, Queens and Staten Island were united with the old city of New York composed of Manhattan Island and the Annexed District. The Annexed District was made up of city land north of the East River and east of the Harlem River. This area became the new Borough of The Bronx and was named for its most notable geographical feature, the Bronx River.

In consolidation, Brooklyn's desire for some independence was the impetus behind elected borough presidents. The office of the borough president was modeled after the elected Commissioner of Street Improvements of the Twenty-third and Twenty-fourth Wards (The Bronx). In fact, the last commissioner, Louis F. Haffen, was elected the first President of the Borough of The Bronx in 1898. This new form of governing was approved by the New York State Legislature and signed by the governor on June 7, 1897. Uncertain about The Bronx as a possible Democratic Party stronghold, Republican Party leaders who controlled the state legislature left the borough as part of New York County, making it the only borough that was not also a county as well. [This was not rectified until January 1, 1914 when The Bronx became the 62nd and last county of the State of New York].[55] The borough was now a political subunit of the enlarged city of New York, the first time such a unique political governance was utilized in the United States.

The new charter retained a strong mayor, and the Board of Estimate for finances.[56] It also established a Board of Public Improvements with the power to order and coordinate public works projects throughout the city. This board consisted of commissioners of city departments. Thus, it was hoped that comprehensive, rational, advanced planning would be promoted.[57]

The borough presidents had restricted powers and could vote only on those issues coming before the Board of Public Improvements that involved their own borough. "Local improvement boards were also established within each borough in districts coterminous with senatorial districts to give each section and neighborhood a voice in the local improvements that affected it. Though advisory, they were an early precedent for [local] decentralization."[58]

The consolidation of New York City wove together the region's diverse municipalities into a single transportation system and real estate market. It

Louis F. Haffen, first Borough President of The Bronx, c. 1900.

The Bronx County Historical Society Research Library.

shifted much of the cost of public works – highways, sewers, bridges, schools, police and fire stations – to Manhattan and its higher tax base.[59]

Yet, there was almost immediate disappointment with the new charter. In addition to Board of Education problems, there was a widespread sense that the boroughs should be allowed to regulate their local improvements. This led to the appointment of a Charter Revision Commission in 1900. The revised city charter of 1901 realigned power in the city by making the mayor and the borough presidents partners in the Board of Estimate and Apportionment. The Charter Revision Commission noted: "It is clear that the vast territory composed within the present City of New York, embracing as it does, districts so essentially different as the crowded east side of Manhattan and the rural districts of Queens demand some subdivision and some degree of local autonomy."[60]

Mr. W. W. Niles, a lawyer who lived in The Bronx in the Bedford Park section, and a leading member of the North Side Board of Trade and counsel to the 1901 Charter Revision Commission, later wrote: "I drafted the chapter relating to borough government and gave the borough presidents a seat and a voice in the Board of Estimate. . . . This was necessary at the time as the boroughs were faring badly under the centralized local government . . . . The boroughs were sadly in need of local improvements and couldn't get them."[61]

The 1901 city charter ended the authority of a strong centralized government. The mayor's power was lessened with the abolition of the Board of Public Improvements and by his sharing control over the Board of Estimate and Apportionment. "The borough presidents were given the responsibility to administer local improvements and public works in their boroughs and were further strengthened by becoming members of both the Board of Estimate and Apportionment, and the Board of Aldermen. They held this dual membership until the Board of Aldermen was replaced by the City Council in the 1936 [City] Charter [revision]."[62]

The administrative functions of the city were thus decentralized at the same time that school reformers were successful in centralizing the public school system.[63]

Until the establishment of Morris High School in 1897, there was no public high school in The Bronx. There were, however, secondary-type schools in existence. Parochial schools included the Academy of Mount Saint Ursula, first established in the Morrisania section and later moved to Bedford Park in 1892 and St. John's High School established in the 1840s, which later became Fordham Prep.[64] This system, however, had a very small number of students and was mostly a conduit for the Catholic colleges.

At the turn of the century, the following schools and training institutions were open: the Catholic Protectory orphanage, which was established after the Civil War as a farm and trade training institute run by the Christian Brothers in the eastern Bronx;[65] the Sacred Heart Academy for Boys at Clason Point run by the Sisters of Charity, which opened in 1883 and which became the Clason Military Academy in 1906;[66] the Lavelle School for the Blind, established in 1904 on Paulding Avenue and 221st Street;[67] the American Female Guardian Society and Home for the Friendless, founded in 1901 on Woodycrest Avenue;[68] the Catholic Orphan Asylum, opened in 1899 on the Bailey estate in Fordham Heights;[69] St. Joseph's Institute for the Care and Instruction of the Deaf and Dumb, begun in 1869 in the Fordham neighborhood,[70] and the Webb's Academy and Home for Shipbuilders in Fordham Heights, founded in 1889 as an old age home for sailors and school for young men to learn the science and profession of shipbuilding and marine engineering.[71]

Higher education was well-established in The Bronx at this point. St. John's College was founded by the Jesuits in 1841 in the Fordham section and, in 1904, became Fordham University.[72] The Academy of Mount Saint Vincent, in the Riverdale section, was a school for girls run by the Sisters of Charity. The school had moved to Riverdale in 1856 after its original site was incorporated into the new Central Park. In 1910, it became the College of Mount Saint Vincent.[73] In 1894, New York University began to build a new campus in The Bronx overlooking the Harlem River valley. Gould Memorial Library and the adjacent Halls of Philosophy and Languages were designed by Stanford White of the famed McKim, Mead and White architectural firm. Attached to the library was an arcade with places for bronze busts and tablets that became the Hall of Fame for Great Americans.[74] This was the first hall of fame in the United States.

As The Bronx developed, additional services were needed in education and health care. In 1900, the Medical Society of the State of New York listed 26 Bronx physicians, and the Westchester County Medical Society listed 140 physicians with Bronx addresses.[75] By 1911, there were thirteen medical facilities in the borough. Seton Hospital was established for tubercular patients in 1892 in Spuyten Duyvil.[76] The Home for Incurables, off Quarry Road and 181st Street, was incorporated in 1866 and run by the Episcopal Church.[77] Fordham Hospital was established in 1892, and, by 1905, occupied a new 15-bed capacity building at Crotona Avenue and Southern Boulevard. It was run by the New York City Department of Charities. Fordham University Medical College accepted its first class in 1905, and was affiliated with Fordham Hospital.[78] Riverside Hospital on North Brothers Island was begun in 1880 for contagious diseases and run by the New York City Department of Charities.[79] Lincoln Hospital and Home, originally incorporated in 1845, was first called a Society for the Relief of Worthy, Aged, Indigent Colored Persons, and then the Colored Home and Hospital, and finally, in 1902, the Lincoln Hospital and Home.

It moved to The Bronx at Concord Avenue between 141st and 142nd Streets in 1898, and was run by the New York City Department of Charities. A training school for Black nurses was established there in 1900.[80] Lebanon Hospital, a private institution founded in 1900, was located at Cauldwell and Westchester Avenues. Its training school for nurses graduated a first class of nine in 1891.[81] Westchester Free Hospital was opened in 1893 at Benson Street and West Farms Road near Westchester Square.[82] The Bronx Eye and Ear Infirmary was established in 1903 as a specialty hospital at 404 East 142nd Street.[83] Bronx Hospital began in 1911 as a dispensary at 1385 Fulton Avenue.[84] The House of Rest for Consumptives opened in 1869 in Tremont. It was here that the first recorded autopsy was performed by Dr. Havilah Sprague in 1874.[85] St. Joseph's Hospital for tuberculosis cases opened in 1888 at 143rd Street between Brook and St. Ann's Avenues, and was run by the Sisters of the Poor of St. Francis.[86] The same order opened St. Francis Hospital in 1906 at 525 East 142nd Street.[87] Union Hospital was begun in 1911 at the former home of Fordham Hospital at Aqueduct Avenue and 190th Street, and was run by the Episcopal Church.[88]

In March, 1901, the Bronx Free Library was founded as a library and adult education organization. It then surrendered its separate existence on January 16, 1904, to the New York Public Library. Its books and good will were given to the Tremont branch, which opened in 1905 at Washington Avenue and East 176th Street. The Bronx Free Library's members acted as an advisory committee to this first library branch in The Bronx. By 1912, other branches of the New York Public Library were located in Morrisania, Mott Haven, Highbridgeville, and Kingsbridge.[89]

By March, 1894, the North Side Board of Trade was established, and the first major newspaper in the area, *The North Side News*, began publishing on April 4, 1897.[90]

Despite the fact that The Bronx was part of the great metropolis, most Bronxites thought of themselves as living in a small village. For example, if asked where he lived, a Bronxite would usually reply Mott Haven, Kingsbridge, or Morrisania. In the 1890s, the small villages were usually only a few blocks long and surrounded by farmlands, orchards, and meadows. The streets were mostly dirt roads, and each village supported only a few stores.[91] The larger towns contained factories, mills and breweries.

The ethnic population of The Bronx at the turn of the century was not very diverse, and most often one ethnic group dominated a village. For example, in Melrose and in Morrisania, where the new Morris High School building was opened in 1904, the dominant population were German immigrants who came to America in the 1860s.[92] Irish dominated in Mott Haven, where many worked in the Mott Iron Works or the Stephens' coal yard. The wealthy Irish doctors settled along Alexander Avenue, which was known as "Irish Fifth Avenue." The Irish were also well represented in

Kingsbridge and Riverdale, where they served as gardeners and servants to wealthy families.[93]

Early in the twentieth century, Black families came to the Morrisania section and into Williamsbridge.[94] At the same time, Jews settled in Mott Haven on land purchased by the Baron de Hirsch Fund.[95] Other Jewish families could be found in the Hunts Point and Morrisania sections as well.

When the original city of New York was located on Manhattan Island, the southernmost tip contained the business section, while the residential section was to the north. As the city grew the business section expanded into the residential area and consequently people kept moving further north. Inevitably as the city grew it expanded beyond the narrow limits of the island.

With this expansion came problems of transportation and the subsequent development of rapid transit. As James Walker described in 1918:

> When Wall Street was the northern limit the traffic problem was simple, but when that limit had been transferred to Twenty-third Street the population had grown to such an extent that it was a difficult matter to provide facilities to take its business men down town in the morning and up town at night. Omnibuses were the first public conveyances following the stage coach days. Then came horse cars, then elevated railroads, then electric trolley cars and finally subways. Each class in its day was overcrowded. This was due principally to the phenomenal growth of the city, which added to the travelling population faster than transportation facilities could be provided.[96]

The Melrose Station of the Harlem River Railroad in the 1870s stands below the grade of the street. The northbound platform is filled with people awaiting the arrival of the next train, which can be seen coming southbound in the center on the other side of the bridge. In the skyline is the village of Morrisania. Today, the site is 161st Street and Park Avenue.
The Bronx County Historical Society Research Library.

By the end of the nineteenth century, there were a number of travel options available to the expanding population of The Bronx which by then had 200,500 people.[97] For local trips within villages, people usually walked, or used a horse and carriage or a trolley. At the southern end of the borough the Suburban Rapid Transit system was available.[98] Known as the Third Avenue El, this elevated rail line was extended to Third Avenue and 177th Street by 1891, and to Bronx Park by 1902. It afforded easy transportation to and from Manhattan and within the borough and provided ease of access to the newly established Bronx Zoo and the New York Botanical Garden.[99] As there was a station close to Morris High School, it was especially convenient for its students.

The first subway lines were extended under the Harlem River to 149th Street and Third Avenue. The work in The Bronx was started in 1901 and the line was operational to West Farms by July, 1905. By 1907, the Broadway IRT line was completed to near Van Cortlandt Park.[100] While the subway and elevated trains ran north and south to and from Manhattan, the horse car lines and then the trolleys were established to connect the subway and elevated lines.[101]

Railroad transportation to Manhattan and points north was also possible by 1905 via the New York Central and New Haven Railroads.[102] The New York Central's Hudson Division ". . . brought the residents of Kingsbridge, University Heights, Morris Heights and Highbridge over the Putnam Bridge crossing the Harlem River to a terminal near the Polo Grounds in Manhattan where they could take the Sixth and Ninth Avenue Els to get downtown."[103] These railroad lines, however, could carry only a small number of passengers in comparison to the rapid transit lines, which were also considerably cheaper with a five-cent fare. The low fare enabled even the poorest person to travel widely in the city.[104]

This transportation revolution was a potent influence on the tremendous growth in the borough's population by dispersing people from overcrowded Manhattan to the open spaces of The Bronx.[105] By 1900, the Borough of The Bronx with its 200,500 inhabitants was larger than every city in New York State but Buffalo, which had a population of 352,387.[106] Even Westchester County, with two cities and twenty incorporated villages only had a population of 133,000 people which was far fewer residents than its neighbor to the south.[107]

New buildings, roads and sewer improvements marked the 1890s. By the end of 1902, *The Annual Report of the President of the Borough of The Bronx* would proudly state that The Bronx had constructed 190,766 miles of sewers, 2,127 receiving basins, and 58.718 miles of various kinds of paved streets since 1874. Over 42 percent of the sewer construction was completed since December 31, 1897, and the bulk of the paved streets were finished since 1894, with an increase of over one hundred percent between that year and 1902. In housing, plans were submitted in 1902 for a total of 882 new buildings worth $6,530,979, and 661 building alterations worth $637,395.[108]

By 1905, the population of The Bronx had increased 300 percent from that of 1890.[109] In 1909, Bronx Borough President Louis F. Haffen would write that ". . . in the few years since 1893, little more than sixteen, the Borough of The Bronx has accomplished this development from village conditions to the population and wealth of a great and progressive city. Since annexation to New York City in 1874, the trans-Harlem territory has shown an increase of 1,300 percent, in population and 2,000 percent, in the value of taxable property. If the Borough of The Bronx constituted a separate city, it would rank as the seventh largest in the United States, and second largest in the State of New York."[110]

Thus, as the twentieth century began, The Bronx could justly claim a record of unparalleled progress and development. The placement of one of New York City's first public high schools in The Bronx had been clearly the correct choice in light of the borough's bright future.

NOTES

[1]New York State Legislature, *An act in relation to the common schools and public schools in the City of New York*, Chapter 387 laws of 1896.

[2]*Ibid.*

[3]New York City Board of Education, *Fifty-fifth Annual Report*, 1896, pp. 54-55.

[4]As early as 1893, the editors of *Educational Review*, complained of the lack of a high school in the "largest and richest city in the country," i.e., New York City. They claimed that this deficiency was compounded by two erroneous attempts to fill the gap between elementary school and college. The first error was in extending the grammar schools by one year, and the second one was for the City and Normal College to overload themselves with high school work. Editorial, *Educational Review* 6 (June, 1893): 98. See also, Editorial, *Educational Review* 13 (May, 1897): 513-515. However, City College regarded the sub-freshman program as a vital link between the ward schools and the four collegiate years and continued its program. Neumann, pp. 47, 48.

[5]New York City Board of Education, *Journal of the Board of Education*, 1896, Special Collections, Milbank Memorial Library, Teachers College, Columbia University, New York; pp. 1572-1573.

[6]*Ibid.*, p. 1573.

[7]*Ibid.*, pp. 1573-1574

[8]New York City Board of Education, *Journal*, 1897, p. 436.

[9]Local residents and businessmen were happy with the decision. An 1897 newspaper editorial congratulated the Taxpayers Alliance and the North Side Board of Trade "for inaugurating and supporting the movement that will give the North Side one of the High Schools." "North Side High School," *Dickson's Uptown Weekly*, 6 March 1897, p. 5.

[10]New York City Board of Education, *Journal*, 1894, pp. 1234-1235.

[11]Archibald Watson Bain, "Co-Education in the Secondary Schools of the United States." Masters Thesis, Columbia University, 1908, p. 16.

[12]Ravitch, p. 100.

[13]The first coeducational college in the country was Oberlin in 1833, and the first coeducational public high school was founded in Providence, Rhode Island, in 1843. Thereafter coeducational high schools were established in other areas, particularly in the midwest, and several eastern academies opened their doors to both sexes. Except in some large cities, by the end of the nineteenth century almost all public high schools were coeducational. Bain, pp. 10-11. Telephone interview with Julie Ramos-Weir, Circulation Librarian, Oberlin College, September 12, 1988. Oberlin opened in 1833 with an enrollment of nine men and fifteen women.

[14]Bain, pp. 11, 25, 35.

[15]*Ibid.*, p. 18, 19.

[16]Editorial, *School Review* 11 (May, 1903): 418.

[17]Lydia F. Wadleigh had been the superintendent of the Normal College. "In Memory of Miss Wadleigh," *New York Times*, 4 November 1888, p. 16. DeWitt Clinton was Mayor of New York City and Senator and Governor of New York State. *The Official Directory of the City of New York: The 1992-93 Green Book* (New York City Publishing Center, 1992), pp. 3, 354.

[18]New York City Board of Education, *Journal*, 1900, p. 778.

[19]New York City Board of Education, *Journal for the School Boards of Manhattan and The Bronx*, 1901, p. 1921.

[20]Albert Ulmann, *New Yorkers from Stuyvesant to Roosevelt* (New York: Chaucer Head Book Shop, 1928), pp. 197-212.

[21]*Ibid.*, p. 109.

[22]New York City Board of Education, *Journal*, 1902, p. 741.

[23]*Ibid.*

[24]For a biography of Morris see Theodore Roosevelt, *Gouverneur Morris* (Cambridge: Houghton Mifflin Co., 1888; reprint edition, Oyster Bay: Theodore Roosevelt Assoc., 1975). Howard Swiggert, *The Extraordinary Mr. Morris* (New York: Doubleday, 1952). Max Mintz, *Gouverneur Morris and The American Revolution* (Norman, Oklahoma: University of Oklahoma Press, 1970).

[25]Shonnard, p. 306.

[26]Stephen Jenkins, *The Story of The Bronx* (New York: G.P. Putnam's Sons, 1912), pp. 84, 269, 360-363. Roosevelt, *Gouverneur Morris,* p. 340.

[27]Lloyd Ultan, Professor of History, Fairleigh Dickinson University, and Director, History of The Bronx Project, interviews with author, Bronx, New York, 19 October 1984, 16 November 1984. Professor Ultan is writing the first comprehensive history of The Bronx. Much of his new information is derived from original source materials, including diaries, newspapers, letters, maps, and reminiscences. Roosevelt, pp. 195-196.

[28]Frank Bergen Kelley, compiler, *Historical Guide to the City of New York* (New York: City History Club of New York, 1912).

[29]Jonas Bronck settled in the area in 1639. His name was given to the Bronx River, for which the Borough of The Bronx was named. Jenkins, p. 26. The murals are located in the school's auditorium.

[30]Lloyd Ultan and Gary Hermalyn, *The Bronx in the Innocent Years* (New York: Harper & Row, 1985), pp. xi, xviii.

[31]North Side Board of Trade, *The Great North Side or Borough of The Bronx* (New York: Knickerbocker Press, 1897), p. 22; Gary Hermalyn, "The Harlem River Ship Canal," *The Bronx County Historical Society Journal* XX (Spring, 1983), pp. 1-23. See also Gary Hermalyn, "The Bronx at the Turn of the Century," *The Bronx County Historical Society Journal* XXVI (Fall, 1989), pp. 92-112.

[32]Lenore Chester, et al., *Borough Representation: The Continuing Debate* (New York: Citizens Union Foundation, 1989), p. 9.

[33]Palmer, p. 266.

[34]David C. Hammack, *Power and Society: Greater New York at the Turn of the Century* (New York: Columbia University Press, 1987), p. 233.

[35]Elizabeth Barlow, *The Forests and Wetlands of New York City* (Boston: Little, Brown and Company, 1969), p. 63.

[36]John Mullaly, *The New Parks Beyond the Harlem* (New York: Record and Guide, 1887), p. 111.

[37]Jenkins, pp. 291-292. See also Gary Hermalyn, "A History of the Bronx River," *The Bronx County Historical Society Journal* XIX (Spring, 1982), pp. 1-22.

[38]George Mazaraki, *The Public Career of Andrew Haswell Green.* Ph.D. Dissertation, New York University, 1966, p. 332.

[39]Hammack, *Power and Society,* pp. 195, 196.

[40]*Ibid.,* p. 198.

[41]Shonnard, pp. 620-622.

[42]Hammack, *Power and Society,* pp. 216, 217; Susan Lyman, *The Story of New York,* (New York: Crown Publishers, 1975), p. 197.

[43]Jenkins, p. 87.

[44]Shonnard, pp. 620-627.

[45]North Side Board of Trade, pp. 30, 31.

[46]Shonnard, p. 621.

[47]Nestor Danyluk, *The Last Years of Westchester Township and the Village of Williamsbridge,* Unpublished article, 1980, The Bronx County Historical Society Research Library, pp. 17, 18, 34. The New York Court of Appeals upheld the annexation legislation.

[48]George Zoebelein, "Boundaries of The Bronx and Its Communities," *The Bronx County Historical Society Journal* III (July, 1966), pp. 51-75. "To Enlarge The City," *New York Times,* May 18, 1895, p. 1.

[49]North Side Board of Trade, p. 31.

[50]Shonnard, p. 2. There have been no major annexations to the city of New York since 1898.

[51]"Greater New York," *New York Tribune,* June 8, 1895, p. 6.

[52]North Side Board of Trade, p. 49.

[53]*Ibid.,* p. 51.

[54]Hammack, *Power and Society,* pp. 220-223. When Greater New York was created in 1898, there were 24, 218 pupils in thirty public grammar schools and one high school in The Bronx. See Table 1 for these schools, their addresses and the number of teachers, students and classrooms.

[55]Hammack, *Power and Society,* p. 225.

[56]*Ibid.,* pp. 224, 225, 228.

[57]*Ibid.,* p. 226.

[58]Chester, p. 9.

[59]Hammack, *Power and Society,* pp. 185, 186.

[60]Chester, p. 10.

[61]*Ibid.,* p. 11.

[62]*Ibid.*

[63]Hammack, *Power and Society,* p. 225.

[64]Vertical File on Schools, The Bronx County Historical Society Research Library.

[65]North Side Board of Trade, p. 130.

[66]*Ibid.*

[67]Vertical File on Schools, The Bronx County Historical Society Research Library.

[68]*Ibid.*

[69]Jenkins, p. 344

[70]North Side Board of Trade, p. 126.

[71]Jenkins pp. 344, 345.

[72]Francis X. Curran, S.J., "Fordham University," *The Bronx County Historical Society Journal* XVI (Spring, 1979), pp. 7-14.

[73]Sister Miriam Ellen Murphy, "College of Mount Saint Vincent," *The Bronx County Historical Society Journal* XVI (Fall, 1979), pp. 79-84.

[74]Jenkins, pp. 346, 347.

[75]Francis J. Loperfido, *A Medical Chronicle of The Bronx* (Bronx, New York: Bronx County Medical Society, 1964), pp. 51-54.

[76]*Ibid.,* p. 149; Jenkins, p. 328.

[77]Jenkins, p. 355.

[78]Loperfido, pp. 134, 136.

[79]Jenkins, p. 12.

[80]Loperfido, p. 142.

[81]*Ibid.,* p. 155.

[82]*Ibid.,* p. 170.

[83]*Ibid.,* p. 150.

[84]*Ibid.,* p. 153.

[85]*Ibid.,* pp. 183, 184.

[86]Jenkins, pp. 12, 13.

[87]*Ibid.*

[88]*Ibid.*

[89]Phyllis Dain, *The New York Public Library* (New York: New York Public Library, 1972), pp. 166, 167; Jenkins, p. 10.

[90]Zoebelein, pp. 64, 65.

[91]Ultan and Hermalyn, p. 2.

[92]Jenkins, pp. 186, 187.

[93]Interviews with Lloyd Ultan.

[94]Adrienne Breeden, *et al.,* "A History of Black People in The Bronx," *The Bronx County Historical Society Journal* XIII (Fall, 1976), pp. 80-88.

[95]The Baron de Hirsch Fund was responsible for settling nearly 80,000 Jews in the United States and Canada between 1900 and 1917. See Stephan F . Brumberg, *Going to America, Going to School: The Immigrant-Public School Encounter in Turn of the Century New York City* (Washington, D.C.: U.S. Department of Education, 1982), p. 69.

[96]James Blaine Walker, *Fifty Years of Rapid Transit 1864-1917* (New York: Law Printing Company, 1918; reprint: New York: Arno Press, 1970), p. i.

[97]See Table 2 for population statistics of The Bronx and New York City between 1855 and 1920.

[98]Until August, 1891, to get from any place in the Annexed District to any place in Manhattan by elevated train would cost two fares, or ten cents, but, on this date, the Suburban line was acquired by the Manhattan Railway Company, and the fare became five cents. Jenkins, p. 243.

[99]*Ibid.*, pp. 242-243.

[100]Robert A. Hall, "New York City Rapid Transit Chronology," Unpublished article, 1945, p. 5, The Bronx County Historical Society Research Library.

[101]Jenkins, pp. 240-246. By 1930, ninety-three percent of its population was within easy access to the subway lines, See Irving Plant, *Population Growth of New York City by Districts* (New York: Consolidated Edison, 1948), p. 26.

[102]*Ibid.*, p. 16.

[103]Ultan and Hermalyn, pp. 12-13; see also Hall.

[104]Plant, pp. 16-19.

[105]Interview with Peter Derrick, Manager of Long Range Planning for the Metropolitan Transportation Authority. See also Peter Derrick, *The Dual System of Rapid Transit: The Role of Politics and City Planning in the Second Stage of Subway Construction in New York City, 1902 to 1913*, Ph.D. Dissertation, 1979, New York University.

[106]David M. Ellis, pp. 356, 387.

[107]Shonnard, p. 627.

[108]New York City, *Annual Report of The President of The Borough of The Bronx for The Year Ending December 31, 1902*, (New York: Mail & Express Co., 1903), pp. 54, 68, 69, 72, 73, 74, 80. In a 1934 city housing report, The Bronx was shown to have 92.3 percent of its buildings built after 1899, and 98.9 percent of its housing to have private bathrooms. Both categories were greater than any other borough in the city and attested to the recent rapid development of The Bronx. Evan Schick, *Neighborhood Change in The Bronx 1905-1960*, Ph.D. Dissertation, 1982, Harvard University p. 18. See Table 3.

[109]See Table 2 for population statistics of The Bronx and New York City.

[110]Louis F. Haffen, *Borough of The Bronx: A Record of Unparalleled Progress and Development* (n.d., but c. 1909), p. 3.

TABLE 1

THE BRONX PUBLIC SCHOOLS IN 1898

SCHOOL	LOCATION	TEACHERS	PUPILS	CLASSROOMS
Mixed High School	157th Street and Third Avenue	23	461	29
P.S. 60	College Avenue and 145th Street	32	806	21
P.S. 61	Third Avenue at 169th and 170th Streets	25	1,716	38
P.S. 62	157th Street and Courtlandt Street	48	2,171	42
P.S. 63	Third Avenue and 173rd Street;	16	817	16
	Annex at Washington and 174th Street			6
P.S. 64	2436 Webster Avenue	*	1,164	24
P.S. 65	Locust Avenue, West Farms	20	858	18
P.S. 66	Church Street, Kingsbridge	18	637	17
P.S. 81	Mosholu Parkway, Bedford Park	19	534	21
P.S. 85	735 East 138th Street	63	2,356	49
P.S. 90	163rd Street and Eagle Avenue	56	2,560	49
P.S. 91	Ogden Avenue, High Bridge	15	534	13
P.S. 97	Second Street;	24	669	14
	Annex at 14th Street and Ave. C, Westchester			2
P.S. 98	Park Avenue and Second Street, Williamsbridge	7	657	15
P.S. 99	Throgg's Neck	*	246	9
P.S. 100	Westchester Turnpike near Classon Avenue	7	221	7
P.S. 101	Matilda Street, Wakefield	22	438	14
P.S. 102	Main Street, City Island	6	204	6
P.S. 115	501 Courtlandt Avenue	25	1,124	21
P.S. 118	Clinton Avenue, Woodlawn	7	124	6
P.S. 133	Fox, Simpson and 167th Streets	15	574	16
P.S. 138	11th St. and White Plains Ave., Williamsbridge	9	256	6
P.S. 139	Pelham Avenue, Bronxdale	5	113	4
P.S. 143	599 East 140th Street	9	332	8
P.S. 145	1787 Weeks Street, Mt. Hope	*		11
P.S. 146	Spuyten Duyvil	7	167	10
P.S. 148	Fifth Avenue and Kingsbridge Road, Eastchester	7	68	3
P.S. 152	Union Avenue and 149th Street	15	399	18
P.S. 154	St. Ann's Ave. between 147th and 148th Sts.	50	2,336	49
P.S. 155	Tremont and Anthony Avenues	17	1,034	21
P.S. 156	Trinity Avenue and 136th Street	5	642	21

31 Schools 33 Locations   Total: 582   24,218   604

Records not available

SOURCE: Mark Price, *A History of the Bronx Public Schools: 1898-1944*,
(The Bronx County Historical Society Research Library, The Bronx, New York).

TABLE 2

THE POPULATION OF NEW YORK CITY, MANHATTAN AND THE BRONX 1855-1920

YEAR	NEW YORK CITY*	MANHATTAN	THE BRONX	PER CENT OF THE BRONX TO ALL NEW YORK CITY*
1855	907,775	629,904	17,079	1.9%
1860	1,174,779	813,669	23,593	2.0%
1870	1,478,103	942,292	37,393	2.5%
1880	1,911,698	1,164,673	51,980	2.7%
1890	2,507,414	1,441,216	88,908	3.5%
1900	3,437,202	1,850,093	200,507	5.8%
1905	4,013,781	2,112,380	271,629	6.8%
1910	4,766,883	2,331,542	430,980	9.0%
1915	5,047,221	2,137,747	615,600	12.2%
1920	5,620,048	2,284,103	732,016	13.0%

New York City figures include all five boroughs.

SOURCE: Walter Laidlaw, compiler and editor, *Population of the City of New York 1890-1930*, (New York: Cities Census Committee, 1932), pp. 49-51.

TABLE 3

CHARACTERISTICS OF HOUSING IN NEW YORK CITY BY BOROUGH AS OF 1934

BOROUGH	BUILT AFTER 1899	WITH PRIVATE BATHROOM	WITH CENTRAL HEATING	WITH HOT WATER	WITH MECHANICAL REFRIGERATION
Bronx	92.3%	98.9%	94.4%	97.2%	48.5%
Manhattan	23.8%	73.6%	63.4%	84.4%	27.6%
Brooklyn	59.4%	89.1%	73.5%	74.7%	23.6%
Queens	84.9%	97.8%	84.4%	90.6%	33.9%
Richmond	81.9%	92.2%	73.5%	84.7%	22.4%

The proportion of housing built after 1899 is given in New York City, Mayor's Committee on City Planning, *City Wide Studies* (New York, 1940); the data on the physical characteristics of housing is adapted from New York City Housing Authority, *et al.*, *Real Property Inventory, Borough of The Bronx:* 32B; *Borough of Brooklyn:* 59A-59B; *Borough of Manhattan:* 18A-18B; *Borough of Queens:* 87A-87B; *Borough of Richmond:* 21A-21B.

SOURCE: Evan Schick, *Neighborhood Change in The Bronx 1905-1960*, (Ph.D. Dissertation, 1982, Harvard University), p. 18.

BUILDINGS AND

SITES

The Initial
Locations

IN SEPTEMBER, 1897, the Mixed High School was opened in Grammar School No. 62 at Third Avenue and 157th Street. The old small brick building had served many purposes, as a school, a factory and a Street Cleaning Department facility. It had been condemned by the Board of Health as unfit for habitation right before it became the Mixed High School.[1] Another shortcoming was the noise resulting from its proximity to the elevated trains and the trolley car lines. It was described rather nostalgically in the first *Morris High School Annual,* published in 1905, as follows: "The building had twenty-three rooms, which were but poorly adapted for the purpose they were put to. It also had a small gymnasium fairly well equipped, but with no lockers or baths. The ceiling was very low and in the summer time Mr. Skeele made it the custom to exercise in the yard for want of proper room and ventilation. This building, which was known to all pupils of Morris as the "main building," was familiarly called the "barn" or the "shanty" by some. This was the beginning of the school that everyone is proud of today."[2]

In an article written for the 1920 *Morris Annual* the first days were described as memorable: "The day before school opened, Mr. Peabody [the physiology teacher] hurried to the building and found that there were no chairs there, only a few bare rooms. Dr. Goodwin delegated him to get chairs and by visiting all the undertakers in the neighborhood, he was able to hire enough chairs for the first day. If you ask Mr. Peabody, he will tell you how on this same day he mistook Herr Althaus [the German teacher] for the boss carpenter, and how he berated him for not having everything prepared."[3]

John Denbigh, Morris High School's second principal and one of the original teachers, described his first days at the new school:

Grammar School No. 62 was the original building of Morris High School
and was located at 3082 Third Avenue at 157th Street.
c. 1890s.

The Bronx Old Timers Collection,
The Bronx County Historical Society Research Library.

The building was undergoing extensive alterations[4] and repairs, which were far from being completed when the teachers and students assembled for the first roll call in what was afterward the school gymnasium. Extremely simple ceremonies marked that first assembly. Dr. Goodwin spoke briefly but inspiringly to the school and then introduced each of the twenty teachers who constituted the original staff to the 400 students who had been admitted. Work began at once, but during the first three months, following the opening of the school, it was very much interrupted by the workmen engaged in the completion of repairs.[5]

As a room was completed a class would move in. Denbigh remembered conducting ". . . recitations in rooms where blackboard slate was being sawed into the right lengths. In spite of the difficulties of such a beginning, teachers and students alike enjoyed those early days, and good work was done."[6]

Years later Herman Elkan, of the Class of 1904, was to recall fondly the first years of Morris High School:

The main building, as we called it, was at 157th Street and Third Avenue. How strange it would seem to our present-day students, with their labora-

Rear view of original building of Morris High School
at 3082 Third Avenue at 157th Street in 1934.
Note the addition of fire stairs on rear of original building connecting the newer structure.

Special Collections, Milbank Memorial Library,
Teachers College, Columbia University.

tories, gymnasiums, lunchroom, cooking room, infirmary and auditorium, to call our little building the main building.

But that little old school house recalls pleasant thoughts. It was presided over by Dr. Edward J. Goodwin, beloved by teachers and pupils alike. How fatherly he ruled, yet how sternly! . . .

Just two things stand out clearly – one, the intimate and personal relations that existed between pupils and teachers. . .

The other things that stands out is the school spirit. Our school – how we loved it, how we worked for it, how we cheered our leaders on![7]

Yet within the first year of operation it was obvious that more room was needed, so an annex for the commercial classes was opened at 173rd Street and Third Avenue.[8] This building was one of the first schoolhouses in The Bronx, and Herman Elkan would recollect, ". . . the desks were marked with the initials of past pupils, narrow halls, poorly lighted and ventilated rooms, a tiny lunchroom. But still it recalls pleasant memories, because of its association with old schoolmates and teachers."[9]

In December of 1898, the high school could not accommodate all the children from the grammar schools who asked to be admitted. Another annex was approved in the newly built P.S. 31 on 144th Street and Mott Avenue (today's Grand Concourse). It was agreed that the high school would not interfere with the needs of the elementary school population which would also use the building. Thus, fifteen rooms of the top two floors were allotted to the Mixed High School.[10] This building was referred to as the "modern building" because it had a regular assembly hall and a gymnasium where all the basketball games and graduation exercises were held.[11]

The Mixed High School was growing so rapidly that in June of 1898 another annex was designated. The Board of Education Committee on Sites and Buildings was requested to prepare the old P.S. 63 to make it temporarily usable for the school. In addition, twelve rooms in the new P.S. 63 were pledged to the Mixed High School.[12] Apparently these last annexes in the old and new P.S. 63 never came to fruition as no further mention was made of them in the *Journals* of the Board of Education, nor in the Morris High School papers. This may have been because there was a serious problem with overcrowding in elementary schools and educators were outraged at the custom of using the elementary schools as high school annexes. Many of the younger children had to attend school on part-time shifts, resulting in their leaving school after 4:00 p.m. when it was often dark. To Alida S. Williams, principal of Public School 33 in Manhattan, a more sensible and fairer solution was to have the high schools double their student sessions and remove the high school classes from the elementary schools.[13]

In June, 1900, the inspectors of the 33rd School District reported that

P.S. 31, Grand Concourse and 144th Street, in October, 1984.
Built in 1899, this structure's top two floors were used as a Morris High School annex
until the new high school building opened in 1904.

The Bronx County Historical Society Research Library.

because of the great increase of students attending the Mixed High School it was necessary to use three different buildings to house the 2,136 pupils. The inspectors found that these sites were totally inadequate. They reported that the building on the original site at 157th Street and Third Avenue was designed as an elementary school and thus was not fitting for a high school because the corridors were very narrow, the rooms too small, and there was but one study hall in the building. The annex at 144th Street and Mott Avenue was also a grammar school, and the inspectors claimed that the space given to the high school had to be reduced as the demand for increased use of the grammar school made it impossible for the high school to retain all the space it had been assigned. Concerning the commercial classes at 173rd Street and Third Avenue, the inspectors asserted that it was an old building, ". . . which has hitherto been condemned and is simply serving as a make shift at present . . . . It is defective in light and ventilation, and not suitable as a school building any longer. It is situated in the yard of a grammar school and at recess times the noise which the grammar students made in their games and play is often very distracting to the high school pupils, making it impossible for them to study at such times."[14]

The inspectors also found that the housing of the high school in buildings so widely separated presented a serious problem. They claimed that it was ". . . a great embarrassment to the Principal in his attempt to administer the general offices of the school and keep in touch with the classroom work of several teachers. . . . The usefulness of the several teachers is being impaired by their being compelled to divide their time between three different places."[15]

The annexes usually handled first-year classes that were ultimately combined at the main building at 157th Street and Third Avenue. It was difficult to maintain unity in the curriculum "where teachers are so widely separated and have so little acquaintance with each other and with each other's plans of work and methods of instruction."[16]

The limited space in all three sites was also a handicap, and the inspectors noted: "The largest number of pupils that can be assembled at any one time in any one of the three buildings is so small (240) that the school is never called together. As a consequence, enthusiasm for the school, a belief in its power and effectiveness and vitalizing contact of the lower classes with pupils more advanced, all of which count for so much in a well ordered secondary school, are notably lacking in the Peter Cooper High School." [Morris High School][17]

The lack of a library and of science laboratories was also reported. The inspection committee concluded that a new high school building in The Bronx was "an immediate necessity." It resolved to ask the Board of Education to proceed as soon as practicable to let the construction start.[18] Apparently because construction did not proceed fast enough, the school board approved a request to construct and equip a physical lab in the annex at 173rd Street and Third Avenue in March of 1901.[19]

In his *Annual Report,* Superintendent Maxwell pressed for the completion of the high school buildings ". . . as the growth of the high school attendance has surpassed all expectations and the present quarters are utterly inadequate."[20]

When the three New York City high schools were opened in 1897, the average daily attendance was 592. By 1901, in addition to the original three main high school buildings, nine annexes were used for high school classes in Manhattan and The Bronx, and the average daily attendance was 5,488.[21] From the very establishment of the high schools, it was apparent that new buildings would have to be built. Even as early as June of 1897 the Board of Education reported that: "When a new building shall have been prepared for a Mixed High School, the old building (Grammar School 62) will be needed for the instruction of Grammar and Primary pupils."[22] It was, however, the case that the new high school construction was to be stretched out for almost six and a half years.

In 1897, the Committee on Sites and Buildings recommended the acquisition of specific locations for high schools. It is interesting that two sites were approved in what was then the twenty-third ward of the city (later part of the Borough of The Bronx). These sites were:

1. A plot on the north side of East One Hundred and Sixty-Sixth Street, running from Boston Road to Jackson Avenue, having a depth of 200 feet on Jackson Avenue and at the northerly line of the plot, to run parallel with East One Hundred and Sixty-Sixth Street.

2. The block bounded by Mott and Walton Avenues, One Hundred and Fifty-Eighth and One Hundred and Fifty-Ninth Streets, north of Cedar Park.[23]

The first plot had been approved by the Committee on High Schools, the city superintendent, and the superintendent of buildings. The second had been approved by the school inspectors and was favored by some of the members of the Committee on Sites. Both sites were submitted to the board for consideration and decision. On June 23, 1897, the board finalized its approval of the Boston Road and Jackson Avenue site for the Mixed High School.[24] The second site would become half of the land upon which the Bronx County Building was erected in the 1930s.

In July of 1897, the board discussed the survey of the approved site and asked the city to acquire the land. The size of the plot for the Mixed High School was 378.04 feet by 218.50 feet by 190.75 feet by 200 feet.[25]

The title to the land was vested in the city as of February 25, 1898. In January of 1899, the School Board for the Boroughs of Manhattan and

The Bronx was urged to complete proceedings for the acquisition of the sites for the Boys' High School, the Girls' High School, and the Mixed High School. The *School Board Journal* stated: "Your Committee [on High Schools] desires to call the attention of the Board to the desirability of completing the proceedings for the acquisition of these sites, in order that it may be known how much will be left for the erection of High School buildings out of the amount authorized to be raised by bonds for the purchase of sites and the erection of three buildings for the accommodation of the schools already established *[sic]*, and your Committee believes that these schools should be hurried to completion as soon as practicable."[26]

The award for the Mixed High School site was $99,320, plus costs of $1,084.49 and interest of $12,232.91, for a total payment of $112,637.40.[27]

In the meantime, the Board of Education, in March of 1898, permitted the Committee on Sites and Buildings to advertise in the *City Record* for bids to build the high schools in Manhattan and the Mixed High School at Boston Road and Jackson Avenue in The Bronx.[28] A similar resolution was passed at the January 15, 1899 meeting indicating that the advertising authorized at the March meeting did not bear sufficient results.[29]

The New
Building

IN DECEMBER of 1898, the *New York Daily Tribune* reported that plans were completed for the new high school in The Bronx. Praising it as a "model high school building" the article exclaimed: "One of the handsomest high schools in New York City will be the Boys' and Girls' High School to be erected in the Borough of The Bronx, on One-hundred-and-sixty-sixth St., between Boston Road and Jackson Ave. The new building will replace the old schoolhouses now used for high school purposes . . . . The school will afford accommodation for about fifteen hundred pupils."[30] These plans were apparently preliminary, as the actual building accommodated 2,500 pupils.[31]

With the site acquired, and the plans and specifications developed, the Committee on Sites and Buildings, in February of 1900, instructed the Superintendent of Buildings to advertise for proposals from contractors to erect the new building for the Mixed High School in The Bronx.[32] The board then announced that the bids for the work were to be opened on November 19, 1900, for the erection of the Mixed High School, to be named Peter Cooper High School. The response to the advertising resulted in eight construction bids. The job was awarded to the lowest bidder, Louis Wechsler, who submitted a bid of $469,383.[33]

At the January 23, 1901, meeting of the Board of Education, it was announced that the Board of Estimate approved the requisition of $469,383 to provide payment for the contract with Louis Wechsler for erecting Peter Cooper High School. This was subject to the concurrence by the Municipal Assembly authorizing the comptroller to issue corporate stock of the City of New York in a manner provided by Chapter 378 of the Laws of 1897. The Municipal Assembly concurred on March 27, 1901, and authorized the comptroller to issue the necessary stock.[34]

The Rogers Estate, c. 1900, was located at Boston Road and 166th Street.
The Rogers family owned this large estate before Jackson Avenue was cut through.
It consisted of stables, barns, orchards and fields. Morris High School
stands on or near the site of the building seen here.

The Bronx County Historical Society Research Library.

The William Cauldwell House, located on the southeast
corner of 166th Street and Boston Road, in 1900.
Cauldwell Avenue was named for Senator William Cauldwell, who
had been head of the Board of Education and who worked for the 1874
annexation of the western section of The Bronx to New York City.
His daughter, Emily, married Thomas Rogers of the
Rogers Estate in a gala 1880s wedding.

The Bronx County Historical Society Research Library.

The building's cornerstone was laid on July 23, 1901, "without much ceremony, and work commenced in earnest."[35] The building of the first public high school in The Bronx was under way.

C.B.J. Snyder, Superintendent of Buildings for the Board of Education from 1891-1923, was the architect of the new school.[36] A resident of The Bronx, Snyder took a special interest in the building, which when completed was hailed as a "model of its kind in the United States."[37]

It was considered by many people to be his masterpiece.[38] Following the dominant architecture[39] of the colleges and universities of the day, Morris High School was designed in the English Collegiate Gothic style,[40] thus reflecting the school's role as the "people's college."

Snyder had never designed a high school before his appointment to design the three new ones for the city in 1897. He had, however, designed many elementary schools

> . . . and he fell back upon this experience, after a thorough investigation of existing high schools. . . In fact, in the first school (Wadleigh) he erected he departed from all known plans for such structures, and made what might be called a glorified, enlarged edition of an H-type elementary building to house the laboratories, lecture rooms, and whatnot, of the higher curriculum operated on the departmental system of instruction. . .
>
> After all, as the architect discovered, the problem of erecting a high-school building in the crowded sections of a populous city differs very little from that of putting up an elementary school under the same conditions, save only in the matter of size and in the internal arrangements of rooms to fit the different course of study.[41]

The H-plan shape had been used successfully by Snyder previously in elementary schools in the city.[42] In order to erect a building to cover most of the available area, the H-design was ideal because it allowed open space for play areas and for air and light in all rooms.[43]

Snyder's technique of adapting the elementary school to the high school design was criticized by architect Felix Clay in 1903. Clay claimed ". . . it is more desirable that the methods of the Secondary School buildings should find their way in to the Elementary Schools, than those of the Elementary School should be adopted in the High Schools, as has hitherto been too much the case; probably owing to the fact that the books published on school buildings treat nearly all questions from the point of view of the School Board."[44]

On the other hand, another architectural critic of the day, Edmund Wheelwright admired Snyder's work in 1901, seeing in his design improvements on the basic European gymnasium (school) models that were used in the Boston secondary schools. For example, Snyder provided for a general cloak room for the pupils' clothing, which Wheelwright saw as "more economical planning than the arrangement of separate

C.B.J. Snyder, Superintendent of School Buildings,
late 1890s.

Office for Metropolitan History.

C.B.J. Snyder's drawing of
Morris High School.
c.1900.

Special Collections, Milbank Memorial Library,
Teachers College, Columbia University.

C.B.J. Snyder's drawing of the
rear view of Morris High School
showing the auditorium, c. 1902.

Special Collections, Milbank Memorial Library,
Teachers College, Columbia University.

wardrobes for each room." Snyder also provided for general study rooms in which more than one class could be accommodated. These innovations, Wheelwright felt, were more "in harmony with the freer spirit which should characterize the secondary schools."[45]

In any case, Snyder was acutely aware of the special needs of school buildings and had written of the problems created by high land values, heavy immigration, and other factors. In a letter he wrote in 1899 he maintained: "It must be admitted that the conditions which we have to confront here in New York are entirely different from those presented by any other city in this or any other country. The density of population and the number of children coming from the blocks and acres of five-story, four-family [per story] tenements in various parts of the city is simply appalling. School buildings accommodating 1,500 children are numerous in the lower East Side, but new ones are being erected all the time, and yet there is a demand for further accommodations."[46] Snyder saw these issues further compounded by the fact that so many of the immigrants did not speak any English to the point that "twenty and more languages and dialects have been represented in one class of the lowest grade," and half of the children could not speak English "beyond the words 'yes,' 'all right,' or 'no.'"[47]

With land costs extremely high in New York City, it was difficult to secure large school sites. Thus, not "one inch of ground area" was allowed to go to waste.[48] Snyder saw the limited land for Morris High School as a problem and a challenge. In 1910, he wrote an article titled "Public School Buildings in the City of New York" in which he commented: "The Morris High School. . . is unfortunately placed upon a street only forty feet in width, the plot having been selected for a small high school, but owing to delays caused by the revision of the city charter and other matters, the final orders were for a building to care for at least 2,500 students, and neither change nor enlargement of the site was possible."[49]

The building Snyder designed, using his usual H-design, was 312 feet wide with wings 104 feet deep and a tower 179 feet high.[50] The size of the plot allowed little open space around the school. The assembly room, or auditorium, was placed at the rear of the building to be easily accessible for the general public for lectures and other purposes. The school was ultimately built to accommodate 2,630 people. It had 2,679,500 cubic feet of space with 46.2 percent of it devoted to classrooms, and the rest to offices, a library with a total of 3,922 volumes in 1904,[51] lecture rooms, lockers, gymnasiums, store rooms and laboratories.[52] In designing the building Snyder took advantage of the grade of the site by building the central part only a few inches over the plot, and placing a high basement on the Jackson Avenue wing where the ground dropped down.[53]

The building rose five stories above the basement, with a central tower of fifty feet square adding another approximately three stories to it.[54] It was

Morris High School Library.

The Morris Annual, 1905.
The Bronx County Historical Society Research Library.

A Morris High School Laboratory.

The Morris Annual, 1905.
The Bronx County Historical Society Research Library.

described by A. Emerson Palmer, Secretary to the Board of Education, as "exceptionally handsome and imposing."[55] In the main part of the building there were seventy-one rooms, with forty-six section rooms ". . . of the usual size, but placed with the long side, of about 28 feet, to the light so that the shorter dimension of 21 feet is the depth of the room, bringing the farthest seats sufficiently near the light. Each room is amply lighted by a large window or rather a group of windows in a single opening, measuring *[sic]* as a minimum an area of 160 square feet."[56]

In the *Annual Report* of the Department of Education for 1902, it was reported that in addition to the section, or classrooms, there were "twelve laboratories for chemical, physiological, biological, physiographical and other purposes and three lecture rooms to be used in connection therewith." A study was provided on each of the four upper floors with a large library on the second floor. There were separate gymnasiums for boys and girls, "each with its running track, shower baths, locker rooms, doctor's examination room, etc., etc."[57] The school also had the most modern equipment and utilities, including electricity throughout, an electric eleva-

Morris High School Gymnasium.

The Morris Annual, 1905.
The Bronx County Historical Society Research Library.

Drawing of Morris High School building
without its central tower, c. 1902.

Special Collections, Milbank Memorial Library,
Teachers College, Columbia University.

tor, an interior telephone system, and a ventilating system referred to as "Plenum" because ". . . a full supply of fresh air is forced by powerful fans into all the rooms, driving out, by pressure, the air that has become contaminated by use."[58] In addition, lunch rooms and bicycle storage rooms were provided in the basement.[59]

While the new high school buildings were being completed, there was debate about the need for adornment on them. The first issue arose over Wadleigh High School[60] and its $100,000 worth of "extra ornament." Snyder's plans, however, ". . . were not revised as no one desired that this City should erect a high school building which would be the subject of scorn and ridicule of the entire country, especially when it was shown that the cost of the completed building per pupil would be less than one half the cost of the high school buildings in other cities."[61]

When the costs for Morris High School came up for the Board of Estimate's approval, the ornament question was again raised, and it was suggested that $5,000 might be saved by eliminating all terra cotta work other than to the window sills and lintels, while another $18,000 could be saved by abandoning the central tower.[62] Such a building, according to Snyder was, "but a faint idea of the [original design] building . . . with the tower eliminated."[63]

The tower, in addition to being the school's "most striking feature," served practical purposes. It contained the ventilating shafts for the building and the boiler chimney "which could not well have been disposed of otherwise without disfiguring the appearance of the building." Further, the upper floors of the tower provided laboratories and work space for professors, which was often overlooked in many high school buildings.[64]

The arguments for the crenelated tower eventually overcame the objections and the ornamental work was permitted "rather than have a plain brick structure." An expenditure of $23,000 for terra cotta on a contract of $469,383 was not considered unreasonable.[65]

The tower was to become a symbol of the strong school spirit that characterized Morris High School students. The *Morris Annual* of 1922 contains the following song about the tower, written by student Hedwig W. D. Hilker, to the tune of "Auld Lang Syne:"

The Morris tower stands straight and strong
Against the city sky,
Above the firm foundation stones
And walls of Morris High.
In sunshine or when stormy gales
Around its turrets blow,
The Tower's quiet steadfastness
Smiles on our world below.
Beyond the strife and stress of life,
Above the Borough's noise,
The tower squares its silent strength
In calm, unvarying poise.
O, Morris tower, we love your way
of reaching toward the sky –
Your four-squared, quiet, steady force –
Dear tower of Morris High[66]

In response to criticism of the cost of the new high schools, C.B.J. Snyder claimed that a comparison with school buildings in other cities showed that the costs per pupil were considerably lower for the New York City schools.[67] Snyder showed that a new Philadelphia high school, which was designed to accommodate 1,500 pupils, cost over $1,000,000. In Boston the cost to accommodate 2,500 pupils was $1,228,000 as compared to $600,000 for the same number of pupils in Morris High School.[68] In comparing grammar school to high school costs Snyder asserted:

> If the grammar or elementary school erected in New York in recent years be taken as a basis, then must be added thereto the sum of, say, $20,000 for extra equipment. This, together with the reduction in the number the building will accommodate as a High School, owing to the fact that more floor space per capita is needed than for an elementary school, would

> bring the cost for two buildings of 1,250 pupils each to about $640,000, plus the cost of the extra six lots of ground – or in all about $700,000.[69]

The final tabulation for the costs of constructing and furnishing Morris High School was well under the amounts Snyder cited for the high schools in other cities.[70] The total cost for construction and for furniture was $652,585.86.[71]

By January, 1904, the building was reasonably complete and all classes were ordered to report to the new site. The pupils and teachers from the original building at 157th Street and Third Avenue moved in on January 25th, and two days later the people from the annexes arrived. As of January 28, 1904, all the pupils and teachers of Morris High School were finally located under one roof.[72]

In the *Morris Annual* in 1905, students proudly described their new buildings:

> It is situated on a plateau on 166th and Boston Road and is a long building with terminal wings, extending 312 feet along 166th Street. To this building, as an attachment to the rear, an auditorium was added, the effect

Auditorium of Morris High School,
showing stage and pipe organ, c.1910.

The Bronx County Historical Society Research Library.

Second floor of Morris High School auditorium,
showing balconies and gothic ceiling, c.1911.

The Bronx County Historical Society Research Library.

being to heighten the artistic appearance and to enhance the architectural
design. The building itself has five stories and basement. It is constructed
of carefully harmonized gray brick with terra cotta trimmings of the same
shade. Passing through the lobby which fronts the elevators (which by the
way are not yet running) we enter a great corridor. This corridor runs
the whole length of the building, and into it open the principal's offices
and a double row of class-rooms. On all floors this is practically the rule of
construction, except that in some cases the street ends are given over to
gymnasiums or laboratories. The auditorium is directly opposite the center
of the corridor and, as far as stage and dressing rooms are concerned, is
part of the main structure. The banked seats in the lower floor and gallery,
about 1300 in number, are under a separate roof, which is on a level with
the second story of the structure.[73]

The building was officially dedicated on June 10, 1904. The auditorium,
with a capacity of 1,700 people, was packed. It was reported that "several
hundred people were unable to get into the school,"[74] and that the stage
was decorated with flags, coats of arms, draperies and palms.[75]

The activities were presided over by Edward J. Goodwin, principal of the school.[76] The opening prayer was offered by Rev. John D. Roach of the Holy Spirit Catholic Church and the high school orchestra played "Romance Sans Paroles." Many addresses were offered in praise of the new high school. Henry A. Rogers, President of the Board of Education, Richard H. Adams, Chairman of the Committee on Buildings, and Frank L. Babbott, Chairman of the Committee on High Schools, all spoke briefly "telling of the pride the Board had in the Morris High School and its teachers and students.[77] Corporation Counsel Thomas F. Delaney spoke on behalf of Mayor George McClellan, and other speakers included Louis F. Haffen, President of the Borough of The Bronx, John H. Eustis, former Park Commissioner of The Bronx, and William H. Maxwell, City Superintendent of Schools.

The most notable speech, however, was given by Nicholas Murray Butler, President of Columbia University and leader of the reform movement which produced the School Reform Law that led to the creation of the first high schools. Butler declared: "This community has come to realize that it cannot escape the responsibility of leadership. It is building slowly, little by little, a city beautiful, a city convenient, a city truly great and everlasting, intellectually and spiritually."[78] Butler placed Morris High School squarely in the American tradition of schools that overcame rather than perpetuated class distinctions. He went on to say:

> There are colleges and universities from Japan to Chile of varying excellence, but the free, public, secondary school is the contribution of the American people to modern theory and modern educational practice. Every secondary school in Europe is by its very nature a class school. There the parents of children who leave home to obtain a systematic education are forced to choose before the youngsters are ten years of age whether they shall take an elementary or secondary course. If, by force of circumstance, they are obliged to decide against that higher training, the doors to which that higher training leads are forever closed to them.
>
> The free public high school of the United States has developed from below, and instead of overlapping the elementary school it is closely connected with and related to it for the very reason that it appeals not to as few as possible but to as many. The essence of a democratic education is an education opening doors so that the pupil, as he goes on, widens the possibility for service and distinction.
>
> Training past the elementary school period is of vital importance in a country like ours. There is no more futile insistence than the one continually harped upon in the public press, that if we would teach only reading and writing and arithmetic we need not do anything else. Reading with nothing to read, writing with nothing to write about, and ciphering with nothing to cipher, are of little importance. If our city is to be great and memorable it will be because we succeed in placing it by the side of Jerusalem, Athens, and Rome as the intellectual and spiritual capital.[79]

Morris High School, c.1905.

The Bronx County Historical Society Research Library.

From its opening day in September, 1897, to June, 1904, the average daily register went from 535 to 1,928 students.[80] This extraordinary jump in attendance was a harbinger of the changes that were taking place in New York City and in the country. The education of the children of America was to become a universal directive. Over the next years, annexes of Morris High School were spun off as separate high schools to meet the large demand. Morris became known as "the Mother of High Schools," as Evander Childs High School in 1913, Theodore Roosevelt High School in 1918, George Washington High School in 1920 and Bronx Vocational High School (later called Alfred E. Smith High School) in 1921, were established.[81]

In its model high school building, the staff of Morris High School taught democratic ideals and became a vanguard for commercial training and academic excellence. The principal architect of this success was a man of great vision and energy, Dr. Edward J. Goodwin.

Looking north up Boston Road in 1904 to Morris High School.

The Bronx County Historical Society Research Library.

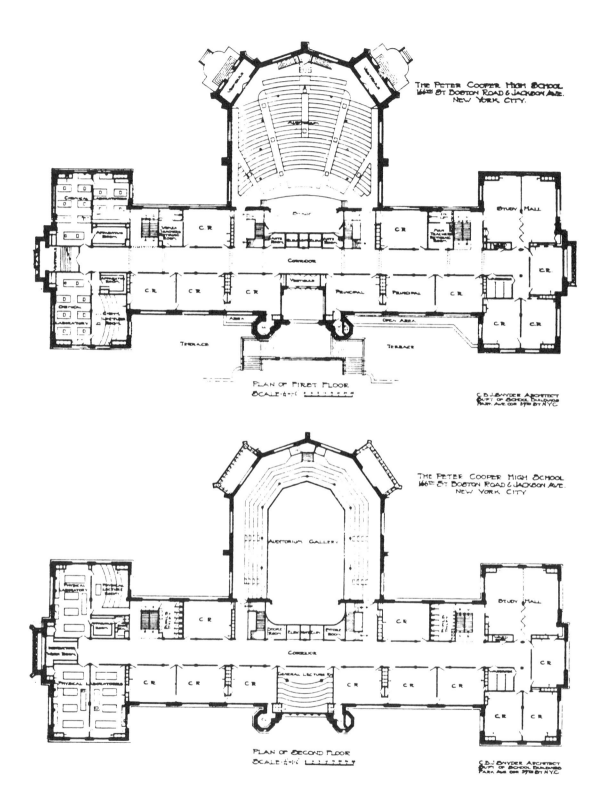

C.B.J. Snyder's plans for Morris High School
depicts first and second floors with the auditorium wing.

The Bronx County Historical Society Research Library

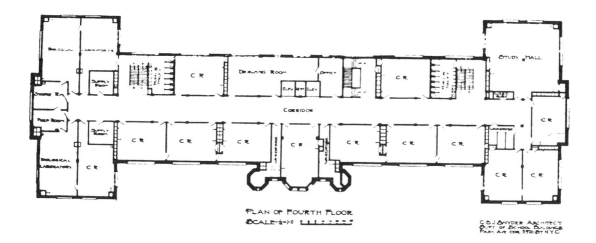

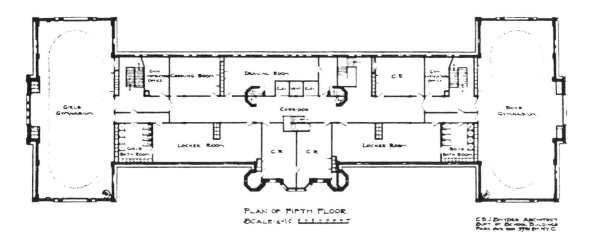

C.B.J. Snyder's plans for Morris High School
depicts H-plan design of fourth and fifth floors.

The Bronx County Historical Society Research Library

166th Street looking east to Morris High School on the hill to the left in 1908.
The backs of the buildings in the middle of the photograph
are between Clay and Teller Avenues.
This was the former site of the Fleetwood Trotting Course
which was in operation from 1870-1898.

The Bronx Old Timers Collection,
The Bronx County Historical Society Research Library.

NOTES

[1] *The Morris Annual,* 1920, The Bronx County Historical Society Research Library, Bronx, New York, p. 40.

[2] *The Morris Annual,* 1905, p. 16. Mr. Otis Skeele was the physical education teacher.

[3] *The Morris Annual,* 1920, p. 40.

[4] Four bids were received "to alter, repair and fix up" the building. The project was awarded to James Hamilton who had bid $21,979. The heating system bid was awarded to E. Rutzler for $16,235. New York City Board of Education *Journal,* 1897, pp. 1187, 1188.

[5] *The Morris Annual,* 1922, pp. 26, 27.

[6] *Ibid.*

[7] *Ibid.,* pp. 22, 27.

[8] *The Morris Annual,* 1905, p. 16.

[9] *The Morris Annual,* 1922, p. 26.

[10] New York City Board of Education, *Journal of the School Board for the Boroughs of Manhattan and The Bronx,* 1898, p. 1599. The school's name remained the Mixed High School until 1900.

[11] *The Morris Annual,* 1922, p. 26.

[12] New York City Board of Education, *Journal of the School Board for the Boroughs of Manhattan and The Bronx,* 1898, p. 1599.

[13] Alida Williams, "New York's School Problem," *Educational Review* 27 (April, 1904): 330-331.

[14] New York City Board of Education, *Journal of the School Board for the Boroughs of Manhattan and The Bronx,* 1900, pp. 588-589.

[15] *Ibid.,* p. 589.

[16] *Ibid.*

[17] *Ibid.,* The names Mixed High School and Peter Cooper High School were used interchangeably at this time.

[18] *Ibid.,* p. 590.

[19] New York City Board of Education, *Journal,* 1901, p. 385.

[20] New York City Department of Education, *Annual Report of the City Superintendent of Schools,* 1900, p. 39.

[21] New York City Board of Education, *Journal of the School Board for the Boroughs of Manhattan and The Bronx,* 1902, p. 1805.

[22] New York City Board of Education, *Journal of the School Board for the Boroughs of Manhattan and The Bronx,* 1897, p. 1190.

[23] New York City Board of Education, *Journal,* 1897, p. 1191.

[24] A *Tribune* article referred to it as the "Rogers property." See "A Model High School Building," *New York Daily Tribune,* 4 December 1898, p. 4; *The Morris Annual,* 1920, discusses the Roger's estate on p. 42. In McNamara's *History in Asphalt,* the Roger's estate is described as quite extensive on Boston Road before Jackson Avenue cut through. It consisted of barns, stables, orchards and gardens, and a large mansion, which stood on the future site of Morris High School. See John McNamara, *History in Asphalt: The Origin of Bronx Street and Place Names* (Bronx, New York: The Bronx County Historical Society, 1984), p. 215. After the Roger's estate was broken up, brick and stone row houses were constructed on the lots adjoining the Morris High School plot. These houses, along with the school and Trinity Episcopal Church of Morrisania (c.1874), now comprise the Morris High School Historic District. Its boundaries are east of Boston Road, including Jackson and Forest Avenues between Home Street and 166th Street. See New York City Landmarks Preservation Commission, *Morris High School Historic District Designation Report,* December 21, 1982, LP-1258, pp. 3, 5; Gary Hermalyn and Robert Kornfeld, *Landmarks of The Bronx* (Bronx, New York: The Bronx County Historical Society, 1990), p. 31.

[25] New York City Board of Education, *Journal,* 1897, pp. 1350-1352.

[26] New York City Board of Education, *Journal of the School Board for the Boroughs of Manhattan and The Bronx,* 1899, p. 124.

[27]New York City Board of Education, *Journal,* 1900, p. 100. It is interesting to note that in February, 1899, the Committee on Sites and Buildings reported the need for iron railings around school buildings to prevent defacement of the stonework. They recommended that all new buildings be so protected, and the motion was so approved. See New York City Board of Education, *Journal of the School Board for the Boroughs of Manhattan and The Bronx,* 1899, p. 196.

[28]New York City Board of Education, *Journal,* 1898, p. 42.

[29]New York City Board of Education, *Journal,* 1899, pp. 76-77.

[30]"A Model High School Building," p. 4.

[31]*Ibid.*

[32]New York City Board of Education, *Journal,* 1900, p. 139.

[33]*Ibid.*, pp. 1653, 1680-1681.

[34]New York City Board of Education, *Journal,* 1901, pp. 84, 383.

[35]*The Morris Annual,* 1905, p. 18.

[36]The Superintendent of Buildings prepared drawings and specifications for new buildings, handled bids and contracts and supervised construction. Frank Rollins, "School Administration in Municipal Government," Ph.D. Dissertation, Columbia University, 1902, pp. 53, 54.

[37]"A Model High School Building," p. 4.

[38]NYC, LPC, LP 1258, p. 5.

[39]New York City Department of Education, *Annual Report,* 1902, p. 189.

[40]The first example using the Collegiate Gothic architectural style is found in Snyder's Public School 31, the 144th Street and Mott Avenue annex of the Mixed High School. Constructed 1897-1899, it represents an important step in New York City's public school architecture. A central entrance tower, gabled bays, arched doorways, and other gothic details were further developed on a larger scale in Morris and Curtis (Staten Island), Flushing (Queens), Erasmus Hall (Brooklyn), and DeWitt Clinton High Schools. New York City Landmarks Preservation Commission, "P.S. 31 Report," July 15, 1986; LP-1435, p. 1.

[41]G.W. Wharton, "High School Architecture in the City of New York," *School Review* 2 (June, 1903): 459. "Renovating a 1902 Novelty" *New York Times,* 19 September 1993, C/WR p. 7.

[42]For a discussion of the rapid development of high school architecture between 1874 and 1903, see William Hatch, "The Modern School Building," *School Review* 2 (June, 1903): 509-520.

[43]John Beverly Robinson, "The School Buildings of New York," *Architectural Record,* 7 (January-March, 1894): 371-372.

[44]Felix Clay, *Modern School Buildings,* (New York: Charles Scribner's Sons, 1903), p. v.

[45]Edmund March Wheelwright, *School Architecture: A General Treatise for the Use of Architects and Others* (Boston: Rogers & Manson, 1901), pp. 211, 187.

[46]New York City Board of Education, *New York City School Buildings, 1805-1956.* Special Collections, Milbank Memorial Library, Teachers College, Columbia University, New York, p. 32.

[47]*Ibid.*

[48]*Ibid.*

[49]A. D. F. Hamlin, C.B.J. Snyder, *et al., Modern School Houses* (New York: Swetland Publishing Co., 1910), p. 48.

[50]*Ibid.*, p. 32

[51]U.S. Commissioner of Education, *Annual Report* 1904-05, Washington, D.C., U.S. Government Printing Office, p. 1911.

[52]Hamlin, Snyder, p. 32.

[53]"A Modern High School Building," p. 4.

[54]New York City Department of Education, *Annual Report,* 1902, pp. 189-190.

[55]Palmer, p. 308.

[56]*Ibid.*, p. 190.

[57]*Ibid.*, pp. 190-191.

[58]*Ibid.*

[59]*Ibid.*

[60]The new Wadleigh High School building was opened on September 17, 1902. Palmer, pp. 307-308. The DeWitt Clinton High School building was occupied on February 19, 1906. New York City Building Board of Education Records Cards, Special Collections, Teachers College Series IV H3f. New York City School Buildings.

[61]New York City Department of Education, *Annual Report,* 1902, p. 188.

[62]See photographs for drawings of the school with and without the tower.

[63]New York City Department of Education, *Annual Report,* 1902, pp. 188-189.

[64]*Ibid.,* p. 188.

[65]*Ibid.,* p. 189.

[66]*The Morris Annual,* 1922, p. 97.

[67]"The Cost of High Schools," *New York Times,* 30 March 1901, p. 9.

[68]To make his point, Snyder prepared a schedule to show the comparison of the costs of New York City high schools with those of other cities. See Table 4.

[69]"The Cost of High Schools."

[70]The school desks were bought through the Superintendent of State Prisons. The right to manufacture the desks was obtained by that department through the purchase of patterns and the payment of royalties to the school furniture manufacturers. The first batch, however, was unsatisfactory and was returned. New York City Board of Education, *Journal,* 1904, p. 137.

[71]See Table 5 "Accounting of Costs of Construction and Furniture for Morris High School."

[72]New York City Board of Education, *Journal,* 1904, p. 137.

[73]*The Morris Annual,* 1905, p. 19.

[74]"Morris High School Dedicated," *New York Daily Tribune,* 11 June 1904, p. 9.

[75]*The Morris Annual,* 1905, p. 17.

[76]"Half-Million Dollar High School Dedicated," *New York Times,* 11 June 1904, p. 6.

[77]"Morris High School Dedicated," p. 9.

[78]"Half-Million Dollar High School Dedicated," p. 6.

[79]*The Morris Annual,* 1905, pp. 20-21.

[80]New York City Department of Education, *Annual Report,* 1898, p. 64. New York City Department of Education, *Annual Report of the City Superintendent,* 1904, p. 57.

[81]"History of Morris High School: Establishment and Building," c. 1960. The Bronx County Historical Society Research Library, Bronx, New York. See Table 6 listing the opening dates for the New York City High Schools through 1942.

TABLE 4

THE COSTS OF BUILDING HIGH SCHOOLS IN 1901

PLACE	BUILDING COSTS	NUMBER OF PUPILS	NUMBER OF PUPILS IN CLASSROOM	COST PER PUPIL
Springfield High	$340,000	650	20	$533
Boston, Dorchester High	300,000	630	42	478
East Boston High	278,000	504	42	552
South Boston High	310,000	672	42	461
New York, 48 classroom building used as High School	369,900	1,500	35	237
Estimated cost of new Girls High School complete	600,000	2,571	35	233

SOURCE: "The Cost of High Schools," *New York Times*, 30 March 1901, p. 9.

TABLE 5

ACCOUNTING OF COSTS OF BUILDING AND FURNISHING MORRIS HIGH SCHOOL

WORK	CONTRACTORS	AMOUNT
General Construction	Louis Wechsler	$469,383.00
Heating/ventilating	United Heating Co.	49,670.60
Sanitary	James Fay	35,545.00
Electric	Frederick Pearce	28,886.00
Fire alarm connection	Commercial Construction Co.	676.00
Telephone system	Frederick Pearce	2,282.00
Grates	Supt. of State Prisons	449.16
Furniture:		
#1. clocks, couches, mirrors, linoleum, shades, tables, typewriter desks, chairs, cabinets, cases, etc.	The Manhattan Supply Co.	8,295.00
#2. library tables, cases, laboratory tables, shelving, cabinets, museum fittings and cases, etc.	C. H. Browne	5,469.00
#3. slate blackboards	Louis Gluck	5,370.00
#4. auditorium seats, chairs, etc.	American School Furniture Co.	5,940.00
#5. teachers' desks, chairs, adjustable desks and seats, etc.	Supt. of State Prisons	8,316.00
Electric elevators	D. H. Darrin Co.	9,000.00
Gym fittings and	Narragansett Machine Co.	10,190.00
locker ventilating	Narragansett Machine Co.	3,400.00
system	Thomas McKeown	690.00
Electric pump	Frederick Pearce	715.00
Alterations for organ	William Werner	1,364.00
Case and pipe organ	W. W. Kimball Co.	6,925.00

Total: $656,565.86

SOURCE: Morris High School: Accounting of costs of buildings and furnishing, 1904, *Building History*, (Board of Education Archives: Special Collections, Milbank Memorial Library, Teachers College, Columbia University, New York).

TABLE 6

OPENING DATES OF NEW YORK CITY HIGH SCHOOLS UP TO 1942
(Alphabetical Listing)

BRONX	DATE OF FIRST SESSION	MANHATTAN	DATE OF FIRST SESSION
Christopher Columbus	Feb. 1, 1939	Benjamin Franklin	Sept. 10, 1934
DeWitt Clinton		George Washington	Feb. 2, 1920
(Originally in Manhattan)	Sept. 13, 1897	Haaren	Sept. 13, 1920
Evander Childs	Sept. 8, 1913	H. S. of Commerce	Sept. 8, 1902
H. S. of Science	Sept. 19, 1938	H. S. of Music & Art	Feb. 1, 1936
James Monroe	Sept. 14, 1925	Julia Richman	Sept. 8, 1913
Morris	Sept. 13, 1897	Seward Park	Feb. 1, 1923
Theodore Roosevelt	Feb. 4, 1918	Straubenmuller Textile	July 6, 1921
Walton	Feb. 1, 1923	Stuyvesant	Sept. 12, 1904
William H. Taft	Feb. 3, 1941	Wadleigh	Sept. 13, 1897
		Washington Irving	Sept. 8, 1902

BROOKLYN		
Abraham Lincoln	Sept. 8, 1930	QUEENS
Alexander Hamilton	Oct. 9, 1899	
Bay Ridge	Feb. 1, 1912	Andrew Jackson	May 10, 1937
Boys	Jan. 5, 1878	Bayside	Feb. 2, 1936
Brooklyn Technical	Sept. 6, 1922	Far Rockaway	Feb. 1, 1929
Bushwick	Sept. 12, 1910	Flushing	May 15, 1875
Eastern District	Feb. 1, 1900	Forest Hills	Feb. 8, 1941
Erasmus Hall	Sept. 14, 1896	Grover Cleveland	Sept. 22, 1931
(Incorporated Aug. 24, 1787,		Jamaica	Dec. 14, 1892
as a private academy.)		John Adams	Sept. 13, 1937
Fort Hamilton	Sept. 8, 1941	Long Island City	Sept. 9, 1939
Franklin K. Lane	Sept. 1923	Newtown	Sept. 9, 1900
Girls	Jan. 5, 1878	Richmond Hill	Feb. 23, 1909
Girls Commercial	Feb. 2, 1920	William Cullen Bryant	Mar. 6, 1889
James Madison	Sept. 14, 1925	
Lafayette	Mar. 23, 1939	RICHMOND
Manual Training	Nov. 14, 1893	
Midwood	Feb. 3, 1941	Curtis	Feb. 11, 1904
New Utrecht	Sept. 13, 1915	New Dorp	Sept. 14, 1936
Samuel J. Tilden	Feb. 3, 1930	Fort Richmond	Sept. 12, 1927
Thomas Jefferson	Sept. 8, 1924	Tottenville	Oct. 5, 1898

OPENING DATES OF VOCATIONAL SCHOOLS

Bronx Vocational H.S., Boys	Oct. 3, 1921	Manhattan H.S.,	
Brooklyn Auto Trade	Oct. 1, 1923	Women's Garment Trade	Sept. 12, 1910
Brooklyn H.S. for		Manhattan Aviation Trade	Sept. 24, 1925
Specialty Trades	Sept. 14, 1925	McKee Vocational H.S.	April 12, 1920
Brooklyn H.S. for Homemaking	Sept. 1, 1925	Metropolitan Vocational H.S.	Feb. 1, 1917
Brooklyn H.S.,		Murray Hill H.S.,	
Women's Garment Trades	Sept. 10, 1930	Building Trades	Mar. 31, 1914
Brooklyn Metal Trade	June 21, 1915	Needle Trades	Feb. 16, 1926
Brooklyn Vocational*	May 24, 1919	New York Printing	May 30, 1925
Central Commercial H.S.	May 13, 1925	New York Vocational	
Chelsea Vocational H.S.	Feb. 1, 1920	H.S. for Boys	Sept. 1909
East New York Vocational H.S.	May 19, 1922	Queens Vocational H.S.	Sept. 13, 1920
Food Trades	Sept. 1938	Samuel Gompers Vocational H.S.	Sept. 1935
Industrial Art	Feb. 13, 1935	Woodrow Wilson Vocational H.S.	Feb. 1, 1942
Jamaica Vocational H.S.	April 2, 1925	Yorkville Women's Service Trade	Sept. 8, 1926
Jane Addams Vocational H.S.	Feb. 21, 1928		

Brooklyn Vocational School was opened May 24, 1919. It was discontinued in 1925 and later made two organizations, the Brooklyn High School for Homemaking and High School for Specialty Trades.

SOURCE: *100th Anniversary of the Board of Education in New York City April 13-20* (Published by The New York Times on the occasion of the 100th Anniversary of the Board of Education of the City of New York, Booklet No. 3., 1942), pp. 25,26.

THE FIRST

PRINCIPAL

Dr. Edward J. Goodwin

T THE TIME the New York City Board of Education established the three original public high schools, they also passed a resolution requiring that the new high schools be run by people with previous experience as high school principals. As a result, no one who was already working in the city's schools was eligible for the high school principal jobs, since there were as yet no high schools in the city. This angered both teachers and principals, who, during their battle against the change in the school law, had anticipated such problems from the reformers.

Residents of the North Side, the Morris High School area, petitioned the Board of Education to rescind the requirement.[1] Evander Childs, then principal of Grammar School 90, was the first nominee for the principalship of Morris. Childs' name, however, was withdrawn, apparently because he had never been the head of a high school.[2] No other reason for the objection to Evander Childs was found. In fact, his name would be given to the second high school established in The Bronx, Evander Childs High School, in 1913.[3]

The demand for experience on the part of the new principals was not arbitrary. The Board of Education was anxious to insure the professionalism of the new high schools, as well as that of the whole school system. It was generally believed that special talents were needed to run a high school. A 1900 article in *School Review* titled "The Equipment of the High School Principal" asserted that the training of a high school principal must produce a man who is a "specialist of specialities." In other words, he must be grounded in the general culture. Further it was clear that: "The daily problems of the principal of a large school are, to some degree comparable to those of the executives of the higher institutions."[4] Rather than a narrowly trained scholar in the classics or science, the high school principal required very broad "intellectual equipment," and perhaps more importantly, needed to be an experienced administrator.[5]

The superintendents of the Board of Education conducted a nationwide search to select the best high school principals they could find for the new positions. In spite of the uproar caused by the Board's standards, they did succeed in recruiting highly professional and experienced individuals to lead the high schools.[6] This was certainly an important ingredient in the immediate success of the new schools. According to Frank Rollins, a teacher at Morris High School who went on to become the first principal of Stuyvesant and Bushwick High Schools: "Whatever may be the formal rule or regulation of the Board of Education, the principal is in fact the administrative and pedagogical head of the school. From the principal more than from any other one person the school takes its character and derives its success or failure."[7]

Edward J. Goodwin was chosen by the Board of Education to be the first principal of Morris High School.[8] Approximately forty-five years old at the time of his appointment, Goodwin was a native of Maine who graduated at the top of his class from Bates College in 1872. After graduation he served as principal in four New England high schools: in Farmington, New Hampshire, from 1872-81; Portsmouth, New Hampshire, from 1881-84; Nashua, New Hampshire, from 1884-87; and Newton, Massachusetts, from 1887-1897.[9]

Newton High School in Massachusetts was well known for its educational innovations. At Newton, a school of about six hundred students, there were four courses of study, which included the general, the classical, the scientific, and the commercial courses. These programs were very much like the first courses of study at Morris High School. The *New York Daily Tribune* reported that: "Boys taking the classical course have in the last ten years gone to Harvard, Yale, Amherst, Williams, Dartmouth, Tufts, and other colleges, and girls have been sent to Wellesley, Vassar, Radcliffe, Smith and Boston University. Not a single applicant for admission to college has been refused from the Newton High School since Mr. Goodwin became its principal."[10]

Mr. Goodwin also lectured quite frequently at his *alma mater* in their pedagogical courses and at other New England schools. One lecture titled *Religion in the Public Schools* given on March 17, 1891, at Bates College, dealt with moral culture as a necessary ingredient for the development of character and true citizenry.[11]

Dr. Goodwin never ceased being a student while he was principal and teacher in the New England high schools as he took courses at Harvard Summer School and at the Massachusetts Institute of Technology. He also wrote many valuable articles for professional periodicals including: For the *School Review* of Chicago, "The Curriculum of a Small High School;" "The

Edward Jasper Goodwin, first Principal of Morris High School, c. 1905.

The Bronx County Historical Society Research Library.

Difficulties and Discouragements in the Early Stages of the Latin Course;" and "Results in the Prussian Gymnasium." For the *Educational Review* (New York City) he wrote: "Electives in the High School; Electives in Elementary Schools;" "Some Characteristics of Prussian Schools;" "The Objections to the Shorter College Course;" "A Comparison of College Entrance Examinations;" and "Some Characteristics of the New York City High School." For the *Bates Student* [Journal] he wrote "Methods of Instruction in Physical Science."

The *Bulletin* of Bates College, which closely followed Goodwin's entire career, described him as an individual whose educational theory and practice ranks him second to no other man in the country. He was considered a great organizer and administrator: "His success as the Principal of the high school at Newton, Mass., won for him national reputation; and when in 1897 public high schools were first established in New York City, Mr. Goodwin was one of the three men selected to direct the work. His school became the largest in the city, numbering several thousand pupils under the instruction of sixty or more teachers. It was one of the largest public schools in the world and by common consent one of the best."[12]

Described as a tall man with a large lean frame, he was ". . . erect, with a high forehead made noticeable by partial baldness, clean shaven, with an unusually strong and determined mouth and chin. His eyes were of a keen and piercing blue, very direct and set well back under rather bushy eyebrows."[13]

A quick and energetic man, "his whole manner decisive and emphatic," Goodwin was a sociable and good-humored person. He was "not urbane," however, because "he was too much in earnest, too intent on the question in hand to waste time on what seemed unessential conventionalities."[14] Goodwin did everything "with zest." He was compared with President Charles Eliot of Harvard University as they both believed in the value of science, in elective courses, and in encouraging students to discover and to follow their aptitudes.[15] Eliot and Goodwin were both fond of quoting from Dr. Thomas Arnold, of Rugby (school), that "a man was no longer fitted to be headmaster . . . when he could not come up the steps two at a time."[16]

Not a man who frequented clubs or accepted social invitations readily or who cared for money, prestige or power as such, Goodwin was a confident, unself-conscious individual. He had the sort of "manner that characterizes the head of a great business." He was remembered as a man who would have been successful in any field he entered.[17] In 1895 he received a doctor of letters from Bates College, for "his conspicuous work in the field of secondary education."[18]

Goodwin was a member of the College Entrance Board, the New York State Examination Board, the Association of Colleges and Secondary

Edward Jasper Goodwin at his
graduation from Bates College in 1872.

Bates College.

Schools of the Middle States, and he was vice president of the Headmasters Association in 1898 and 1901, and became president of that association in 1917.[19]

Early on, Goodwin was in the mainstream of educational reform. He authored an article on electives in the high school for *Educational Review* in February 1893, that produced such a reaction to his ideas that the editors commented on it in a glowing editorial.[20]

In 1894-1895, Goodwin took a leave of absence for eight months to study the Prussian (German Empire) school system, which had been praised by some American educators. He visited several schools and, in December, 1896 reported his findings in an *Educational Review* article.[21] The schools he described were plain and devoid of ornaments, with very orderly and subdued students. Goodwin admired some of the Prussian practices, but criticized others. He praised the physical educational classes and the frequent recesses for physical activity throughout the school day. The children's respect for the teachers impressed him as well. On the teaching of religion in the schools, which was the Prussian practice, however, Goodwin was somewhat ambiguous. He indicated that it was ". . . worthy of note that the responsibility of teaching religion to the children is put upon the schools instead of being assumed by the Church, or altogether neglected."[22]

Initially the German children's reserved and disciplined manner made an impact on Goodwin. He observed that this was characteristic of the Germans generally. He saw that: "The people on the streets were as quiet, orderly, and undemonstrative as the children in the schools."[23] Goodwin's conclusion was: "Discipline is a national characteristic. Its roots strike deep into the soil of the social and political institutions of the country, and these in turn are the outgrowth of royal authority and demand submission and conformity."[24]

Goodwin criticized some of the incentives in the Prussian system, which encouraged disciplined, submissive, and studious students. Parents had to pay an annual tuition fee, which Goodwin felt applied pressure to be good in school. If the student did not succeed in the competitive gymnasium by the time he was twenty years old, he had to do a year of military service. In addition, there was no profession or "career of honor" open to a person who did not graduate from the gymnasium. The incentive was to succeed in the gymnasium.[25]

There was also system-wide discrimination in Prussia against females. Their high school education ended at sixteen years of age, and the female schools were less rigorous and demanding than those of the males. Goodwin was critical of this practice, citing how different the situation was in the United States. "In the higher education of girls there is a marvelous difference between the schools of Prussia and those of the United States. With the exception of a private school of about forty girls, recently established under the patronage of the Empress Victoria, there is no school in Berlin where a girl may study Latin or Greek, or take what we call advanced high school courses in mathematics and science."[26]

On the other hand, Goodwin felt that the teachers in the Prussian system were much more competent, educated and mature compared to the American teachers. The reason behind this, he felt, was that the teachers were highly respected in Germany and rewarded for their services. They had to fulfill rigorous requirements to enter the teaching force, which included graduation from both the gymnasium and the university. In addition, they had to have two years of teaching experience without pay before they could be certified. But after receiving certification, they were given a position for life, a good salary, and a generous pension program.[27]

Not only were the Prussian teachers "men of maturity, scholarship and skill," according to Goodwin, but they worked a longer school day and week than American teachers. Goodwin felt that this longer educational time was a great advantage in that it allowed for additional guidance by the teacher, and thus helped the students learn more quickly. Much of the work the American student did as homework was done in the Prussian classroom. Goodwin saw this as a two-edged sword. He felt that the German students knew more subject matter from books, but the American students, because they worked alone more, were "more independent in their thinking, more self-reliant in their methods of work," and had "unequalled power in getting usable information from books."[28]

The German schools were more proficient in their language instruction and taught languages quite early in the schools, a practice which Goodwin praised. He found, however, that their science instruction was quite lacking and "in no case did their methods of instruction compare favorably with ours."[29] Indeed, he felt that the Germans were using antiquated methods of science instruction with no direct student involvement in experiments.[30] Despite some superior scholarship, Goodwin felt that it was hard to believe that the Prussian system was "altogether wise and beneficent." He discussed the advantage of the American system over the Prussian one:

> It was a favorite saying of President Mark Hopkins that moral character is conditional upon the privilege of making a free choice. If this be true, and if the safety of our republic and the perpetuity of its institutions be dependent upon the moral power of its citizens, little is to be gained for the country's good from the discipline of a school in which boys obey instinctively or from the force of habits which they have no part in forming. Men trained in such a way make ideal soldiers, but not the best citizens.[31]

Shortly after his return from the Prussian tour, Goodwin was called upon to help develop the plans for the proposed high schools in New York.[32] He was credited with having developed the high school curriculum.[33]

Goodwin's philosophy was that ". . . education was an end in itself and a process of actual living here and now, and that the motivation of study or of any kind of child activity must not only be of interest, but the particular kind of interest that rises from the connection of the study or activity with the child's daily life."[34] He advocated the project method and was particularly interested in the use of exhibits as a teaching and learning tool. Not only did exhibits provide an enjoyable learning experience for students, but they also were instructive for visitors, especially the parents. Goodwin cited the example of a botanical exhibit in which the students acted as interpretive guides for visitors to their experiments which included ". . . plants growing under a variety of conditions, magnified cross-sections revealing structure, tests for starch and sugar in foods, cultures, fermentations, distillations, yeast plants and bacteria under the compound microscope, etc., etc."[35] Goodwin felt that the "far-reaching" results of such exhibits "outweighed all its cost in time and effort."[36]

The student project approach was also clear in the development of *The Morris Annual* that first appeared in 1905. This ninety-six page journal, fully illustrated, with original poetry and articles, was apparently the work of the student editors, who were helped by the faculty. In addition, the many extra curricular programs at Morris, including an original class play, and activities by several literary societies, attest to the emphasis on personal involvement outside the classroom. The intellectual training of the high school student should, Goodwin claimed, "enable him to master the arts of inter-communication and give him the conventional view of the world."[37]

Goodwin saw the true goals of high school as social and intellectual development rather than solely the accumulation of information.

> As the student emerges from the school and takes up the duties of life, he more and more loses his hold upon the facts of geography, history, language, mathematics, and science which have been taught him with so much solicitude; but the intellectual training which he gets from study, and the ideals of character and conduct, the outlook upon life – its duties and opportunities – which he gets from the teacher, are permanent acquisitions which may contribute more toward his ultimate success and service-ableness than any knowledge he has obtained from his school-books.[38]

For this reason, Goodwin believed that teachers needed to be "cultured, broadminded and socially responsive." Further, the teachers needed to be involved in the community and home life of the students so they did not lose "the true vision of education" and thus "believe that the acquisition of knowledge is the real purpose of the school."[39] High school teachers could not, however, be expected to be sociologists. Such expertise was for Goodwin in the realm of higher education "whose business it is to define the ends of education and to train teachers to accomplish them."[40]

An advocate of teachers' colleges, Goodwin described the mission of such schools in the following way:

> It cannot be amiss to say that it is the privilege and the duty of the university to establish such programmes of study as shall give their students who intend to become teachers not only a just and comprehensive view of the actual condition and needs of our heterogeneous population, but also of the educative means and processes by which the school may be better adapted to promote the physical, intellectual, and moral vigor of the children and so to transform them into successful bread-winners and good citizens.[41]

Goodwin noted that, in New York State, both Columbia and Syracuse Universities had established colleges for teachers while twelve other colleges maintained teacher training departments.[42]

The role of public education, according to Goodwin, was "gradually changing and enlarging," and it was clear that ". . . in our large centers of population the school has come to be our chief reliance for welding together our racially mixed population and for promoting ideas of civic duty and social development."[43] Goodwin saw that certain changes in society made new demands on the schools and stated: "Deplore it as we may, the church no longer occupies the place of commanding influence which it once held, and, under our changed industrial conditions, the influence of the home, as an educative agency, has been seriously impaired."[44] As a consequence the school had to take up the slack resulting in increased demand for training students to be wage earners. Goodwin felt that secondary schools were focusing too much on a liberal education and those students who aspired to go to college, and "too little upon those who must be relied upon to promote the nation's mechanical, industrial, and commercial activities." Most of the children who left high school without graduating belonged to the wage earning class. Goodwin argued that the system of secondary education was "radically defective" since it did not provide for wage earners. He felt the burden was on the teachers who had to ". . . enlarge their vision of education, and help adapt the activities and teaching of the school to the actual needs of our children and our industries."[45]

On the other hand, Goodwin supported the needs of his students who wished to go on to college. He was involved in setting up the College Entrance Examination Board, known as the CEEB.[46] In a 1903 article he discussed the results of a study he conducted comparing the standardized CEEB exams with those of specific colleges. He found the CEEB exams more comprehensive and was particularly pleased that they provided a uniform and scientific method of examining students. A long sought educational reform, the CEEB simplified the task of preparing students for college exams. Instead of working with individual students to help them pass a test at the college of their choice, the whole school could be directed according to the CEEB's syllabi.[47]

Goodwin felt that another means of aiding his students was through their parents. It was his opinion that it was the duty of the principal to be open to the parents from whom he "may often get much needed and valuable information about his own school." Goodwin followed that practice by setting aside an hour or more a week for private conferences with parents. He reported that: "As an outcome of these conferences, which increased in number and length from year to year, perplexing cases of discipline were amicably settled, misunderstandings were cleared up, elective studies were adopted to the proposed destination of students, and, best of all, the school thereby obtained a stronger hold upon the community's confidence and co-operation."[48]

Strongly in favor of professional centralized control of the schools, Goodwin was critical of local school board control, as it was administratively inefficient and subject to political influence. Nevertheless, he believed that strong parents' associations were "the most effective and permanent means of promoting close relationship and sympathy between the school and the home," a tie that could only help the student. In Goodwin's view these parents' organizations were a wave of the future as they were growing rapidly in large cities and were valuable in developing a sense of responsibility in parents, especially from the neighborhoods of the poor.[49]

With his deep concerns and obvious dedication, Goodwin was an immensely popular figure with both faculty and students. On the 25th anniversary of the school, John Denbigh recalled: "Dr. Goodwin was an inspiring leader; he quickly gained the confidence and respect of the whole Board of Education and was – more than any other one man – responsible for the thorough foundation upon which the structure of public secondary education was laid in the City of New York."[50]

Goodwin's tenure at Morris lasted until he saw the high school properly set up in its new building. In the winter of 1903-04, the New York State educational system was reorganized.[51] On May 1, 1904, Goodwin was appointed Second Assistant Commissioner of Education for secondary schools in New York State in the new and more powerful system.[52] He was now in charge of the state secondary school system and, according to State Commissioner of Education Andrew Draper, brought "wide reading, deep thinking and ample experience" to the position.[53]

When Goodwin left Morris High School the students reported: "Coming as it did when the school was getting used to its new home, his loss would have been irreparable. So, although he accepted the appointment, Dr. Goodwin stayed with us more or less until June, when it was with great sorrow we parted with him."[54] The dedication ceremonies for the new Morris High School building in June of 1904 "were made an occasion for paying him [Goodwin] a high tribute for his services as a principal during the last seven [eight] years."[55]

City Superintendent Maxwell would write in his 1904 *Annual Superintendent's Report:*

> No man has done more to bring about the development of our city high schools to their present efficiency than Dr. Goodwin. In transferring his wide experience, his sound scholarship, and his rare organizing ability to the special service of the State, he has not lost his interest in our city schools. In his present wide sphere of influence he will do much to elevate the high schools not only of this State but of this City, where his counsel and encouragement will always be welcome.[56]

On June 20, 1904, the Chairman of the Board of Superintendents nominated John H. Denbigh as the new principal of Morris High School, subject to his obtaining the necessary license. The Board of Education's Committee on High Schools and Training Schools agreed and submitted the nomination to the Board of Education for approval, which it gave on July 11, 1904.[57] Denbigh, who was in charge of the mathematics department at Morris High School at the time of his appointment, had not previously served as a high school principal.[58]

Mr. John Denbigh was the head of the Mathematics department
on the original faculty. He became First Assistant, and in 1904
was appointed second Principal of Morris High School.

The Bronx County Historical Society Research Library.

John Denbigh had quite a different background from Edward Goodwin. His biography in *The Morris Annual* of 1905 depicted him as an English-born, naturalized American citizen, who attended Bath College and later Brasenose College, Oxford where he received honors in mathematics and athletics. Denbigh's professional career entailed four years as a head housemaster in a large boarding school called Rosall, "one of the more modern of the English Public Schools of the Rugby and Marlborough type."[59] After teaching in England for four years, Denbigh came to this country in 1895, and became assistant master at the Trinity School for Boys in New York City. Goodwin brought him on as the head of the mathematics department at Morris High School when the school opened in 1897.

Although he was Goodwin's choice for the position of principal of Morris High School and later his successor at Packer Collegiate Institute, Denbigh seems to have been quite the opposite in personality.[60]

During Denbigh's tenure as principal, Edward Goodwin was warmly remembered. The first *Morris Annual* in 1905 was dedicated to Dr. Goodwin with the following comments:

To Dr. Edward J. Goodwin,
Second Assistant Commissioner of Education
of the State of New York
Admired for his Learning
Honored for his Justice
Loved for his Kindness
This Book is Dedicated by the Students of
The Morris High School,
once his pupils, always his friends[61]

On June 28, 1905, Dr. Goodwin was conferred his second honorary doctorate of letters, by Amherst College. The presentation stated that Dr. Goodwin was "Superintendent of the Department of High Schools in the State of New York, an inspiring teacher, a broad and discerning organizer, recognized in academic circles as a first authority on secondary education."[62]

Edward Jasper Goodwin, educator, died at the age of eighty-two on April 29, 1931.[63] On May 29, 1931, twenty-five hundred students, teachers, alumni and former members of the faculty of Morris High School attended memorial exercises for Dr. Goodwin, which were held in the school auditorium. He is buried in Dunstan Cemetery in Scarborough, Maine.[64]

Edward Goodwin put into practice the educational reforms of his time through his imprint on the curriculum for the new high schools. A noted molder and leader of teachers, he gathered about his side an experienced and caring faculty. Nearly 90 percent of that faculty had a college degree, an unheard of figure at the turn of the twentieth century when the average United States high school faculty had less than 50 percent.[65] At least five of the Morris teachers became principals in seven high schools.[66] In addition, many of Goodwin's hand-picked faculty by 1905 were spreading out to other schools and projects.[67] Under Dr. Goodwin's leadership Morris High School became an exemplar for public secondary education.

DEDICATION
OF THE
NEW BUILDING
OF THE
MORRIS
HIGH SCHOOL
JUNE 10
1904

Program for the Dedication
of the New Building
on June 10, 1904.

Morris High School Collection.
The Bronx County Historical Society
Research Library.

Order of Exercises

Edward J. Goodwin,

Principal of the School

The Presiding Officer

Prayer . The Reverend John D. Roach

Chorus . . . . High School Students

"Larghetto" : Beethoven

Addresses

The Honorable Richard H. Adams

Chairman of the Committee on Buildings

The Honorable Henry A. Rogers

President of the Board of Education

The Honorable Frank L. Babbott

Chairman of the Committee on High Schools

High School Orchestra

"Romance sans Paroles" : L. Gregh

Order of Exercises

Address

The Honorable George B. McClellan

Mayor of the City of New York

Chorus . . . . High School Students

"Berceuse" : Hadley

Addresses

Nicholas Murray Butler, LL. D.

President of Columbia University

The Honorable John H. Eustis

The Honorable Louis F. Haffen

President of the Borough of The Bronx

William H. Maxwell, LL. D.

City Superintendent of Schools

Chorus . . . . High School Students

"America"

Benediction

The Reverend Gustavus Tuckerman

Dr. Frank Rollins, c. 1906, was head of the 173rd Street annex
of Morris High School until 1904, when he became the first
Principal of Stuyvesant High School and in 1910
of Bushwick High School.

Stuyvesant High School.

Gilbert Blakely was on the original faculty
of Morris High School in the English department
until he left to become the first Principal of
Evander Childs High School, c. 1914.

Evander Childs High School and
The Bronx County Historical Society Research Library.

NOTES

[1] "Another High School Head Chosen by the Board of Education," *New York Daily Tribune*, 20 May 1897, p. 5.

[2] "New Educational Ideas," *New York Daily Tribune*, 23 May 1897, p. 3.

[3] New York City, Board of Education, Bureau of Reference, Research and Statistics, "Year of organization of high schools," 1948, Special Collections, Milbank Memorial Library, Teachers College, Columbia University, New York. See Table 6.

[4] S.O. Hartwell, "The Equipment of the High School Principal," *School Review* 9 (March, 1902): 160-166.

[5] *Ibid.*, p. 162.

[6] Herbert Shapiro, "Reorganization of the New York City Public School System, 1890-1910," Ph.D. Dissertation, Yeshiva University, 1967, p. 79.

[7] Frank Rollins, p. 73.

[8] Of the first high school principals, Dr. Goodwin, Mr. John T. Buchanan of Clinton, and Mr. John G. Wright of Wadleigh, only Dr. Goodwin is listed in *Who Was Who*, or had a *New York Times* obituary.

[9] *The Morris Annual*, 1905, p. 11. *Bates College General Catalogue*, 1864-1930 (Lewiston, Maine: Bates College, 1931) p. 38.

[10] "New Educational Ideas," p. 3.

[11] *The Bates Student*, (Lewiston, Maine: Bates College, April, 1891, 19:4), p. 103.

[12] Bates College Bulletin, (Lewiston, Maine: Bates College, May 15, 1905), pp. 23, 24.

[13] Marjorie L. Nickerson, *A Long Way Forward: The First Hundred Years of the Packer Collegiate Institute* (Brooklyn: Packer Collegiate Institute, 1945), p. 143.

[14] *Ibid.*

[15] *Ibid.*, p. 153.

[16] *Ibid.*

[17] *Ibid.*, p. 143.

[18] *Ibid.*, p. 142. "Commencement Day at Amherst" *Springfield Republican*, June 28, 1905, p. 1. Dr. Goodwin was honored as an inspiring teacher and recognized in academic circles as a first authority on secondary education.

[19] Nickerson, p. 145.

[20] Edward Goodwin, "Electives in the High School: An Experiment," *Educational Review* 5 (February, 1893): 142-152. Editorial, *Educational Review* 5 (May, 1893): 513-514.

[21] Edward J. Goodwin, "Some Characteristics of Prussian Schools," *Educational Review* 12 (December, 1896): 453-465.

[22] *Ibid.*, p 456.

[23] *Ibid.*, p. 457.

[24] *Ibid.*

[25] *Ibid.*, pp. 458-459. A gymnasium was a secondary school in the Prussian system.

[26] *Ibid.*, p. 465. *Bates Student,* December 1896, 24:10, pp. 264, 265.

[27] Goodwin, "Some Characteristics of Prussian Schools," p. 460.

[28] *Ibid.*, p. 462.

[29] *Ibid.*, p. 463.

[30] *Ibid.*

[31] *Ibid.*, p. 457.

[32] *The Morris Annual*, 1905, p. 11.

[33] "Elastic Courses of Study," *New York Daily Tribune*, 20 June 1897, p. 1.

[34] Nickerson, p. 139.

[35] Edward J. Goodwin, "The School and The Home," *School Review* 16 (May, 1908): 328.

[36] *Ibid.*

[37]*Ibid.*, p. 323.

[38]*Ibid.*, p. 321.

[39]*Ibid.*, pp. 320-321.

[40]*Ibid.*, p. 324.

[41]*Ibid.*, pp. 324-325.

[42]*Ibid.*, p. 325.

[43]*Ibid.*, p. 322.

[44]*Ibid.*

[45]*Ibid.*, pp. 322-323.

[46]According to John Denbigh, the second principal of Morris High School, probably no man, with the exception of Dr. Nicholas Murray Butler, had more to do than Dr. Goodwin with the inception of the much needed College Entrance Examination Board. Nickerson, p. 142.

[47]Edward J. Goodwin, "A Comparison of College Entrance Examinations," *Educational Review* 26 (December, 1903): 440-456.

[48]Goodwin, "The School and The Home," p. 325.

[49]*Ibid.*, pp. 326-328.

[50]*The Morris Annual,* 1922, p. 9.

[51]Until 1904, the state system was generally confused as the lines of responsibility were blurred between two agencies, the Regents and the Department of Public Instruction. The 1904 Unification Law provided for a new system that created a "unified Department of Education with the Board of Regents as the governing body and the Commissioner of Education as the Administrative Officer." The Regents were granted sole jurisdiction over the colleges, universities, professional and technical schools, libraries, museums and other agencies, and the Commissioner of Education was in charge of the elementary and secondary schools. Andrew Sloan Draper was chosen as the state's first Commissioner of Education. New York State Department of Public Instruction, *Fiftieth Annual Report of the State Superintendent,* Year ending July 31, 1903. Transmitted to the Legislature, April 15, 1904 (Albany: Oliver A. Quayle, 1904), Milbank Memorial Library, Teachers College, Columbia University, New York. See also Harlan Hoyt Horner, compiler and editor, *Education of New York State 1784-1954* (Albany: University of the State of New York, 1954), pp. 16-21.

[52]Goodwin left the state system in 1908 to become the third president of Packer Collegiate Institute. This private Brooklyn secondary school for girls of socially prominent families was founded in 1845. See Nickerson.

[53]Andrew S. Draper, "The New York Secondary School System" *Addresses by the Commissioner of Education* (Albany: New York State Education Department, 1904), p. 56.

[54]*The Morris Annual,* 1905, p. 21.

[55]"Half-Million Dollar School Dedicated," p. 6.

[56]New York City Department of Education, *Annual Report of the City Superintendent of Schools,* 1904, pp. 63-64.

[57]New York City Board of Education, *Journal,* 1904, p. 1529.

[58]*The Morris Annual,* 1905, p. 29.

[59]*Ibid.,* p. 15.

[60]Marjorie Nickerson, in her history of Packer Collegiate Institute, stated: "It is interesting that he (Denbigh) should have twice followed Dr. Goodwin. The two men had in common certain foundation stones of character and some ethical, intellectual and educational convictions. But, in background, tastes, methods of work, and temperament, they were very different." Nickerson, p. 174.

[61]*The Morris Annual,* 1905, p. 5.

[62]"Commencement Day at Amherst," p. 1.

[63]*Who Was Who 1897-1942,* Vol. I (Chicago: Marquis, 1943), p. 469.

[64]Obituary, Edward Goodwin, *New York Times,* 30 May 1931, p. 8; New York City Department of Health Death Certificate, No. 3244, 30 April 1931.

[65]John Franklin Brown, *The Training of Teachers for Secondary Schools in Germany and The United States* (New York: Macmillan Co., 1911), pp. 232-233. See Table 9 for a complete listing of Morris teachers in 1901.

⁶⁶In 1904 Dr. Frank Rollins, who had been in charge of the difficult 173rd Street Morris annex for the previous five years, assumed the principalship of the new Stuyvesant High School. Dr. Rollins was later to continue to follow in Dr. Goodwin's footsteps, when in 1908 he became the assistant state commissioner for education. Then, in 1910, Dr. Rollins became the principal of the new Bushwick High School in Brooklyn. See *The Morris Annual,* 1905, p. 29; Obituary, Frank Rollins, *New York Times,* 12 May 1920, p. 5. Later, in 1913, Gilbert Blakely, another teacher from the original faculty of Morris, became the first principal of Evander Childs High School when it was spun off from Morris. See *The Morris Annual* 1914. Erza Sampson, who was the acting principal of Newton High School when Dr. Goodwin took his Prussian tour, became the principal of the Morris Evening High School in 1905. See *The Morris Annual,* 1908, p. 11. Irving Heikes also became the Morris Evening High School principal and was on the original faculty in the mathematics department. See Interview on April 18, 1991 with Monroe Lovinger, graduate of Morris Evening High School. Neither Blakely, Heikes, Rollins, nor Denbigh had previous experience as high school principals. Clearly, the original rule that required the principal of a high school to have previous experience as the head of such a school was now abandoned. There was no discussion of why the rule was changed in the Board of Education *Journals.* It seems, however, that by this time a cadre of professional administrators, with proven abilities, had been trained within the system especially at Morris High School. For even the High School Teacher's Association of New York City organized in 1900 was run by Frank Rollins at Morris High School! See *High School Teachers Association Yearbook,* 1906-07, p. 5.

⁶⁷George J. Smith who organized the English Department in 1897 resigned in 1898 and became one of the Board of Examiners with the New York City Board of Education. William C. Waters, an inspiring Latin teacher accepted a professorship at New York University. Dr. Rollins took four Morris teachers with him to the new Stuyvesant High School. Three others joined the new Commerce High School; one teacher went to Newton, Queens, Eastern District and Orange, New Jersey high schools. *The Morris Annual,* 1905, p. 28-30. John Arent, a 1901 Morris graduate came back to the school as an English teacher from 1911-1919. In 1924 he became the principal of Curtis High School on Staten Island. *The Morris Annual,* 1923, p. 12.

THE

CURRICULUM

Original Course Of Studies: 1897

THE CURRICULUM for New York City's three new high schools was prepared with the help of the three men who were to be their principals. Edward J. Goodwin, John T. Buchanan, and John G. Wright were charged with the practical implementation of the courses of study. Their work was of great interest to New Yorkers and was lauded in a *New York Daily Tribune* article in June of 1897: "The three men selected to supervise the work of establishing schools of this rank in the metropolis are experts in secondary educational methods, and the task, which they have performed to the satisfaction of the High School Committee of the Board of Education, as well as to that of the Board of Superintendents, could scarcely have been performed by men less skilled in high school work."[1]

In preparing the curriculum the faculties of City College and Normal College were consulted. This was particularly important since one of the roles of the high schools was to serve as an "intermediate school between the elementary and the city college courses." There was some controversy over the admission of fourteen year olds to the sub-freshman year at the colleges. Students were going straight from the grammar schools into the colleges.[2] The two city colleges had not expanded in the previous twenty years and could not handle the increasing demand for education above the elementary school level. These colleges, however, did offer instruction "of both secondary and more advanced grade" to a limited number of grammar school graduates.[3]

The business community was also pressing for additional training for non-college bound students. The new high schools, therefore, were clearly to be considered the "people's college" as they originated partially in response to the demand for a more educated student who was going directly to work after high school.[4]

In response to these demands, the Committee on High Schools formulated a general plan for the new curriculum that was intended to:

1. Reduce the work of the highest grade of the Grammar Schools so that it can be completed in six months, and start the high school work at the beginning of the eighth year of school.
2. Take in work now done in the present "Supplementary grade."
3. Take in the work now done in the sub-freshman classes, and in part that done in the freshman classes of the two city colleges.[5]

According to the 1897 *Journal of the Board of Education:* "This plan contemplates the ultimate absorption of the sub-freshman or introductory classes of the two colleges into the high schools, but this is to be accomplished gradually, and it is believed, without causing any undesirable disturbance in the work of those institutions."[6] Four different courses of study were developed for the three new high schools.[7] These included a general course, a City/Normal College course, a commercial course, and a classical course.

The general course of study, according to the 1898 Department of Education brochure furnished to those pupils who desired admittance to the three public high schools was ". . . designed to meet the demands of those boys and girls whose school life is to end with the secondary school. It seems desirable, therefore, that it should recognize two classes of subjects, one including those deemed essential in every well ordered system of secondary education, the other comprising a large list of electives so grouped as to constitute a curriculum that shall be both elastic and comprehensive."[8]

The three principals who were helping design the courses of study felt that the general course could be arranged to "suit individual tastes and preferences because of the large number of electives in the last two years." They reported that "the great feature of this course of study is its elasticity."[9]

The general course reflected many of the recommendations of the National Education Association (NEA) Committee of Ten for its three non-classical programs, *i.e.* Latin-scientific, modern languages, and English. But they were offered by the general course in a way that allowed the student to select many subjects. The required courses were four years of English, history, music, drawing, and physical training; two years of mathematics and science; and one year of civics. All foreign languages were elective, and a student could choose additional studies in mathematics, history, English, and the sciences.

The elective courses were only run if there were twenty-five students for first year courses, twenty for second year courses, fifteen for third year courses, and ten for fourth year courses. In addition, girls were expected to take "sewing once a week for the first year, and cooking once a fortnight for the second year."[10]

The City College and Normal College preparatory course, on the other hand, was ". . . designed to meet the requirements of admission to the College of the City of New York (for boys) and the Normal College (for girls)."[11] In the 1901 Department of Education circular, this course was also specified as preparatory for the training school for teachers.[12] This was a three-year program, and was adapted from the general course to fit the needs and the requirements of those students who wished to prepare for the city's colleges.

The commercial course was made up of two classes of subjects. "The first class is identical with the required subjects of the general course and is designed to furnish the student with a substantial foundation of general training; the second class is intended to supply the pupil with such technical knowledge of bookkeeping, commercial law, etc., as will enable him to meet the demands of ordinary business life."[13] Because they were in the "commercial metropolis of the country," the principals regarded the commercial course to be of special importance. They designed it ". . . to give those going into business a sound education – something different entirely from what is given in the so-called business colleges."[14] The commercial course required: four years of English, history, music, physical training, and a modern language; three years of drawing; two years of mathematics and science; and one year of civics. The rest of the demanding schedule was devoted to commercial subjects with no electives.

The classical course was arranged so that students would be able to gain admission to the major colleges in the country.[15] This program was basically what the NEA Committee of Ten recommended for its classical program. The course required four years of English, Latin, and physical training, three years of history and either the Greek, French or German language. The mathematics requirements were algebra in the first and third years, and geometry in the second and fourth years. The science requirements were physiology in the first year and physics or chemistry in the fourth year.

The curriculum originally used in Morris High School, therefore, represented a kind of tracking system. College-bound students received a specifically designed program to get them to their destination. There was even a different program for students attempting to pursue study in the city's colleges. Students not college-bound were offered two separate, but nonetheless rigorous, plans.

In order to gain admission to Morris High School, or any of the public high schools in New York City, a pupil had to provide a certificate from their grammar school principal. There was, in addition, a special form that grammar school principals submitted to the district superintendent evaluating each student's performance in the various subjects and recommending whether a diploma of graduation should or should not be awarded.[16]

It seems, however, that these very detailed forms emphasizing performance were filed in the district superintendent's office, rather than being used by the high schools to assess the attainments and abilities of the incoming freshmen from the grammar schools. Apparently there was no consultation between the high schools and the elementary schools concerning their common students. For entrance to the high schools, only the grammar school principal's certification was required.[17] Once in the high school, then, the students usually started out without a history, except for the name of the school they came from and the certification of the grammar school principal. It was regrettable that the grammar school records were not used. Louis Blan, in his contemporary 1908 masters thesis, at Columbia University, pointed out that using these records could possibly have lowered the drop-out rate in the high schools by encouraging the staff to channel the students into courses appropriate to their abilities and backgrounds.[18]

For those students who were not entering high school directly from grammar school special examinations were given. For admission to the first year class, students were examined in arithmetic, grammar, geography, spelling, and United States history. Admission to the second year required passing examinations in algebra, physiology, English, the history of Greece and Rome, drawing, and either Latin, French, German, or Spanish. If a student wanted to enter at the third or fourth year, a suitable examination was provided.[19]

Standardized Course
Of Studies:
1902

THE COURSE of studies set forth at the beginning of the high schools in 1897 remained generally the same through 1901.[20] In 1902, however, after the charter revision that strengthened the centralized Board of Education, the high school course of study was standardized to one program and remained unchanged for many years.[21] Superintendent Maxwell instituted the standardized high school curriculum so that students who transferred from one school to another "would not waste time and energy adapting to the different curriculum."[22] Another more important reason was that Maxwell felt that standardization was a means by which excellence could be achieved throughout the system.

The uniform course of study for all the New York City public high schools became effective in the beginning of the 1902 school year.[23] This program reflected the combination of required and elective courses recommended by the NEA Committee on College Entrance Requirements in 1897.[24] According to Maxwell: "The chief feature of interest in connection with this course is that it offers a judicious combination of the old fixed course for all pupils and the purely elective system."[25]

The fixed program was the same for all students, and the electives were offered to accommodate individual needs. These elective choices increased as the student advanced to the upper grades. The new program required four years of English and the study of foreign languages, either Latin, German, or French, for four years. Three years of mathematics were required, *i.e.* algebra and geometry, but a third year of bookkeeping could be substituted. The science requirements now covered three years, with biology in the first year, physics in the third, and chemistry or physiography or biology in the fourth year.

There was also a change in the history curriculum, which reflected the

American Historical Association's Committee of Seven report.[26] This report recommended that at least four blocks of history be offered in high schools, *i.e.* ancient history, medieval and modern history, English history, and American history and civics.[27] The 1902 course of study followed this closely and required three years of history, *i.e.* Greek and Roman, English history, and English and American history and civics, with medieval and modern history as a fourth year elective.[28]

Further requirements in the 1902 course of study were drawing, art, music, and declamation, although not all of these subjects had to be taken every year. Physical training, on the other hand, was required for two periods a week each year.[29]

The Board of Superintendents had a syllabus prepared for each subject in the 1902 curriculum. Edward Goodwin asserted that this was done because:

> It was thought necessary to define and describe the work to be done in each subject from term to term, because the number of sections in a class must be condensed at the end of each half year because a pupil rarely completes a piece of work with the teacher with whom he began it, because of the migratory character of the population occasions frequent transfers from school to school, and because the manifest policy of the City Superintendent is to unify the work of the several high schools and to bring them to an approximately uniform standard of excellence.[30]

The overall purpose of the standardized curriculum, according to Goodwin, was to offer students the opportunity to prepare for whatever might be their destinations after high school. He emphasized that the proportion of required subjects, compared to electives, was very large, and maintained: "No one can be graduated who has not had four years of successful work in English, three years in history, three years in mathematics, three years in a foreign language, one year of biology and two additional years of sciences or a third foreign language for two years."[31] Goodwin noted that the number of lessons per week that were now required was similar to that of the German schools. The new program had twenty-six classes per week during the first year, twenty-five in the second, at least twenty-four in the third, and not less than twenty-one in the fourth year.[32]

The rules for conducting the classes, their fifty-minute length and other requirements were succinctly defined in the 1902 course of study brochure. The minimum number of students required before an elective class was formed remained the same.[33] The difference was that electives now became an essential element to the course of study for all high school students in New York City.

Goodwin was an early advocate of the elective system. As principal of Newton High School, he had organized the curriculum along similar lines. Newton was one of the first public high schools in the United States and used electives as early as 1886. Goodwin found that the students at Newton avoided Latin when given the option, with thirty-nine percent choosing it in the freshman year, but only six percent choosing it in the senior year. The students also avoided mathematics, with seventy percent of the freshmen not taking algebra and seventy-seven percent not taking geometry.[34] Yet, Goodwin felt that electives should be used on the elementary level as well.[35]

The advocates of electives took two different approaches, either elective courses of study or elective subjects. The four programs of study recommended by the Committee of Ten were an example of the electives by course approach, as was the 1898 curriculum at Morris High School. Under this arrangement a student chose a course, but the subjects on that course were prescribed, although there may have been some allowance for a few elective subjects. On the other hand, the electives by subject approach was exemplified by the Newton High School program, the NEA Committee on College Entrance Requirements proposal, and by the 1902 standardized curriculum at Morris High School.[36] This kind of program called for a required core of subjects for all students and allowed them to select others from a list.[37]

Electives was a hotly debated educational issue of the day. Electives in the high schools was the central topic at the annual meeting of the Association of Colleges and Preparatory Schools of the Middle States and Maryland held at Columbia University in November of 1903.[38] Superintendent Maxwell led the discussion and described three possible positions. The first position was that there should be no options at all, "only one uniform course for all students." This option remained the choice in private schools that were primarily geared for getting their students into colleges. The second position involved the permitting of student choice for the whole course of study, which Maxwell referred to as "elective chaos." The middle position was to require some courses and to allow some electives. Maxwell was in favor of the middle course, but with few electives. He reasoned that the course of study should be designed with the principles of the NEA Committee of Ten in mind, that is: ". . . every subject studied in the high school should be studied with sufficient intensity and for a sufficient length of time to provide a substantial mental training. . . every subject which is taught at all in a secondary school should be taught in the same way and to the same extent to every pupil so long as he pursues it, no matter what the probable destination of the pupil may be, or at what point his education is to cease."[39] While on one hand Maxwell standardized the curriculum of all the city's high schools, he was also in favor of a diversity of pursuits for high school students. Thus, the elective system allowed for the accommodation of individual needs and aptitudes. In a speech before a group gathered in Carnegie Hall to celebrate his twenty-five years of service in the New York schools, Maxwell said:

> . . . it has been my aim to diversify work in the high schools so that they will not only lead to the gates of the university, but that they will lead to that particular higher training, whether commercial, scientific, or philosophical, for which the individual student's abilities are adapted. For, as I have never tired of preaching to our teachers, there is no waste of human energy, and, consequently, of material resources comparable to the waste involved in setting men and women to work for which they are not fitted.[40]

Nevertheless, there was no diversity allowed in the amount of time a student had to devote to school work in order to get a high school degree. To graduate from Morris High School a student had to have satisfactorily completed all the required work and have taken at least 3,000 periods of study that required preparation, which excluded drawing, art, music, and physical training. All work had to be completed in not less than three years, and no more than six years. Allowances were made on the last point for pupils transferring from other high schools.[41]

After sample testing in the previous year, from July 31, 1902 on, all graduating students at Morris High School were required to take an exam conducted by the College Entrance Examination Board. This exam covered all high school subjects and was necessary for graduation from high school and for admission to the colleges.[42] All students who passed this exam were given a "diploma of graduation." Students who did not take the exam but who complied with all the other conditions were given a certificate of completion."[43]

City Superintendent Maxwell saw several advantages to uniform testing. He believed the cost was insignificant, and certification by a high-level association raised the value of the diploma. More importantly, Maxwell saw such exams as a fine test of the high schools themselves. Weak schools would be exposed, as would weak areas in the curriculum, and thus could be remedied. Under the guidance of a strong principal a strong high school, like Morris, would earn a good reputation. Further, Maxwell wrote:

> The pupils in the high schools would have a certificate to strive for worthy of their ambition. And, finally, if, as I believe they would, the pupils of the high schools should demonstrate the exalted character of their training by passing the examinations of a board whose decisions none could gainsay, the board of education would have a perfect defense of its high school policy, and the high schools would have a perfect defense of their work, against the attacks of those self-seeking politicians who strive for a little cheap notoriety by attacking the high schools – the "colleges of the people."[44]

However, the College Entrance Examination Board was unable to give the necessary exams to all the candidates for graduation from the high schools.[45] Therefore, in June of 1903, an exam prepared by the high school principals and teachers was given under the direction of the city superintendent of schools.[46]

SCHOOL BOARD FOR THE BOROUGHS OF MANHATTAN AND THE BRONX

Park Ave. and 59th St., New York

June, 1900

ADMISSION TO THE HIGH SCHOOLS

(This blank is to be filled out *by the pupil.*)

1. Name in full

2. Date of birth

3. Name of parent or guardian

4. Residence of parent or guardian

5. Number of Grammar School or other school } from which you come.

*6. Name the High School you wish to attend

7. Name the course of Study you wish to } pursue in the High School.

†8. If you select the General Course, choose from the five subjects—Latin, French, German, Spanish, and Biology—the two you wish to take.

9. If you select the Commercial Course, name the modern language you wish to pursue.

††10. If you select the Classical Course, name the College for which you wish to prepare, and the modern language you wish to pursue.

---

* The main building of the Boys' High School is located at No. 60 West Thirteenth Street, the Girls' High School at No. 36 East Twelfth Street; the Mixed High School at 157th Street and Third Avenue.
† Candidates for the Classical Course of the City College, for the Normal College, and for the Training School for Teachers, are to take Latin and Biology the first year. Candidates for the Scientific Course of the City College are to take French and Biology the first year.
†† The Classical Course is not intended to prepare pupils for either the City College or the Normal College.

SIGNATURE OF PARENT OR GUARDIAN

• •

This is to certify that

a pupil in P. S. has satisfactorily completed the work of Grade 7 B and in my opinion is qualified to enter the High School.

Principal,

P. S.

NEW YORK, June 1900.

Original Admission Form to the high schools.

The Morris High School Collection.
The Bronx County Historical Society Research Library.

In 1904, Goodwin called attention to the city superintendent's ". . . most recent and unique scheme for the uniform examinations for graduation from the high schools and for admission to the two training schools for teachers."[47]

The plan was based on a numerical system. The idea was similar to what is today called a point or credit system. A subject taken four or five times a week was equal to 100 credits. To get a diploma, a student had to pass subjects aggregating 1,200 credits. Goodwin explained that the grade for passing decreased as the number of subjects "presented for examination increases beyond the minimum." Everyone had to take an English examination, but all the other subjects were optional. A preliminary examination was given to each student at the end of the third year if the student had satisfactorily completed the examination subjects and aggregated 500 credits.[48]

Goodwin claimed that the standard of scholarship of city superintendent's examinations was equal to that of the College Entrance Examination Board's tests. He based his findings on a comparative study of the score results from both tests taken by Morris High School students.[49]

In his conclusion to a 1904 article on the New York high schools, Goodwin praised Maxwell for his work and provided some interesting background to the recent changes and to the great victories of the educational professionals. Goodwin wrote:

> To summarize what I have said, the board of superintendents in New York City is in virtual control of the schools; in addition to scholarship and insight, the City Superintendent has courage and executive ability commensurate with his great legal authority; the politicians have folded their tents and withdrawn from the ground occupied by the schools; the teacher's tenure of office, salary, and pension are insured by statute law; the principal has the largest liberty in the selection of text-books and supplies, and has all the influence he deserves in the appointment and promotion of his teachers; the great size of the schools, the rapid shrinkage of classes, and the semi-annual reorganization have caused the creation of departments and have made syllabuses a necessity; the sentiment in favor of encouraging the college to ascertain for itself the qualifications of the candidates that knock at its gate for admission is quite unanimous; and the City Superintendent's unique scheme of uniform written examinations for graduation is likely to have a far-reaching effect in setting the standard of scholarship for the public secondary schools of the Empire State.[50]

Maxwell, for his part, in 1904 said: "There are no better public high schools in America than those which now exist in the Boroughs of Manhattan and The Bronx."[51] Under a strong and indomitable city superintendent, the energetic and able principals at Morris, DeWitt Clinton and Wadleigh High Schools had fulfilled the long-held hopes and aspirations of the education reform movement.

NOTES

[1]"Elastic Courses of Study," *New York Daily Tribune,* 20 June 1897, p. 1.

[2]At the time the original public high schools were established, Manhattan and The Bronx had seven-year programs in the elementary school while Queens, Brooklyn, and Richmond had eight-year programs. See Palmer, pp. 305-306.

[3]New York City, Bureau of Reference, Research and Statistics, "Brief Historical Sketch of the High Schools of New York City," September, 1926, Special Collections, Milbank Memorial Library, Teachers College, Columbia University, New York, p. 1.

Usually the terms "secondary" and "high" school were used interchangeably. But there was a distinction, which reinforced the argument of those who called for more levels of schooling. An elementary, or primary school was the first school introduced to the child: the one in which the elements of subjects were taught. Logically, a secondary school was the second school of the child. The term "high" implied a higher level of education that went beyond secondary schooling. See E.W. Coy, "What is a Secondary School?" *Journal of Proceedings and Addresses of the Thirty-Fifth Annual Meeting of the National Educational Association, July 3-10, 1896* (Chicago: University of Chicago Press, 1896), pp. 613-618.

[4]Shapiro, p. 74.

[5]New York City Board of Education, *Journal,* 1897, p. 576.

[6]*Ibid.*

[7]For the 1898 Course of Study Program for the new high schools, see Table 7. For a general historical review on the development of the curriculum in secondary schools see Edward A. Krug, *The Secondary School Curriculum* (New York: Harper & Bros., 1960). An interesting perspective on the New York City high school curriculum is offered in Moses Stambler's "The Democratic Revolution in the Public High Schools of New York City, 1898-1917," Ph.D. Dissertation, New York University, 1964.

[8]New York City Department of Education, Courses of Study for the High Schools of the Boroughs of Manhattan and The Bronx, 1898, *Morris High School Scrapbook: 1897-1914,* Morris High School Collection, The Bronx County Historical Society Research Library, Bronx, New York.

[9]"Elastic Courses of Study," p. 1.

[10]New York City Department of Education, Courses of Study for All High Schools, 1898, *Morris High School Scrapbook: 1897-1914,* p. 5.

[11]*Ibid.* p. 8.

[12]New York City Department of Education, Courses of Study for the High Schools, 1901, p. 5.

[13]New York City Department of Education, Courses of Study for All High Schools, 1898, p. 8.

[14]"Elastic Courses of Study," p. 1.

[15]New York City Department of Education, Courses of Study for All High Schools, 1898, p. 8.

[16]Louis B. Blan, "The Elective System in Secondary Education with Special Reference to the New York City Public High Schools," Masters Thesis, Columbia University, 1908, pp. 34-37. See pages 141-143 for this form.

[17]See page 137 for the official form for admission to the New York City public high schools.

[18]Blan, pp. 34-38.

[19]"Elastic Courses of Study," p. 1.

[20]New York City Department of Education, Courses of Study for the High Schools, 1901, p. 2.

[21]See Table 8 for the 1902 Course of Study.

[22]New York City Department of Education, *Annual Report of the City Superintendent,* 1898-99, p. 103.

[23]In 1903 Maxwell adopted a standardized course of study and an eight-year length for all the elementary schools in the city system. Maxwell felt that the shorter seven-year program in Manhattan and The Bronx presented problems for those students. Of particular concern was the fact that these students were graduating earlier and therefore going to high school at a younger age, which involved much more pressure and put them at a disadvantage. Palmer, pp. 305-307.

[24]Krug, *The Shaping of the American High School,* pp. 141-143.

[25]Editorial, "City Superintendent Maxwell," p. 16.

[26]For a discussion of the American Historical Association Committee of Seven see Hazel Whitman Hertzberg, *Social Studies Reform: 1880-1980* (Boulder: Social Science Education Consortium, 1981), pp. 12-16.

[27]Edgar Dawson, "The History Inquiry," *Historical Outlook* 15 (June, 1924): 239-250.

[28]Maxwell had followed through on his 1898 proposal to adopt the American Historical Association Committee of Seven recommendations for the high schools. See New York City Department of Education, *Annual Report of the City Superintendent,* 1898-99, p. 104.

[29]New York City Department of Education, Course of Study for All High Schools, 1902.

[30]Edward J. Goodwin, "Some Characteristics of the New York City High Schools," *Educational Review* 28 (October 1904): 260-261.

[31]*Ibid.*

[32]*Ibid.*, p. 262.

[33]New York City Department of Education, Course of Study for All High Schools, 1902, p. 268.

[34]Goodwin, "Electives in the High School: An Experiment," pp. 142-145.

[35]Edward J. Goodwin, "Electives in Elementary School," *Educational Review* 8 (June, 1894): 12-21.

[36]Krug, *The Shaping of the American High School,* p. 191.

[37]According to Krug, "the high point of electivism was probably reached between 1900 and 1905." An extreme elective system was introduced in Galesbury, Illinois as early as 1895. In this program all subjects were elective. The motivation behind this action was the forty percent drop-out rate in the freshman year. By the time the first class graduated under the elective plan, school attendance had "increased from 234 to 518 pupils." In 1900, Chicago set up a plan which had very few constants, only two in English, two in a foreign language, one in algebra, one in history, and one in science. Boston's plan began in 1901 and was radical in that all subjects were elective except for gymnastics or military drill, hygiene, and music. Krug further reports on two 1901 studies on the topic. One revealed that elective programs tended to require certain core subjects. The other study showed that of forty administrators of large city school systems, only two favored free electives without any constants, but three advocated a few constants. Fifteen of the respondents preferred election by courses and eleven advocated limited or no electives. The conclusion of this study was that superintendents were hesitant to advocate a very large number of electives in secondary schools. See Krug, *The Shaping of the American High School,* pp. 194-196.

[38]William H. Maxwell, "The Elective System in Secondary Schools," *Proceedings of the 17th Annual Convention of the Association of Colleges and Preparatory Schools of the Middle States and Maryland,* Columbia University, New York, November 17-18, 1903, University of the State of New York, Bulletin 310-317, Milbank Memorial Library, Teachers College, Columbia University, New York, pp. 7-39.

[39]Maxwell, "The Elective System in Secondary Schools," pp. 7, 8, 13.

[40]William H. Maxwell, "My Ideals as Superintendent," *Educational Review* 44 (December, 1912): 454.

[41]New York City Department of Education, Courses of Study for All High Schools, 1902, pp. 6-7.

[42]New York City Department of Education, *Annual Report of the City Superintendent,* 1901, p. 99.

[43]New York City Department of Education, Courses of Study for All High Schools, 1902, pp. 6-7.

[44]New York City Department of Education, *Annual Report of the City Superintendent,* 1901, p. 100.

[45]New York City Department of Education, *Annual Report of the City Superintendent,* 1902, p. 71.

[46]New York City Department of Education, *Annual Report of the City Superintendent,* 1904, p. 52.

[47]Goodwin, "Some Characteristics of the New York City High Schools," p. 262.

[48]*Ibid.*

[49]*Ibid.* pp. 263-4.

[50]*Ibid.*, p. 264.

[51]Editorial, *Educational Review* 27 (January, 1904): 21.

DEPARTMENT OF EDUCATION

THE CITY OF NEW YORK

[GRAMMAR SCHOOLS]

ESTIMATE OF GRADUATING PUPIL'S ATTAINMENTS

Term ending January
June   190

Borough of_____ **District No.**_____**P.S.**_____

Name of pupil_____

Date of birth_____**Residence**_____

ESTIMATE OF PUPIL'S ATTAINMENTS

Note - Satisfactory ("a", excellent; "b(plus)," very good; "b", good) - Unsatisfactory ("c," poor; "d," bad)

Class standing_____ Principal's estimate_____

I recommend   )

                the said pupil for graduation from this school.

I do not recommend   )

Approved   )
Disapproved   ) _____   _____
          District Superintendent   Principal

Grammar School Estimate of Graduating Pupil's Attainments, page 1.
This three page form was submitted by the grammar school principal to the district superintendent.

The Bronx County Historical Society Research Library.

	I Indicate ability by a small letter in this column.	**II** Put general estimates in CAPITALS in this column.

I. READING

1. Amount of literature read in class during the
    term now closing ....
2. Power to interpret the matter so read ....
3. Amount of literature memorized ....
4. Ability to read aloud accurately and intelligently
    new reading matter ....
5. Power to give understandingly the substance of a
    paragraph, after a single reading ....
6. Use of library books ....
7. Power to understand and explain the meaning of words ....
8. Skill in the use of a dictionary ....

    General estimate ....

II. GRAMMAR

1. Ability to explain the meaning and grammatical
    structure of sentences in the usual forms ....
2. Ability to distinguish the language forms -
    words, phrases, and clauses - to show their use
    and force in sentences of ordinary difficulty,
    and to classify them as parts of speech, etc. ....
3. Ability to distinguish and give the various
    inflected forms of ordinary words ....
4. Ability to use a text-book as a book of reference ....
5. Power to use grammar to correct errors in the
    pupil's own discourse oral and written ....

    General estimate ....

III. COMPOSITION

1. Skill in talking intelligently and grammatically
    on subjects within the pupil's knowledge. ....
2. Power to arrange his thoughts in order and
    to write them grammatically ....
3. Ability to write from given data,
    letters correct in both form and substance ....
4. Estimate of rapidity and legibility of handwriting ....

    General estimate ....

IV. SPELLING

1. Power and habit as a speller ....
2. Ability to write from dictation, paragraphs of
    ordinary difficulty.......................................
3. Skill in applying rules for spelling to the
    inflected and derived forms of words ....

    General estimate ....

V. MATHEMATICS

1. Power to use the four simple rules with reasonable
    rapidity, employing the customary short methods ....
2. Ability to solve problems that involve fractions,
    common and decimal ....
3. Power to solve ordinary problems, including industrial
    measurements, percentage, etc ....
4. Ability to analyze processes ....

Grammar School Estimate of Graduating Pupil's Attainments, page 2.

	I	II
	Indicate ability by a small letter in this column.	Put general estimates in CAPITALS in this column.

5. Knowledge of the metric system
6. Ability to apply algebra and geometry to
   the solution of problems . . . .

    General estimate . . . .

VI. HISTORY

1. Knowledge of the time and sequence of events in
   United States history . . . .
2. Knowledge of the main causes that have brought our
   country to its present condition . . . .
3. Comprehension of the Declaration of Independence, of
   Washington's farewell address, and
   Lincoln's Gettysburg speech. . . . .
4. Knowledge of the leading events in English history . . . .

    General estimate . . . .

VII. CIVICS

1. Knowledge of the most important provisions of
   the United States Constitution and of the
   organization of state and municipal governments . . . .

    General estimate . . . .

VIII. GEOGRAPHY (as completed in 7B)

1. Mastery of a school textbook . . . .
2. Knowledge of the important physical features of the
   continents, of the United States, of New York State . . . .
3. Power to locate the chief countries of the world,
   their great cities and foreign possessions, and
   to give and recognize their chief productions . . . .
4. Knowledge of the chief transcontinental and ocean
   routes of commerce . . . .
5. Knowledge of the causes of dew, rain, snow, wind
   and other ordinary physical phenomena, and
   knowledge of the relations of place to climate . . . .

    General estimate . . . .

IX. SCIENCE

1. Number of experiments performed by teacher in science . . . .
2. Number of experiments performed by pupil in science . . . .
3. Pupil's knowledge of such experiments . . . .

    General estimate . . . .

X. ELECTIVES

1. Character of work done in
   French, German, Spanish, or Italian . . . .

NOTE: The pupil's rating in column I should be made by the teachers of the graduating classes under the direction of the principal, and the general estimates in column II should be made by the principal.

Grammar School Estimate of Graduating Pupil's Attainments, page 3.

The Bronx County Historical Society Research Library.

TABLE 7

COURSES OF STUDIES FOR THE HIGH SCHOOLS OF THE BOROUGHS OF MANHATTAN AND THE BRONX IN 1898 GENERAL COURSE

FIRST YEAR REQUIRED SUBJECTS		SECOND YEAR REQUIRED SUBJECTS	
English	3	English	3
History	2	History	2
Physiology	2	Physics	3
Algebra	4	Geometry	4
Drawing	1	Drawing	1
Physical Training	2	Physical Training	2
Music	1	Music	1
	Total: 15		Total: 16

ELECTIVE SUBJECTS *Two electives required*		ELECTIVE SUBJECTS *Two electives required*	
Latin	4	Latin	4
French	4	Greek	4
German	4	French	4
Spanish	4	German	4
Biology	4	Spanish	4
		Physiography	4

THIRD YEAR REQUIRED SUBJECTS		FOURTH YEAR REQUIRED SUBJECTS	
English	3	English	3
History	2	History	2
Civics	2	Drawing	1
Drawing	1	Physical Training	2
Physical Training	2	Music	1
Music	1		Total: 9
	Total: 11		

ELECTIVE SUBJECTS *Three electives required*		ELECTIVE SUBJECTS *Four electives required*	
Latin	4	Latin	4
Greek	4	Greek	4
French	4	French	4
German	4	German	4
Spanish	4	Physics	4
Chemistry	4	Solid Geometry and	
Algebra and Plane Geometry	4	Plane Trigonometry	4
English	4	English	4
History	4	History	4
Art	4	Art	4
Economics and Astronomy	4	Psychology and Ethics	4

TABLE 7 CONTINUED

COURSES OF STUDIES FOR THE HIGH SCHOOLS CONTINUED

CITY COLLEGE AND NORMAL COLLEGE PREPARATORY COURSE (ADAPTED FROM GENERAL COURSE)

FIRST YEAR		SECOND YEAR	
English	3	English	3
History	2	History	2
* Latin	4	French and German, or	
or		Latin and one of the following:	
†French	4	Greek, German, French	8
‡Algebra	4	‡Plane Geometry	4
Physiology	2	‡Physics	4
Biology	3	Drawing	1
Drawing	1	Music	1
Music	1	Physical Training	2
Physical Training	2		

THIRD YEAR	
English	3
History	2
French and German, or	
Latin and one of the following:	
Greek, German, French	8
‡Algebra and Plane Geometry	4
‡Physiography	4
Drawing	1
Physical Training	2

* *Candidates for the College of The City of New York, who elect Latin for the first year, may choose Greek, German or French as the second language for the second and third years; those who elect French the first year must take German as the second language for the second and third years.*

†*Candidates for the Normal College must take Latin in the first year, and Greek, German or French as the second language for the second and third years.*

‡*One of these periods is to be given to exercises in this subject, for which no special preparation has been made by the student.*

TABLE 7 CONTINUED

COURSES OF STUDIES FOR THE HIGH SCHOOLS OF THE BOROUGHS OF MANHATTAN AND THE BRONX IN 1898

COMMERCIAL COURSE   CLASSICAL COURSE

FIRST YEAR		FIRST YEAR	
English	3	English	3
History	2	Latin	5
Physiology	2	Algebra	5
Algebra	3	History	2
Drawing	1	Physiology	2
Physical Training	2	Elementary French or German	4
Music	1	Physical Training	2
French or German or Spanish	4	**Total: 23**	
Biology	4		
Total: 22			

SECOND YEAR		SECOND YEAR	
English	3	English	3
History	2	Latin	5
Physics	3	Greek or French or German	5
Geometry	3	Geometry	3
Drawing	1	History	2
Physical Training	2	Elementary French or German	2
Music	1	Physical Training	2
French or German or Spanish	4	**Total: 22**	
Bookkeeping and Arithmetic	4		
Total: 23			

THIRD YEAR		THIRD YEAR	
English	3	English	3
History	2	Latin	5
Civics	2	Greek or French or German	5
Drawing	1	Algebra	3
Physical Training	2	History	2
Music	1	Elementary French or German	2
French or German or Spanish	4	Physical Training	2
Bookkeeping and Arithmetic	4	**Total: 22**	
Stenography and Typewriting	4		
Total: 23			

FOURTH YEAR		FOURTH YEAR	
English	3	English	3
History	2	Latin	5
Physical Training	2	Greek or French or German	5
Music	1	Geometry	2
French or German or Spanish	4	Physics or Chemistry	5
Commercial Law and		Physical Training	2
History of Commerce	4	**Total: 22**	
Stenography and Typewriting	4		
English Composition	4		
Total: 24			

SOURCE: New York City, Department of Education, Courses of Studies
for the High Schools of the Boroughs of Manhattan and the Bronx - 1898;
Morris High School Scrap Book, 1897-1914.
(The Bronx County Historical Society Research Library, The Bronx, New York).

TABLE 8

COURSE OF STUDY FOR ALL HIGH SCHOOLS IN 1902
Except Manual Training and Commercial High Schools

DEPARTMENT OF EDUCATION THE CITY OF NEW YORK

FIRST YEAR
REQUIRED SUBJECTS

English	5
Latin or German or French	5
Algebra	5
Biology, including Physiology, Botany and Zoology in different parts of the year	5
Total:	20

SECOND YEAR
REQUIRED SUBJECTS

English	3
Latin or German or French	5
Plane Geometry	4
Greek and Roman History	3
Total:	15

ELECTIVES
Greek	5
German	5
French	5
Spanish	5
Chemistry	5

THIRD YEAR
REQUIRED SUBJECTS

English	3
Latin or German or French	5
English History	2
* Physics	5
† Geometry and Algebra (second course)	3
Total:	18

ELECTIVES
Greek	4
German	4
French	4
Spanish	4
Stenography and Typewriting	4
Bookkeeping	3
Economics	3

FOURTH YEAR
REQUIRED SUBJECTS

English	3
A foreign language	4
‡ Chemistry or Physiography or Biology	4
English and American History and Civics	4
Total:	15

ELECTIVES
Physics, as in third year	5
Greek	4
Latin	4
German	4
French	4
Spanish	4
Mathematics	4
Stenography and Typewriting	3
Economics	3
Domestic Science (sewing, cooking and household economy)	3
Commercial Law and Commercial Geography	3
Additional Latin or Greek or English	3
Medieval and Modern History	3

* *A student preparing for college, who has already taken two foreign languages, may substitute a third foreign language for science specified. At least one period a week of Physics shall be devoted to unprepared work.*

† *Bookkeeping may be substituted for Geometry and Algebra.*

‡ *A student preparing for college, who has already taken two foreign languages, may substitute a third foreign language for science specified.*

SOURCES: New York City, Department of Education, *Course of Study for All High Schools -1902*, Morris High School Scrap Book, 1897-1914, (The Bronx County Historical Society Research Library, The Bronx, New York).

THE

FACULTY

Professional
Standards

WRITING ABOUT American high schools in 1909, John Franklin Brown noted: "It is better to sacrifice at any other point than to accept a mediocre or poor teacher."[1]

Edward Goodwin agreed, but put it in his own way, "It should never be forgotten that the educative process depends quite as much upon the teacher's personality and point of view as upon the subject of study."[2] In order to prepare students for the "duties and opportunities" of life, a teacher, according to Goodwin, must be broadly educated.[3] Thus, for his faculty Goodwin carefully chose experienced and well-educated individuals.

The academic backgrounds of the teachers of Morris High School were quite impressive. In the 1901 listing of teachers, their schools and certifications, there was a significant representation of graduates from major colleges and universities. Of the sixty-five teachers listed, forty, or 61.5 percent, had a college education, not specifically teacher training. When the graduates of the Normal Schools are included, the number of college graduates jumps to fifty-eight people or 89.2 percent. Of the remaining seven teachers, five received professional training leaving only two teachers with neither college nor professional training. A faculty so well educated was extraordinary.[4] Even by 1911, John Franklin Brown reported: "Taking the country over, it is probably true that not more than fifty percent of the high school teachers are either graduates of a four-year college course, or have training equivalent to that required for such graduation; and that a much smaller number, probably not more than five percent, have adequate pedagogical training . . . ."[5]

None of the Morris teachers went to the New York or Brooklyn Training Schools for Teachers, although twenty-five did receive professional training at other schools. Five of the teachers graduated from New York Normal

Morris High School faculty in June, 1902.
Dr. Goodwin is in center of photo, sixth from left in second line.
John Denbigh is in the first line, second from right.

The Morris High School Collection.
The Bronx County Historical Society Research Library.

Schools, and another eleven from normal schools not in New York State. Only one person held a New York State certificate issued by the New York State Superintendent of Public Instruction, while two teachers held "college graduate" certificates from the state. These latter certificates were not diplomas of graduation from a college, but rather special forms of license to teach, issued to graduates of colleges.[6] In addition, five female and four male teachers on the Morris High School faculty had received their basic education in Europe. All five women and two of the men taught foreign languages, and the other two men taught history and mathematics.[7]

The issue of teachers' qualifications, licenses, and hiring practices was a subject of dispute between the borough boards and the city superintendent. The problems were not settled until after the revised charter of 1901 created the powerful centralized board. The early Morris High School faculty was, of course, hired before that time. Yet the teachers reflected an extremely high standard of education. The people employed to teach at Morris had credentials that were in keeping with the reform ideal of having educational professionals in their secondary school system. As Superintendent Maxwell wrote in his first *Annual Report:*

> Now, if I am right in holding that the pupils in the elementary schools are radically different in character from the pupils in the high schools, and that the knowledge to be taught in the elementary school differs from the knowledge to be taught in the high school as empiricism differs from science, it follows that the high school teacher should be not only more extensively and scientifically informed than it is reasonable to expect or require the elementary school teacher to be, but that he should have undergone training which is needed to fit him to deal as a teacher with adolescent pupils to impart organic instruction.[8]

As early as 1898-99, Maxwell set down qualifications for teachers' licenses. Although he was not supported by the borough boards, Maxwell insisted on examinations for high school teachers. He felt that this would make the high schools of the city of New York the best in America.[9] Therefore, to secure a license as an assistant teacher in a high school, the candidate had to be a graduate of a college or university, and either have two years of teaching experience in college or secondary schools (five years, if teaching in Manhattan and The Bronx), or have two years post-graduate work in the area to be taught and in the science of education. For teaching commercial subjects, the arts, or manual training, the requirements were less stringent. Each applicant was to pass an oral and a written examination, which varied according to the subjects to be taught, but always included the science of education.[10] It is not known if new faculty at Morris High School actually took these examinations; however, under Principal Goodwin it is likely that they did.

There was special consideration given to teachers who wished to teach more than one subject.[11] The Committee on High Schools for the Boroughs of Manhattan and The Bronx reported in 1898 ". . .the teachers of the high schools have asked in what way licenses may be extended to cover other subjects than those for which they are appointed."[12] As a result the following resolution was approved for incorporation into the By-Laws: "Any teacher in the high schools desiring to secure a license to teach permanently a subject or subjects other than those for which he was appointed, may, on the recommendation of the principal of the school, apply to the City Superintendent for a license to teach in such additional subjects."[13]

In order to be appointed a teacher in the New York City school system it was necessary to be on the eligible lists. According to Frank Rollins, one of the original teachers at DeWitt Clinton who later joined the Morris High School faculty, the use of the eligible lists compelled ". . . the consideration of each candidate approximately in order of standing on the eligible list,

Josie A. Davis came to Morris High School with Dr. Goodwin.
She was a First Assistant and Latin teacher on the original faculty.

The Morris Annual, 1923.
The Bronx County Historical Society Research Library.

and seems designed to protect the interest of the candidate, and to relieve
the superintendents and the Board of Education from political influence
or social pressure in the interests of any applicants for positions."[14]

When the first faculty was chosen for the Mixed High School, there were
no eligible lists since they did not come in until Maxwell initiated them in
1898-99. In any case, the rule for enforcing the list in standing order was
not effective until the Davis Law in 1900, so any qualified teacher on the
list could be appointed. This would account for the fact that Goodwin was
able to bring along Ezra W. Sampson, Josie A. Davis, Frank Rollins[15] and
Abby Barstow Bates[16] to New York from Newton High School, as they
probably would not have registered for such a list.[17]

In addition to the concern about the qualifications of teachers and how
they were to be chosen, another issue was raised regarding their salaries.[18]
New York, according to Maxwell, paid the highest salaries in the country in
1904. He wrote:

> Now, I do not say that these salaries [in New York City public schools],
> which I believe are the highest in the world for elementary school work, are
> salaries that may be paid, or ought to be paid, in every city and village in

Abby Barstow Bates was brought by Dr. Goodwin
from Newton High School as the original history teacher.
She continued to direct the history and economics
departments until she retired in 1926.

The Morris Annual, 1926.
The Bronx County Historical Society Research Library.

the country for the simple reason that the cost of living in New York City is probably higher than in any other city of the country: but I do say that if we are to get the right kind of people to teach in our schools and if those people are to have the necessary opportunities for culture, for improvement, for getting breadth of mind thru travel or thru going to the summer school or the university, we must pay all over this country proportionately high salaries.[19]

This indicates that Maxwell felt that the teachers in New York City were doing well in regard to their salary levels. Indeed, by this time, the Davis Law was in effect and the city's teachers were being paid according to the legally determined schedule. National Education Association statistics for 1904 indicated that the annual salary range for women teachers in New York City was between $700 and $2,500, and for men it was between $900 and $3,000. In comparison, the average salary range for the twenty-eight cities studied was between $768 and $1,816. The upper limit for male teachers in New York City was the second highest in the country, and was exceeded only by Boston teachers with a maximum of $3,060.[20]

Of the sixty-nine teachers on the Morris High School faculty for the year 1903-04 the average salary was $1,863, which was higher than the upper limit average in the twenty-eight cities cited in the NEA report.[21] The highest salary of $3,500 was paid to the two men in charge of the annexes, Frank Rollins and Ezra Sampson.[22] Only two people received salaries under $1,200, with the lowest wage of $745.83 paid to a female teacher. The lowest male teacher's salary was $962.50. The highest salary for a female teacher was $2,500, compared to $2,916.67 for the highest paid male. There were twenty-seven male teachers, with an average salary of $2,206, and forty-two female teachers, with an average salary of $1,761.[23]

The total amount of salaries paid at Morris High School for the year 1904, including the teachers and the principal was $133,518.42. When the school opened in 1897 with twenty-one teachers on the faculty, the total salaries were $39,600 with the average salary at $1,647.62, or $214.96 a year less than the average in 1904. The minimum salary level in 1897 was $1,200, which went to seven female teachers. In 1904 the salary minimum was $745.83. This lower 1904 figure may have reflected the Davis Law schedule or it may have been because a lower grade of teacher was hired when a new teacher replaced an experienced one or perhaps it was a combination of both these factors. In 1897, there were ten men and eleven women on the faculty. By 1904, there were fifteen more women than men on the Morris faculty. The average female teacher's salary in 1897 was $1,381, compared with an average of $1,940 for the males. The highest 1897 salary of $3,000 went to two male teachers.[24]

Dr. Goodwin's salary, which did not change from its initial level in 1897 through 1904, was $5,000 a year.[25] In comparison, the Secretary of the

Martha Freeman Goddard was a Biology teacher
at Morris from 1901-1911.

The Morris Annual, 1913.
The Bronx County Historical Society Research Library.

Board of Education, A. Emerson Palmer, received $4,000 per year while C.B.J. Snyder, the superintendent of school buildings, and William Maxwell, city superintendent, were both paid $8,000 a year.[26] Public school principals received $3,000 per year.[27] Substitute teachers were paid $3.00 a day, but they had to have at least two years of experience before they could qualify.[28] Interestingly, the salary of school superintendent for the Borough Boards of Manhattan and The Bronx, John Jasper, was $7,500, only $500 lower than that of the city superintendent.[29]

Some of the custodial staff at Morris High School were better paid than some of the teachers in 1904. The janitor at the new Morris High School building received $1,800 per year, and the one at the old building received $1,794.[30] The boiler fireman and the coal-stoker received $912.50.[31] The elevator attendant received $750 a year, while the cleaners earned $480.[32] The clerk of the school earned $900 per year.[33]

Despite the high salaries for New York City teachers, and particularly for

Morris High School, when compared with other occupations, teachers were not paid as much as might be expected given the high qualifications demanded for their positions. The *School Review* asserted that teachers' salaries made ". . . a poor showing in comparison to such trades as marble-cutters, bricklayers, plumbers, metal-lathers, and stonesetters, whose average earnings range from $902 to $1,500 . . . . Were the pay in our high schools better, we should not be losing so many good men each year to insurance, book-selling, and other more remunerative business occupations."[34] The teachers being lost to "more remunerative business occupations" were usually male. Yet the issue that was to cause the most reaction during this period was salary discrimination based on gender.

The equal pay movement began in New York City, and was led by Grace Strachan, a New York City public school teacher who rose to the position of district superintendent.[35] As was the case at Morris High School, most of the teachers in the New York City school system were women. By 1907, for example, there were 12,000 female teachers and only 2,000 male teachers. The female teachers, following the provisions of the Davis Law, were systematically paid less than the male teachers. In trying to rally support for equal pay for women, Grace Strachan asserted: "The people should realize the injustice of the presumption which underlies a system that starts a woman teacher at $600 and a man teacher at $900, and raises the woman's pay $40 a year and the man's pay $105."[36]

The general argument for the split pay schedules was that men required a "necessary wage," as they were to be considered the heads of households. Women, on the other hand, did not require the same amount, as it was ". . . assumed that the woman teacher is a bird of passage - a schoolmarm one day and a blushing bride the next, while the man will be on the job for life."[37] City Superintendent Maxwell, a supporter of the Davis Law, favored the sex discrimination of the salary schedule. He relied on sociologist Herbert Spencer's theories of innate differences between the sexes to validate his position. Maxwell claimed that male models were needed, particularly for the poor immigrant population. Since men had the option of many other means of employment which were not available to women, the men had to be paid more in order to keep them in the schools. According to Maxwell, if it was necessary and important to employ men in the schools, then ". . . it follows that the educational authorities must pay salaries to men sufficient to obtain the requisite supply of men teachers of ability and culture. If, however, it is not necessary to pay the same salaries in order to obtain a sufficient supply of women teachers of refinement and culture, it is difficult to see what reason can be advanced for increasing the educational expenses to the extent involved in equalizing the salaries."[38]

The issue was not a new one, nor did it begin with the Davis Law, although that legalized the inequity.[39] By the turn of the century, perhaps

The faculty through the eyes of student artist,
Joseph Wiseltier.

The Morris Annual, 1905.
The Bronx County Historical Society Research Library.

because of the Davis Law, the proponents for equal pay began to gain strength. In Brooklyn, "equal pay was the law," but that, too, changed with the Davis Law in 1900, which fixed and regulated the salaries of all teachers in New York City and provided that ". . . the salaries of all principals and teachers shall be regulated by merit, grade of class taught, length of service, experience in teaching or by a combination of these considerations."[40]

To Grace Strachan, the law had ". . . a new consideration, that of sex is given an insulting and, to the women teachers, degrading prominence, in that it is made the basis for dividing the salary schedule for the same grade and class of work into two unfair and inequitable lists."[41]

The disparity in salary schedules between the sexes applied only to the teachers in the city's regular schools. The Board of Education maintained one pay schedule for all other positions, including the principals and teachers in special school programs, such as recreation, vacation, and evening schools. Sexual discrimination in salaries was also not the rule for principals of high schools, district superintendents, the city superintendent, associate city superintendents, and the board of examiners.[42]

Under the Davis Law, the sexual discrimination in salaries was greatest at the elementary school level. It was not as wide at the high school level, where the highest number of male teachers were found. This in itself caused a problem as certification requirements and duties were identical. Thus comparisons were easily made.[43]

Teaching was one of the few professions open to young women at the turn of the century. May Doherty of the Morris High School Class of 1913 exemplified this situation. Miss Doherty recalled that she became a teacher because her mother was one and she encouraged her daughters to follow suit. According to Miss Doherty, there were twelve women teachers in two generations of her family. She reported that there really was no other field open to educated women, "only the telephone company or a department store."[44]

The issue was reduced to two propositions, "Are women as fit in every way as men, for the position of teacher in the public schools? . . . Granted their fitness, is it economically sound to make their salaries equal?"[45] The first case was fairly easy to prove, and was not central to the debate. Everyone seemed to agree that women were as capable of being teachers as men were, although some people, like Maxwell, wanted to insure that there were enough men teachers. Most of the controversy then centered on the economic issue.

Among Grace Strachan's associates was Elizabeth H. du Bois, Ph.D., a Latin teacher who was a member of the original Morris High School faculty. Dr. du Bois contributed an article to Strachan's book, *Equal Pay for Equal Work*, [46] in which she raised the question: "Is a man, because he has

Ezra W. Sampson was a close friend of Dr. Goodwin, and was Acting Principal
of Newton High School when Dr. Goodwin went on his Prussian tour.
He moved with Goodwin to Morris as First Assistant and
Physical Geography teacher on the original faculty.
In 1905, he became the Principal of the Morris High School
Evening School. He retired in 1913 at the age of seventy.

The Morris Annual, 1913.
The Bronx County Historical Society Research Library.

a family, or may have a family, to receive money for that family rather than for his services?"[47] The claim was that eighty percent of the male high school teachers were married, but du Bois counter-claimed that in one high school ninety-one percent of the women teachers had family obligations. Du Bois, therefore, concluded that: "The case of the men teachers seems from first to last a piece of special pleading. What if they lack knowledge of their subject, ability to make all clear, a high sense of honor – they are fathers, or may be. This is taking the city's money under false pretenses. Just as between a man and a woman physician, income from practice is a matter of special fitness, so it should be between men and women teachers."[48]

The equal pay movement gained momentum with equal pay bills being introduced in the New York State Legislature in 1907, 1908, 1909, and 1911. Finally, in 1911, Chapter 902 amended the Greater New York Charter and guaranteed equal pay for women teachers.[49]

Another sexual discrimination issue involved the Board of Education's practice, as mandated by its by-laws, of not hiring married women as teachers. The by-laws also required the termination of employment of women when they married. This discrimination can be observed in *The Morris Annual* for 1905 in which there is a listing of twenty-eight former members of the faculty. Each teacher was cited for his or her contributions to the school, and gave the reason for leaving. Five teachers went on to the new Stuyvesant High School, including Frank Rollins, who became its principal. Three teachers went to the High School of Commerce, and four more to other high schools. Another three teachers went to teach in colleges or universities and one became a member of the Board of Examiners. All of these people were male teachers. Of the eleven women who left Morris High School, nine departed because they were getting married. One left for health reasons, and one went on to teach at a private school.[50] In 1904, in lieu of a court decision against such discrimination, the Board of Education changed its by-laws to provide for the employment of married women teachers. As a result, "a large number of women teachers were married in the next few months and continued to teach."[51]

On another financial matter, New York City public school teachers were provided with a pension plan. City Superintendent Maxwell felt that this was "one of the reasonable compensations of a teacher, who cannot possibly become rich on his or her salary." By 1904, the New York City teachers' pension plan provided from $600 to $1,000 per year after thirty years of service, and up to $1,500 for principals. The pensions were paid largely from the city's excise monies.[52]

Permanent tenure was also granted to New York City public school teachers, including those at Morris High School, at the turn of the century. However, this was one benefit that Maxwell, who argued for higher salaries, pension plans and teacher input into the curriculum, did not fully support.

Marie M. Diedrich taught French
at the High School from 1901-1915.

The Morris Annual, 1915.
The Bronx County Historical Society
Research Library.

Marie P. Lippert was an original faculty member.
She taught German until retiring in 1915.

The Morris Annual, 1915.
The Bronx County Historical Society Research Library.

He felt that there should be some limit on the tenure system in New York City. The city superintendent cautiously wrote: "Quite possibly we have gone too far in the direction of permanent tenure in New York City, where we have made the tenure of the teacher a life tenure after a probationary period of three years; possibly that is going too far."[53]

In order to attain their goals, Maxwell felt that teachers could organize into societies, but not into unions. In fact, he found the idea of a strike by teachers inconceivable, because he felt: "Poverty may come, persecution may come, [but] the true teacher will never desert his holy mission to childhood. No possible conditions will ever justify a teacher strike. Yet if they join a trades-union they are bound to strike when so ordered. The true solidarity of teachers is as far removed from trade-unionism as a profession from a trade."[54] The type of teachers' organization that Maxwell suggested was one which had a "code of professional ethics that will set a standard of professional honor and professional duty," and ultimately this code would "transcend school-board ordinances and statutory enactments."[55]

The High School Teachers Association of New York City was just such a group. Organized in 1900, it's objective was "the advancement of secondary education and the promotion of teachers' interests."[56] Membership was open to any teacher in a public high school in New York City, who signed the constitution and paid dues. The first president was Frank Rollins of Morris High School, who served for two terms.[57] The organization's *Yearbook* reveals that the main concerns of the group were the curriculum and the promotion of the students, ideals that were quite in keeping with Maxwell's vision.

NOTES

[1]John Franklin Brown, *The American High School* (New York: Macmillan Co., 1909), p. 193.

[2]Goodwin, "The School and The Home," p. 321

[3]*Ibid.*

[4]The earliest complete listing of teachers, including their schools and certifications was in the year 1901. See Table 9.

[5]John Franklin Brown, *The Training of Teachers*, pp. 232-233.

[6]New York City, Board of Education, Office of the Borough Superintendent for Manhattan and The Bronx, Letter to the principals of schools concerning teacher qualifications, June 12, 1901, The Bronx County Historical Society Research Library, Bronx, New York.

[7]*The Morris Annual*, 1905, pp. 30, 72-74.

[8]New York City, Department of Education, *Annual Report of the City Superintendent*, 1898-99, p. 93.

[9]*Ibid.*, pp. 98-99.

[10]*Ibid.*, p. 82.

[11]As far as can be determined one teacher taught two subjects at Morris High School. L. Marie Peirce taught both English and history. *The Morris Annual*, 1905, p. 29.

[12]New York City, Board of Education, *Journal of the School Board for Manhattan and The Bronx*, 1898, p. 1401.

[13]*Ibid.*, p. 1462.

[14]Rollins, p. 81.

[15]*The Morris Annual*, 1913, p. 13; 1926, p. 19. *New York Times* Obituary, 12 May 1920, p. 5, Rollins, p. 107.

[16]*The Morris Annual*, 1926, p. 4.

[17]The original Morris faculty was a very select group that came from a larger group of seventy-five who were chosen out of five hundred by competitive examination. *The Morris Annual*, 1920, p. 41.

[18]For a listing of the salaries paid to the original twenty-one teachers at the Mixed High School in 1897 see Table 10.

[19]William H. Maxwell, "The Teacher's Compensations," p. 471.

[20]Editorial, *School Review* 13 (March, 1903): 266-267.

[21]In 1900 the Board approved $500 salary increments for teachers in the annexes as they were doing "special service." See New York City Board of Education, *Journal of the School Board for Manhattan and The Bronx*, 1900, p. 1040.

[22]*The Morris Annual*, 1905, p. 16.

[23]New York City Board of Education, *Journal*, 1903, pp. 2191-2193.

[24]Miss Josie A. Davis, chairman of the Latin department until 1923, was hired at a salary of $2,000 in 1897, and by 1904 her salary had increased to $2,500, which was the highest for the women in both years. New York City Board of Education, *Journal*, 1897, pp. 1474-1476, *Journal*, 1903, pp. 2191-2193.

[25]New York City Board of Education, *Journal*, 1897, p. 1474, Journal, 1903, pp. 2191-2193. See also Editorial, *School Review* 13 (March, 1903): 267.

[26]New York City Board of Education, *Journal*, 1898, p. 506.

[27]New York City Board of Education, *Journal*, 1897, p. 2157.

[28]New York City Board of Education, *Journal of the School Board for Manhattan and The Bronx*, 1898, p. 167.

[29]New York City Board of Education, *Journal*, 1901, p. 1252.

[30]Janitors had to be at least thirty years old and married, and they had to live within 500 yards of the school. New York City Board of Education, *Journal*, 1898, p. 2243, *Journal*, 1901, p. 3197.

[31]New York City Board of Education, *Journal*, 1904, pp. 2709, 3298.

[32]*Ibid.*, pp. 301, 637, 828, 128.

[33]New York City Board of Education, Minutes of the Committee on High School and Training Schools, October 20, 1902, Special Collections, Milbank Memorial Library, Teachers College, Columbia University, New York.

[34]Editorial, *School Review* 13 (March, 1903): 266-267.

[35]Robert E. Doherty, "Tempest on the Hudson: The Struggle for Equal Pay for Equal Work in the New York City Public Schools, 1907-1911," *History of Education Quarterly*, Winter, 1979, pp. 427-428.

[36]Grace Strachan, *Equal Pay for Equal Work: The Story of the Struggle for Justice Being Made by the Women Teachers of the City of New York* (New York: B.F. Buck, 1910), p. 450.

[37]*Ibid.*, p. 450.

[38]Maxwell, *A Quarter Century of Public School Development,* pp. 246-248.

[39]As early as 1862, at a Board of Education session, Susan B. Anthony proposed an equal salary resolution which was rejected. Strachan, p. 23.

[40]*Ibid.*, p. 23.

[41]*Ibid.*, pp. 23-24.

[42]*Ibid.*, p. 25. See also Palmer, pp. 405, 410, 415, 416.

[43]Doherty, "Tempest on the Hudson," pp. 416-417.

[44]May Doherty, Morris High School Class of 1913, telephone interview with author, January 22, 1985. Ms. Doherty, who is not related to Robert Doherty, was a New York City Public School teacher for thirty-five years.

[45]Strachan, p. 508.

[46]*Ibid.*, pp. 508-509.

[47]*Ibid.*, p. 508.

[48]*Ibid.*, p. 509.

[49]Doherty, "Tempest on the Hudson," pp. 427-428.

[50]*The Morris Annual,* 1905, pp. 28-30.

[51]Palmer, p. 315.

[52]Maxwell, "The Teacher's Compensations," pp. 474-475.

[53]*Ibid.*, p. 470.

[54]Maxwell, "The American Teacher," p. 157.

[55]*Ibid.*

[56]High School Teachers Association of New York City *Yearbook 1906-7* (New York: Ed. J. Smith Co., 1907), p. 5.

[57]*Ibid.*, p. 2.

TABLE 9

TEACHERS OF MORRIS HIGH SCHOOL
QUALIFICATIONS AND SCHOOLS ATTENDED AS OF 1901

CODE EXPLANATION:

(a) *Issued N.Y. State certificates by the New York State Superintendent of Public Instruction*
(b) *Issued "College graduate" certificates by the New York State Superintendent of Public Instruction*
(c) *Issued Training School or Training Class certificates by the New York State Superintendent of Public Instruction*
(d) *Graduated from New York State Normal Schools*
(e) *Graduated from Normal Schools outside of New York State*
(f) *Graduated from Normal College of the City of New York*
(g) *Graduated from New York Training School for Teachers or the Brooklyn Training School for Teachers*
(h) *Attended a Normal or Training School or Class without graduating*
(i) *Received professional training from any institution not mentioned above*
(j) *Graduated from the College of the City of New York*
(k) *Graduated from other colleges*
(l) *Not included in any of the above*

CODE	TEACHER	SCHOOL / CERTIFICATION
k	Ackerly, Jennie	Vassar College
k	Althaus, Edward	Royal Military Academy, Berlin
f	Armand, Emma C.	City of New York Normal College
d	Baltz, Frank P.	Potsdam Normal School
k	Bates, Abby B.	Boston University
i	Barnum, Grace E.	Mt. Holyoke College / Posse Normal School of Gym
i, k	Blakely, Gilbert S.	Dartmouth / Harvard
a, e, k	Bevier, Marie	Jersey City Normal School / Poughkeepsie Female Collegiate
k	Breckenridge, Wm. E.	Yale
k	Burt, Clara M.	Wellesley / Columbia
k	Carr, Agnes	Smith
k	Constatine, Harriet L.	Wellesley
k, i	Cunningham, Celeste	Women's College, Columbia, S.C. / National Conservatory
k	Cutler, Sanford L.	Amherst
k	Davis, Josie A.	Boston University
i, k	Denbigh, John H.	Columbia University / Oxford
d	DeWitt, Louise L.	Geneseo State Normal
i, k	Diedrich, Marie M.	Geneva, Switzerland
e, k	du Bois, Elizabeth H.	Philadelphia Normal / Cornell
f, i, h	Falk, Anna A.	Teachers College
k	Foster, Harold E.	William's College
k	Foster, Walter E.	William's College and Post-Graduate Study
d, k	Freeston, Mary C.	Oswego / Posse Normal School of Gym
l	Gaylord, Harriet E.	
h, k	Goddard, Martha F.	Clark University, Worcester, Mass. / Wellesley
k	Goodwin, Edward J.	Bates College

Continued on next page —

TABLE 9 CONTINUED		
CODE	TEACHER	SCHOOL / CERTIFICATION
e, k	Heikes, Irving A.	Millersville, Pa. / Lehigh University
f, i	Hixon, Kate B.	Barnard / Cornell
h, k	Howell, Logan D.	University of North Carolina
i, k	Hussey, George B.	John Hopkins University / University of Chicago / Columbia
e, k	Johnston, Mary	Ontario School of Pedagogy / University of Toronto
f	Knox, Charlotte G.	City of New York Normal College
e	Konermann, Helene V.	Schleswiger Lehrerinnen Seminar, Germany
i, k	Lance, Frances C.	Wellesley
k	Laughlin, Hugh C.	Ohio State University / University of Nebraska
h, i	Leighton, Margrarette	Salem Normal School, Mass. / Institute of Technology, Mass. / Harvard
i, k	Lippert, Marie P.	Konigliches Lehrinnen Seminar, Berlin
h, k	Lyman, Roce C.	Smith
i, k	Lyman, Grace G.	Smith
f, i	Mendum, Georgiana	Glenmore Summer School / Harvard
f, i	Merington, Ruth	National Academy of Design, N.Y. / Academie Julien, Paris
d, k	Miller, Myrtle H.	Cortland State Normal School / Cornell
h, k	Morrey, William T.	Inter. State Summer School, Columbus, Ohio / Ohio State University / New York University
k	Mullen, Loring B.	University of Wooster, Ohio
e	Mussey, Dela P.	Mass. Normal Art
i	Parker, Jacob	Possee Normal School of Gym
k	Peabody, James E.	Williams / Harvard
i, f	Pierce, L. Marie	New York University Law School
b, d, k	Pingrey, Cora E.	Cortland State Normal School / Wellesley
i, k	Pyle, Willard R.	State Normal School, West Chester, Pa. / University of Michigan
k	Pyne, Henry R.	Columbia University
i, k	Rollins, Frank	Harvard / Columbia / Wesleyan
e	Sampson, Ezra W.	Bridgewater, Mass.
e	Schoeede, Emma J.	Konigliches Lehrerinnen Seminar, Cassel, Germany / University of Marburg, Germany / Cornell / Columbia
i	Skeele, Otis C.	Possee Normal School of Gym
i	Smith, Harriet K.	Harvard
k	Sohon, Michael D.	Lehigh / Johns Hopkins
k	Stevens, William S.	New York University / Washington College
i, k	Tildsley, John L.	Princeton / University of Halle, Prussia
i, k, b	Trask, Thomas C.	Yale
i, k	Wahl, Emanuel M.	Halle, Strassburg / Leipsic
e	Walker, Suzanne A.	Bridgewater, Mass. / Normal School in France and Germany
l	Williams, Edward M.	
c, i	Winslow, Isabel G.	Boston Normal School / Radcliffe
e	Woodward, M. Laura	Albany State Normal

SOURCE: Morris High School (Peter Cooper High School), List of teachers with qualifications and school attended, June 19, 1901, (Morris High School Collection, The Bronx County Historical Society Research Library, The Bronx, New York).

TABLE 10

SUBJECTS TAUGHT AND ANNUAL SALARY OF THE MIXED HIGH SCHOOL TEACHERS IN 1897

FIRST ASSISTANTS	SUBJECT	SALARY
Mr. Ezra W. Sampson	Physical Geography	$3,000
Mr. G. J. Smith	English	3,000
Miss Josie A. Davis	Latin	2,000
SECOND ASSISTANTS		
Mr. Edward Althaus	German	2,000
Mr. Gilbert S. Blakeley	English	1,800
Mr. John H. Denbigh	Mathematics	1,800
Mr. Michael D. Sohon	Chemistry	1,800
Miss Abby B. Bates	History	1,800
Miss Elizabeth H. du Bois	Latin	1,800
THIRD ASSISTANTS		
Mr. Charles L. N. Reed	History	1,500
Mr. Henry R. Pyne	Greek	1,500
Mr. Irving A. Heikes	Mathematics	1,500
Mr. James E. Peabody	Physiology	1,500
Miss Marie L. Bevier	Botany	1,200
Miss Jennie Ackerly	Mathematics	1,200
Miss Emily Faber	French	1,200
Miss Marie L. Lippert	German	1,200
Miss Georgiana Mendum	English	1,200
Miss Mary C. Freeston	Physical Training	1,200
Miss Dela P. Mussey	Drawing	1,200
Miss Harriet K. Smith	Stenography	1,200

SOURCE: New York City, Board of Education, *Journal for the Board of Education, 1898,* (Special Collections, Milbank Memorial Library, Teachers College, New York), pp. 1476-1477.

THE

STUDENTS

The
People's College

THROUGHOUT THE COUNTRY the number of students attending public high schools was steadily increasing at the close of the nineteenth century. By 1899-1900, the total number of students attending such schools was 530,425, or .7 percent of the total population.[1] For New York City, the number of public high school students was increasing at a high rate as well, although the percentage of the population attending the schools was much lower than for the country as a whole. In 1899-1900, for example, the city superintendent reported that there were 17,018 students enrolled in the public high schools, or .5 percent of the total city population of 3,474,202.[2]

Not only were the numbers of high school students increasing, but the percentage of high school students compared to the total city public school population was rising as well.[3] The greatest increase was in the 1898-99 enrollment for Manhattan and The Bronx, which showed 2,307 additional students for an 89 percent increase in one year, the second year the new high schools were in operation.[4]

When Morris High School opened as the Mixed High School in September of 1897, the average daily register was 535 students, according to the first *Annual Report* of the Department of Education.[5] The official 1897 Mixed High School register book, however, records 524 pupils entering the first year.[6] Of those students listed in the official register book, 324 have only minimal information recorded, *i.e.* name, when admitted, address, and one year or less of grades, indicating that they either left at the end of the year or before the year was over. There may have been more students like this, which would account for the discrepancy between the two register figures, or perhaps the register book was filled in from a previous list with certain names omitted.[7]

The other two hundred students, however, had full data recorded for them, including home address, when admitted, date of birth, last school attended, vaccination date, name of parent, as well as a spread sheet listing the course of study and the grades for each year attended. In addition, there were indications of whether or not the student graduated, and/or went on to another school. There is some reason to question the last items as some students who had no notation that they graduated from the school were on the graduation lists. It is likely, therefore, that such information was not faithfully kept up. The available data, however, does provide unique background material on the first students.

Based on the registration data for the two hundred fully registered students, a profile of the original Morris High School student body has been developed. What follows is an analysis based on the original source material of the Mixed High School register for 1897-98 and the graduation lists.

Of the 200 students studied, a slight majority, 109, resided in The Bronx, 88 lived in Manhattan and 3 in Brooklyn. It is to be expected that over half of the students lived in the borough where the school was located. Given the access to the school from Manhattan via the new rapid transit lines, it is not surprising that so many came from Manhattan, particularly from the nearby Harlem and Washington Heights areas. Brooklyn is another matter, and even three students from there is unusual, not only because of the travelling involved, but because it had fine high schools.

Of the first students who attended the Mixed High School, 162 came to it from the public grammar schools of New York City. With the exception of one student who transferred from City College in the second year, the remaining 37 came from private schools. Almost all of these private schools were located outside New York City, indicating that the families of these students had moved into the city or that Bronx families now decided to use the public high school. The age of the students on admission in 1897 ranged from thirteen to twenty-two years, but most of the students were thirteen or fourteen years old, with one twenty years old and one twenty-two years old.

Of the first 524 students on the Mixed High School register, 72 graduated, at least 326 left during or at the end of the first year, another 85 left in the second year, 34 left in the third year, and 7 left before completing the fourth year.[8] Of the 14 percent of the students who graduated, one, a transfer student, graduated after only two years. Thirty-one students graduated after three years, most of whom probably went on to the City or Normal Colleges (this group included 27 females and 4 males), and 40 students graduated in the fourth year (15 females and 25 males).

The breakdown of the various courses of study was fairly even for the students entering in 1897. The City/Normal College program was the highest with 56 students and by far most of them were females as indicated by the

The Alpine Literary Society in 1904-1905.

The Morris Annual, 1905.
The Bronx County Historical Society Research Library.

number of graduates who went on to Normal College for females. The lowest registration, with 42 students, was for the general program.

A 1904 study by the U.S. Commissioner of Education offered the opportunity for a comparison between the number of male and female students preparing for college at Morris High School with the statistics of the country as a whole.[9] The 1904 graduating class of Morris High School had a lower percentage of female college preparatory students, 13.33 percent at Morris versus 27.45 percent for the country.[10] On the other hand, the percentage of male students preparing to go to college was much higher at Morris High School: 67.76 percent at Morris versus 45.65 percent for the country.

Compared with the national average, the percentage of students enrolled in the classical course was higher at Morris, yet the percentage enrolled in the scientific program was lower. This could be explained by the fact that the standardized curriculum did not clearly distinguish between "classical" and "scientific" programs because of the elective system.

From the start of Morris High School, there were more female than male students. Of the first 200 full registrants, 122 were females and 78 were males. By 1904, female students had risen to 1,811, and the number of male students to 1,123. This was not unusual as the number of females in high schools throughout the country was significantly greater than the number of males. Yet, in universities and colleges males out-numbered females.[11]

Of the Morris High School male students who entered in the opening term of the school, and for whom an indication of a further school attended was available, one went to City College, two to Cornell, and two to New York University. Two males left for further business school without graduating. Twenty-five females, however, went to the Normal College, and six to training schools.

The full schedules and conservative grades listed in the official Mixed High School Register book for 1897 indicate that the students had rigorous programs. Yet, there was more than just class work at the school. By the 1904 school year, many academic, artistic and sports organizations were in full operation.[12] Among the organized activities available to Morris High School students was the Special Sketch Club, which made posters and illustrations for various classes and societies. There were also five literary societies, which apparently had different approaches. The Irving Literary Society was the oldest, but seemed defensive about being "dull." The Philologian Literary Society was very proud of its debating record. The Goodwin Literary Society, named in honor of the school's first principal, was for first year students only. The Acorn Literary Society was organized at the 173rd Street Annex. Its motto was "great oaks from little acorns grow." Finally, there was the Alpine Society, which was organized by students who felt that

The Acorn Literary Society, 1904-1905.

The Morris Annual, 1905.
The Bronx County Historical Society Research Library.

the other literary societies were not "earnest, serious, helpful."[13]

There were several music clubs for the students as well. The Morris Mandolin Club played at special events. The Girls' and Boys' Glee Clubs aimed "to teach its members to sing and appreciate good, classical music." The Morris High School Orchestra, which played at graduations, had thirteen violins, two flutes, two clarinets, two cornets and three pianos.[14] In addition, there were two secret organizations at Morris High, one for boys, Phi Nu Epsilon, and one for girls, Phi Kappa Sigma.[15]

The Morris High School Printing Office was begun in January, 1897, with a $30 surplus from the "annual fund" appropriated for the purchase

The Morris High School Boys' Glee Club.

The Morris Annual, 1905.
The Bronx County Historical Society Research Library.

The Morris High School Orchestra.

The Morris Annual, 1905.
The Bronx County Historical Society Research Library.

The First Annual Social Meeting ticket of
the Peter Cooper High School Alumni Association,
dated December 27, 1901.

Morris High School Collection.
The Bronx County Historical Society Research Library.

of second-hand type and a foot-power press that could print forms 5½ x 10 inches. The boys of the printing squad "furnished programs and tickets for the Alumni Reunions, Musical Clubs, Oratorical Contests and Debating Societies, and blank forms for school and regents examinations, records, notices and many other purposes."[16]

By the school year of 1904, the Morris High School Athletic Association, which was organized in 1897, had succeeded in establishing a full complement of teams. The football team, first formed in 1898, was in full swing with "encouraging" results, although it suffered from a shortage of boys, and a loss of its coach the year before. Baseball was Morris High's "strongest sport" and, indeed, it was known as a "baseball school." The basketball team, organized in 1898, was quite successful as well, and played teams from as far away as Jersey City. In addition, there was a track team, a midget football team, and other midget sport teams, which had size and weight limits to encourage all students to enjoy team sports.[17]

In 1899 the Athletic League of the Metropolitan District was created with Morris, Clinton, Commercial, Manual Training, Flushing and Jersey City

The Morris High School Baseball Team.
The Morris Annual, 1905.
The Bronx County Historical Society Research Library.

High Schools. Morris won the baseball and track championships in 1899 and the football championship in 1900 and 1903. One of the league's founders was Henry R. Pyne, the Greek language teacher at Morris.[18]

Athletics for the girls was much more limited, and initially there were no female teams. But in the winter of the first year, twenty girls formed the Atalanta Club in order to get more physical training than provided for in the curriculum. According to the *Morris Annual* of 1905:

> They formally chose their officers, they joyfully paid their membership dues – and then – they began to make a reputation for themselves as a hard working, social body.

> All through the winter they showed firm little hands, going from blister to callous as they traveled ladders, climbed ropes, and "chinned" themselves. They made up as far as possible in jumping, vaulting, and run-

ning for the years that had passed with a steady stream of "Don't run," "Don't climb," "Don't jump," "It is unladylike." And they rejoiced that now they were in a position where time, place, and dress all favored these pleasures.[19]

The girls were the "cheerleaders" for their "brothers" on the teams at games, where they were "properly chaperoned."[20] Everyone in the school seemed to support the teams. Herman Elkan of the Class of 1904 would write: ". . . and those football games at Manhattan Oval! One hundred percent of the school was there – boys and girls – to watch our boys trim Clinton."[21]

An Alumni Association was begun in 1901 with the aim to: ". . . foster a spirit of cooperation among fellow graduates, and to revive and preserve those friendships which began in high school . . . (and) to constitute a

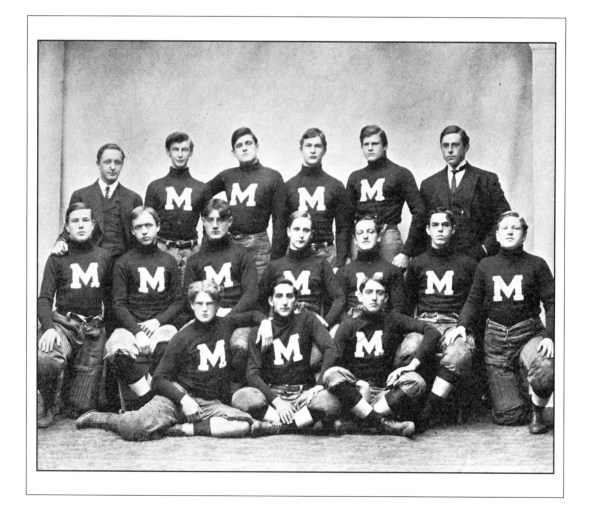

The Morris High School Football Team.

The Morris Annual, 1905.
The Bronx County Historical Society Research Library.

Henry Rogers Pyne was the original faculty's
Greek teacher. He helped to establish the
athletic programs at Morris High School.

The Morris Annual, 1911.
The Bronx County Historical Society Research Library.

material and moral support of its high school."[22]

The Morris High School Organization was formed in 1904, stating that: "Any person over eighteen years of age having attended Morris High School for the period of one year is eligible for membership subject to the approval of the membership committee."[23] The idea was to afford the opportunity of meeting former instructors and friends outside of the school and to foster a genuine spirit of sociability and friendliness.[24] This association organized dances for its members.

These groups give some indication of the spirit that grew around Morris High School and which was recalled by so many of its students. As a 1904 graduate, and later a teacher at Morris, recalled: "And that spirit must not

The Morris High School Basketball Team.

The Morris Annual, 1905.
The Bronx County Historical Society Research Library.

Morris High School Track Team.

The Morris Annual, 1905.
The Bronx County Historical Society Research Library.

Morris High School Midget Football Team.

The Morris Annual, 1905.
The Bronx County Historical Society Research Library.

die. That spirit that has been carried down through a decade and more must go on. It is to you, the present holders of the trust, that we, the old guard, look to carry it forward, unsullied and undimmed."[25]

This kind of spirit was also in evidence in those who travelled to the school from far-off locations. Herman Weiss Johnston, class of 1908, who later graduated from City College of New York, recollected that getting to the school was an involved series of public transports. Living in the northeast Bronx, he began attending Morris in September, 1903:

> "At that time, the trolley car to Mt. Vernon. . . would stop for me right in front of our house. This car took me to Mt. Vernon. From there I took another trolley down White Plains Avenue to Bedford Park and the 3rd Avenue elevated train to 166th Street and 3rd Avenue. Then it was only a short three-block walk to Morris High School. There were several other routes that I used but they all averaged one and a half to one and three-quarters hours. I had to leave home on the 6:50 [A.M.] trolley in order to get to school on time.[26]

It is of special note that a number of the original faculty at Morris High School enrolled their kin in the new school. Ezra W. Sampson, one of Dr. Goodwin's most valued friends and first assistant who came with Goodwin in 1897 from Newton, Massachusetts, registered two of his sons in the school.[27] Edwin Sampson transferred from Newton High School and took the general course of study,[28] graduating in June of 1901.[29] Winslow Sampson graduated in 1902. Both Sampsons went to Harvard.[30] Marion Osgood Skeele, the daughter of Otis C. Skeele, the physical education teacher, wrote the early Morris High School song.[31]

Frank Rollins brought his daughters to the school as well. Rollins had been the master at Newton High School from 1893 to 1897 when he went to New York as a first assistant at DeWitt Clinton High School, and later joined Morris as head of one of the annexes.[32] Ethel Rollins transferred from Claflin Grammar School in Newtonville, Massachusetts and took the classical program for four years,[33] graduating in 1901.[34] In 1904, Mabel Rollins graduated and followed her sister to Cornell.[35]

Edward Althaus, Jr., son of the original German teacher, graduated in 1901 and went to Cornell. His sister, Amalie Louise Althaus, graduated in 1903 with a Barnard Trustee Scholarship and later joined the Morris faculty as a German teacher working alongside her father.[36]

Perhaps the best indication of the confidence that the new principal had in the school was that he enrolled his son in the opening term. Norman Goodwin was admitted as a second-year student and graduated in 1900, in the first graduating class. He went on to Cornell University.[37]

The students of Morris High School seemed extremely fond of their teachers. This was reflected in the written articles for *The Morris Annuals* and in their memories. In a recent interview, May Doherty, Class of 1913,

Edward Althaus was on the original Morris faculty
as a Second Assistant and taught German
until his retirement in 1920.

The Morris Annual, 1920.
The Bronx County Historical Society Research Library.

Charlotte Knox was on the Morris faculty
as an English teacher by 1901.

The Morris Annual, 1926.
The Bronx County Historical Society
Research Library.

spoke of John Denbigh as a "nice looking man," and a "good principal."[38]
Roslyn (Wax) Eisenstein, a student during the 1920s, and later a teacher
there, recalled Charlotte Knox, who was on the faculty in 1901 and by the
1920s had become dean of girls, as an "austere, stern, strict disciplinarian
with little or no sense of humor," but who was very fair. Ms. Knox was
remembered for being "dressed well in a tailored suit," and that "her standards of dress and behavior were followed by her students." Mrs. Eisenstein
also recalled Edith Read, who taught biology for over 25 years as a "lovely,
warm, gentle, soft-spoken lady and an excellent teacher."[39] Armand
Hammer, class of 1916, also recalled his years at Morris High School with
fondness and nostalgia."[40]

Irene C. (Jurs) Brock, a 1914 graduate, who was a member of the danc-
ing club, thought Mr. Denbigh "fair and square. . . a nice man, stately and
well-bred," and Mr. Althaus as a "lovely man" and Edith Read, as "very popular."[41] Murvin Becker, who entered Morris at 13 years of age in 1906,
remembered that people called Morris High School "the greatest high
school in the world." He was proud to walk the half hour each way between
his home in the Tremont section of The Bronx and school. In 1909 he was

Marie L. Bevier was the original Botany teacher
on the first Morris faculty. She retired in 1913 after
forty-four years of teaching.

The Morris Annual, 1913.
The Bronx County Historical Society Research Library.

a member of the school's Greater New York Championship Baseball Team. Mr. Becker's recollections of his teachers were remarkable in their lucidity, warmth and directness. He brought forth vivid images of Ezra Sampson as a "calm, bearded, level-headed person, who could handle any crisis" and Gilbert Blakely and Abby Bates as "wonderful teachers," Otis Skeele as a "grand fellow," the French teacher, Marie Bevier, as "stiff necked," and Mr. Denbigh and Miss Davis as "very austere individuals, never to be taken lightly." After graduation, he became a teacher in the New York City public school system, and for 32 years taught at Morris.[42]

John M. Avent, president of the Class of 1901, who became an English teacher at Morris High School from 1911-1919, and, principal of Curtis High School in 1924, wrote tenderly at a later date of the early teachers in the days when "Every one knew every one else." Avent remembered: "It was no uncommon thing to have the same English, Latin, history or mathematics teacher for three or four years: it was possible to go through high school with the same set of teachers!"[43]

On the occasion of the twenty-fifth anniversary of Morris High School, Evelyn Schwab of the Class of 1922, wrote in the *Annual*:

> Morris, that eminent bulwark of education, that mighty influence on the thousands of young lives that enter its portals, is just a quarter of a century old. Relatively few changes have taken place within its walls in those twenty-five years. From a small frame structure on Third Avenue in 1897 to the beautiful building of the present day, Morris activities and Morris traditions have practically remained the same. Morris, from the very beginning, has established a record by her splendid achievements in scholarships . . . .
>
> . . . Morris, to her credit, has always stood for hard work, fair play, honor, truth and service. These, then, are the things for which we must strive. . . Toward this end we are aided by the immeasurable influence of our teachers, whose aim it is to build up our minds and our souls; and while teaching us to be loyal and faithful students are, at the same time, instructing us in the principles of loyal and faithful citizenship.[44]

John McDonough Avent, a Morris graduate of 1901
and later an English teacher at Morris High School,
became the Principal of Curtis High School in 1924.

The Bronx County Historical Society Research Library.

The Morris High School faculty, 1904-1905.
Principal John Denbigh is in center of photograph
to the left of the woman with the large hat.

The Morris Annual, 1905.
The Bronx County Historical Society Research Library.

HIGH SCHOOLS
BOROUGHS OF
MANHATTAN AND
THE BRONX

FIRST ANNUAL

GRADUATING EXERCISES

FRIDAY MORNING, JUNE 29, 1900

AT TEN O'CLOCK

HALL OF
THE BOARD
OF EDUCATION
PARK AVENUE & 59TH STREET

The First Annual Graduating Exercises Program in 1900.

Morris High School Collection.
The Bronx County Historical Society Research Library.

ORDER OF EXERCISES

🙢

Music

READING OF SCRIPTURE

Music

INTRODUCTORY REMARKS

> HON. JAMES P. LEE, CHAIRMAN,
> Committee on Special and High Schools

Music

ADDRESS

> HON. ABRAM S. HEWITT

Music

PRESENTATION OF CLASSES

> JOHN JASPER, BOROUGH SUPERINTENDENT

Music

PRESENTATION OF DIPLOMAS BY

> HON. MILES M. O'BRIEN, PRESIDENT OF THE SCHOOL BOARD

Music

SINGING OF AMERICA

> In which the audience is requested to join.

GRADUATES

THE WADLEIGH HIGH SCHOOL

FOUR YEAR COURSE

Edith Hill
Helen L. King
Anna G. Ware

Ida E. Lewis
Florence M. Mills
Minna J. Morgenthau

Hattie Neuman
Bessie L. Swan
Jeannette M. Wick

THREE YEAR COURSE

Blanche W. Adams
Irene M. Ahearn
Edith C. Ahern
Elsie L. Baese
Sadie R Barnett
Ernestine Birnbaum
Anita S. Boddicker
Rosetta C. Borger
Margaret M. Brennan
Elizabeth A. Brownlee
Muriel Burger
Mary F. Butler
Anna M. Cahill
Katheryn E. Cahill
Maud A. Cahill
Agnes M. Callahan
Ida Degner
Elizabeth A. Duffy
Jessie H. Duncan
Bessie Feigin
Mary C. Finley
Frances Flynn
Grace Ganzenmuller
Julia Goldberg
Frances Golovensky
Mildred Gomez
Adelaide Gosman
Frances E. Gottler
Harriet L. Griffin
Millie F. Hag

Nellie G. Haller
Annie Hamill
Lilie E. Harned
Sarah R. Hanson
Lucie W. Hoelz
Elizabeth Hoffman
Anna E. Hume
Amy A. Hurley
Amelia Hymanson
Florence A. Jeffery
Lillian Joseph
Fannie Kahn
Carrie Kaplan
Mary H. Kasl
Ida Kaufman
Rosemary E. Kehoe
Caroline G. Kelly
Helen E. Knauff
Janet Kraft
Editha Kudlich
Katherine C. Lengemann
Edna M. Levi
Beatrice Lewis
Ella M. Loughran
Kate A. Loughran
Kathryn A. McFarland
Catherine Mackie
Bessie K. Marsh
Edith E. Menken
Florence M. Nash

Mary R. O'Donnell
Helen G. O'Hare
Gertrude M. Patterson
Juliette Pons
Tina Rappaport
Helen Regan
Sarah C. Regan
Dorothea A. Reichert
Anna Riley
Mary E. Rooney
Elsie N. Rose
Lillie C. Rose
Lillie F. Rosenblum
Frances R. Sarasohn
Mary Schleifstein
Ethel S. Schwarz
Eugenie Serber
Rebecca Serber
Marie V. Shannon
Mildred A. Sherman
Marion F. Smith
Louisa F. Snyder
Ada J. Stern
Ida M. Tankard
Rose Tiernan
Sara Todd
Rebecca Trachtenberg
Clara M. Warren
Florence E. Wilson

THE DE WITT CLINTON HIGH SCHOOL

THREE YEAR COURSE

William Anthony Aery
Max Winkler Amberg
Henry Amster
Harry Arranow
Samuel Blumberg
Edward Dudley Bryde
William Buxman
Marcus Louis Chasins
Bernard Cohen

Abraham Moses Davis
Leo Feibel
Edward Augustus Fitzpatrick
Millard James Friedberg
Highland Garnet Handy
Walter Robert Johnson
Frederick Lask
Elias Lieberman
Harold Neuhof
Edward Stuart Peck

Joseph Rothkowitz
Harry Schimmel
Morris Schneiderman
Walter Le Roy Shipman
Max Slutzky
Stephen Moore Smith
Arthur Sidney Unger
Jacob Walz
James Wilzin

THE PETER COOPER HIGH SCHOOL

FOUR YEAR COURSE

May Elizabeth Brockman
Norman Goodwin
Frederick Reid Heath

Irving Isaac Lewine
Lansing Yates Lippincott
Clarence Paul Oberndorf

Howard MacMillan Richard
Jacob Anthony Weber

THREE YEAR COURSE

Mary Accurso
Gertrude Claire Archer
Florence Cleora Bartholomew
Mary Cecilia Barrett
Estelle Bruner
Mary Magdalen Buzak
Marietta Irene Chambers
Emma Mary Regina Dennerlein
Mae Feust
Sarah Gold
Natalie Florine Hodgman

Lillie Hogenauer
Blanche Mayette Katz
Caroline Elizabeth Keil
Meta Alvina Kiefer
Jeanette Therese Krellenstein
Isaac Kroll
Rita Levy
Naomi Levy
Henrietta Louise Loasby
Emma Hardy Mathewson
Florence Wallace Mathews
May Ella McCarthy

Thomas McGreevy
Fannie Augusta Meierdiercks
Sybil Kent Morse
Anna Katherine Pergolie
Esther Rubin
Loretta Mary Shea
Caroline Silberstein
Kathryn Genevieve Stone
Margaret Madeline Tucker
Caroline Louise Vogel
Kenneth Whittemore Wright

The First Annual
Graduating Exercises
Program in 1900.

Morris High School Collection.
The Bronx County Historical
Society Research Library.

SCHOOL BOARD

MILES M. O'BRIEN, President
WILLIAM J. ELLIS, Secretary

Richard H. Adams
Charles C. Burlingham
Vernon M. Davis
William T. Emmet
Edward F. Farrell
John B. Harrison
Joseph J. Kittel
James P. Lee
John M. Linck
George Livingston

Patrick F. McGowan
Thaddeus Moriarty
Alfred Hennen Morris
John G. O'Keeffe
Waldo H. Richardson, M.D.
Henry A. Rogers
Abraham Stern
Morris E. Sterne
Thomas W. Timpson
Edward G. Whitaker

COMMITTEE ON SPECIAL AND HIGH SCHOOLS

JAMES P. LEE, Chairman

Vernon M. Davis
Edward G. Whitaker
Edward F. Farrell,
Alfred Hennen Morris

George Livingston
Charles C. Burlingham
Waldo H. Richardson, M. D.
Morris E. Sterne

BOARD OF SUPERINTENDENTS

JOHN JASPER, Chairman

James Godwin
George S. Davis
Henry W. Jameson
John L. N. Hunt
Thomas S. O'Brien
Alfred T. Schauffler
Edward D. Farrell
James Lee

Edgar Dubs Shimer
Matthew J. Elgas
Gustave Straubenmüller
Albert P. Marble
Clarence E. Meleney
Seth T. Stewart
Andrew W. Edson
Arthur McMullin

The First Annual Graduating Exercises Program in 1900.

Morris High School Collection.
The Bronx County Historical Society Research Library.

NOTES

[1]See Table 11 for the national secondary student population figures from 1889 through 1904.

[2]New York City Department of Education, *Annual Report of the City Superintendent,* 1901, pp. 21, 33.

[3]See Table 12 for the enrollment in the high schools of the city for seven years, with the percentage increase over the previous year. For comparison, the total city public school population figures are offered.

[4]Pupil statistics can by very confusing. A good deal depends upon when the statistics were drawn during the year and whether the figure represents enrollment, average attendance, or average daily register. For example, the 1904 New York City Department of Education, *Annual Report* shows an average register for Bronx high schools of 2,218 (p. 9), but this does not agree with the 1904 City Superintendent's *Annual Report* which indicates a 1,925 average daily register for Bronx high schools (p. 39). Another example of such a discrepancy is found in the City Superintendent's *Annual Report* for 1904, which lists 3,355 enrolled students in the Bronx high schools (p. 40), while the U.S. Education Commissioner's report for 1904 lists 2,934 students in Morris High School, the only high school in The Bronx (See Tables 12 and 14).

[5]New York City Department of Education, *Annual Report,* 1898, p. 64.

[6]Morris High School (Mixed High School) Register 1897-98, Morris High School Collection, The Bronx County Historical Society Research Library, Bronx, New York.

[7]See Table 13 for a tabulation of the data from the Morris High School Register.

[8]The drop-out problem was nationwide. In 1900, only 11.9 percent of the pupils enrolled in the country's public high schools graduated. In addition, only 10.2 percent of the fourteen to seventeen year olds were even enrolled in secondary schools across the country. See Krug, *The Shaping of the American High School,* pp. 172-173.

[9]See Table 14.

[10]This did not include the Normal College, a destination of many Morris High School female students.

[11]For an analysis of the male/female enrollment in secondary schools and colleges see Table 15.

[12]For a discussion of the value of play and sports by a turn of the century educator see Otho Winger, "Practical Application of Aristotle's Principle, Catharsis," *Education* 28 (March, 1908): pp. 401-410.

[13]*The Morris Annual,* 1905, pp. 35, 57-62.

[14]*Ibid.,* pp. 62-67.

[15]*Ibid.,* pp. 68-69.

[16]*The Morris Annual,* 1912, p. 105.

[17]*The Morris Annual,* 1905, pp. 38-40, 44-47, 50. The term 'midget' refers to students under the average size; e.g. the midget relay team was for students under 110 pounds.

[18]*The Morris Annual,* 1912, p. 80. *The Morris Annual,* 1911, p. 82.

[19]*The Morris Annual,* 1905, p. 51.

[20]*Ibid.,* pp. 51-52.

[21]*The Morris Annual,* 1922, p. 26.

[22]*The Morris Annual,* 1905, p. 75.

[23]*Ibid.,* p. 70.

[24]*Ibid.*

[25]*Ibid.,* pp. 26-27.

[26]Margaret R. Johnston, *Memoirs of Herman Weiss Johnston, 1889-1969.* (Published by author, 1977), p. 26.

[27]*The Morris Annual,* 1905, p. 16. *The Morris Annual,* 1913, p. 13.

[28]Morris High School Register, 1897-1898, p. 155.

[29]Graduation brochure, 1901, *Morris High School Scrapbook*: 1897-1914, The Morris High School Collection, The Bronx County Historical Society Research Library, Bronx, New York.

[30]*The Morris Annual,* 1906, p. 90.

[31]*The Morris Annual,* 1905, p. 23.

[32]Rollins, p. 107.

[33]Mixed High School Register, 1897-98, p. 145.

[34]Graduation brochure, 1901, *Morris High School Scrapbook.*

[35]*The Morris Annual,* 1912, pp. 13-14.

[36]*Ibid. The Morris Annual,* 1911, p. 64.

[37]Morris High School Register, 1897-98, p. 378.

[38]May Doherty, interview.

[39]Roslyn (Wax) Eisenstein, Morris High School Class of 1929, telephone interview with author, December 1, 1984, letter to author, January 10, 1985. In 1934 she worked at the Brook Avenue Annex of Morris High School and was paid $7 per day. Mrs. Eisenstein graduated from Hunter College and taught at Morris High School from 1934-1939.

[40]Armand Hammer, Morris High School Class of 1916, letter to author March 6, 1986.

[41]Irene C. (Jurs) Brock, Morris High School Class of 1914. Taped interview with James Musto, III, December 20, 1991. Ms. Brock lived one block from the school at 759 Home Street and took a General Course of Study. She later went to teacher training school on 126th Street and was a teacher in the New York City public school system for over 30 years. Her first pay as a teacher was $15 per week.

[42]Murvin Becker, Morris High School Class of 1910. Telephone interview with author, May 24, 1993. Mr. Becker was born on June 19, 1893 and entered Morris in 1906. After graduation, he attended the New York Training School for Teachers, and taught in P.S. 11, P.S. 45, and then in 1922 joined the Morris faculty where he remained for thirty-two years. Mr. Becker taught civics, history, and economics. As the baseball team coach for many years, he coached Hall of Famer, Hank Greenberg. Alma Becker, Murvin's sister also graduated from Morris and became an elementary school teacher.

[43]*The Morris Annual,* 1922, p. 22.

[44]*Ibid.,* pp 17-18.

TABLE 11

SECONDARY STUDENTS AND PERCENT TO
TOTAL U.S. POPULATION 1889-1904

YEAR	IN PUBLIC INSTITUTIONS		IN PRIVATE INSTITUTIONS		IN BOTH CLASSES	
	SECONDARY STUDENTS	PERCENT OF POPULATION	SECONDARY STUDENTS	PER CENT OF POPULATION	SECONDARY STUDENTS	PER CENT OF POPULATION
1889-90	221,522	.36%	145,481	.23%	367,003	.59%
1890-91	222,868	.35	147,567	.23	370,435	.58
1891-92	247,660	.38	154,429	.24	402,089	.62
1892-93	256,628	.39	153,792	.23	410,420	.62
1893-94	302,006	.45	178,352	.26	480,358	.71
1894-95	361,370	.53	178,342	.26	539,712	.79
1895-96	393,729	.56	166,274	.23	559,003	.79
1896-97	420,459	.59	164,445	.23	584,904	.82
1897-98	459,813	.63	166,302	.23	626,115	.86
1898-99	488,549	.66	166,678	.23	655,227	.89
1899-1900	530,425	.70	188,816	.25	719,241	.95
1900-1901	558,740	.72	177,260	.23	736,000	.95
1901-2	566,124	.72	168,636	.22	734,760	.94
1902-3	608,412	.76	168,223	.21	776,635	.97
1903-4	652,804	.80	169,431	.21	822,235	1.01

SOURCE: United States Commissioner of Education, *Annual Report*, 1904-05,
(Washington, D.C.: U.S. Government Printing Office), p. 1732.

TABLE 12

PUBLIC HIGH SCHOOL ENROLLMENT FOR THE CITY OF NEW YORK 1897-1904

YEAR/ BOROUGH	HIGH SCHOOL ENROLLMENT	PER CENT OF INCREASE OVER PREVIOUS YEAR	TOTAL CITY ENROLLMENT*	PERCENT OF HIGH SCHOOL TO TOTAL ENROLLMENT
1897-1898			** Total city enrollment includes*	
Manhattan & Bronx	2,591		*high schools, grammar schools,*	
Brooklyn	7,068		*and kindergartens.*	
Queens	497			
Richmond	191			
Total: 10,347			470,491	2.2%
1898-1899				
Manhattan & Bronx	4,898	89.0%		
Brooklyn	7,782	10.1		
Queens	737	48.3		
Richmond	314	64.4		
Total: 13,731		32.7	493,849	2.8%
1899-1900				
Manhattan & Bronx	7,622	56.0		
Brooklyn	7,973	2.5		
Queens	1,019	38.0		
Richmond	404	28.0		
Total: 17,018		24.0	523,419	3.2%
1900-1901				
Manhattan & Bronx	8,383	10.0		
Brooklyn	8,800	10.4		
Queens	1,369	34.3		
Richmond	461	14.1		
Total: 19,013		11.8	559,218	3.4%
1901-1902				
Manhattan & Bronx	9,525	13.6		
Brooklyn	9,782	11.2		
Queens	1,528	11.6		
Richmond	626	35.8		
Total: 21,461		12.9	588,614†	3.6%
1902-1903†			*†For the first time pupils who transferred within*	
Manhattan	9,601 }	23.7	*the city were not counted twice. According to*	
Bronx	2,184 }		*Superintendent Maxwell, this mistake was*	
Brooklyn	9,538	2.5	*inevitable as long as the boroughs were under*	
Queens	1,786	16.9	*separate boards.*	
Richmond	592	5.4	[Annual Report of City Superintendent, 1903, p. 33]	
Total: 23,701		10.4	575,568	4.1%
1903-1904				
Manhattan	11,319	17.9		
Bronx	3,355	53.6		
Brooklyn	10,467	9.7		
Queens	1,893	6.0		
Richmond	760	28.4		
Total: 27,794		17.3	622,201	4.5%

SOURCES: New York City, Department of Education, *Annual Reports of the City Superintendent, 1899-1904.* For 1897-1898 there was no *Annual Report of the City Superintendent,* however, Superintendent Maxwell presented a summary of statistics gathered by the borough superintendents at the July 19, 1898 meeting of the Board of Education. See New York City, Board of Education, *Journal,* 1898, p. 406.
(Special Collections, Milbank Memorial Library, Teachers College, Columbia University, New York)

TABLE 13

STUDENTS REGISTERED AT THE MIXED HIGH SCHOOL
IN 1897

RESIDENCE	NUMBER OF STUDENTS
Bronx	109
Manhattan	88
Brooklyn	3
Total:	200

ELEMENTARY OR PREVIOUS SCHOOL	NUMBER OF STUDENTS
Public (all elementary)	162
Private	38
Total:	200

AGE AT ENTRANCE	
Thirteen years	15
Fourteen years	61
Fifteen years	63
Sixteen years	32
Seventeen years	13
Eighteen years	5
Nineteen years	0
Twenty years	1
Twenty-one years	0
Twenty-two years	1
Unknown	9
Total:	200

COURSE OF STUDY	
General	42
Classical	52
City / Normal College	56
Commercial	50
Total:	200

YEAR LEFT SCHOOL WITHOUT GRADUATION	
First	* 2
Second	85
Third	34
Fourth	7
Total:	128

MALES	78
FEMALES	122
Total:	200

* *Note: does not include the 324 students not fully registered.*

GRADUATES	MALES	FEMALES	TOTAL
First year	0	0	0
Second year	1	0	1
Third year	4	27	31
Fourth year	25	15	40
Total:	30	42	72

SCHOOLS ATTENDED AFTER GRADUATION	MALES	FEMALES	TOTAL
Normal College	0	25	25
City College	1	0	1
Training Schools	0	6	6
Colleges / Universities	4	0	4
Total:	5	31	36

SOURCE: Morris High School (Mixed High School), Register 1897-1898.
Morris High School Collection,
(The Bronx County Historical Society Research Library, The Bronx, New York).

TABLE 14

COLLEGE PREPARATORY STUDENTS IN PUBLIC HIGH SCHOOLS OF THE UNITED STATES: 1903-1904

COURSE	TOTAL NUMBER OF STUDENTS	PER CENT OF TOTAL	MALE STUDENTS	PER CENT OF TOTAL MALE	FEMALE STUDENTS	PER CENT OF TOTAL FEMALE
Classical	34,307	5.40%	15,043	5.65%	19,264	5.21%
Scientific	26,300	4.14	15,974	6.01	10,326	2.79
*Total:	60,607	9.54	31,017	11.66	29,590	8.00
Graduating in 1904	75,476	11.87%	27,921	10.50%	47,555	12.86%
College prep students in graduating class	25,801	34.18†	12,747	45.65†	13,054	27.45†

STATISTICS OF MORRIS HIGH SCHOOL 1903-1904

Classical	308	10.50%	158	14.07%	150	8.28%
Scientific	58	1.98	49	4.36	9	.50
**Total:	366	12.47	207	18.43	159	8.78
Graduating in 1904	124	4.23%	34	3.03%	90	4.96%
College prep students in graduating class	33	26.61†	21	67.76†	12	13.33†

* Total number of students in high schools 635,808: 266,039 boys, 369,769 girls.
** Total number of students in Morris High School 2,934: 1,123 boys, 1,811 girls.
† Per Cent of graduates, either male or female.

SOURCE: United States Commissioner of Education, *Annual Report*, 1904-5, (Washington, D.C.: U.S. Government Printing Office), pp. 1730-1911.

| | TABLE 15 | | | | | |

COMPARISON OF MALE-FEMALE ATTENDANCE
IN HIGH SCHOOLS AND ABOVE

	1902-1903			1903-1904		
INSTITUTIONS	MALE	FEMALE	TOTAL	MALE	FEMALE	TOTAL
Public high schools	245,771	346,442	592,213	266,039	369,769	635,808
Public normal schools	1,672	4,372	6,044	2,150	3,243	5,393
Public universities and colleges	7,552	2,603	10,155	8,835	2,768	11,603
Private high schools	50,434	51,413	101,847	51,599	51,808	103,407
Private normal schools	4,683	3,268	7,951	4,198	3,618	7,816
Private universities and colleges	29,749	13,890	43,639	30,073	14,555	44,628
Private colleges for women	......	5,809	5,809	......	4,800	4,800
Manual training schools	4,037	4,940	8,977	5,641	3,139	8,780
Total:	343,898	432,737	776,635	368,535	453,700	822,235

SOURCE: United States Commissioner of Education, *Annual Report*, 1904-5, (Washington, D.C.: U.S. Government Printing Office), p. 1728.

Front view of Morris High School tower, c. 1906.

The Bronx County Historical Society Research Library.

THE MORRIS HIGH SCHOOL

BOROUGH OF THE BRONX

Fifth Annual Graduating Exercises

MONDAY EVENING, JUNE TWENTY-SEVENTH

NINETEEN HUNDRED AND FOUR

AT EIGHT O'CLOCK

The Program for the Fifth Annual Graduating Exercises.
held on June 27, 1904 at the new school building.

Morris High School Collection.
The Bronx County Historical Society Research Library.

Order of Exercises

READING OF THE SCRIPTURES - - - The Reverend Gibson Harris

IMPROMPTU VALSE - - - - - - - - *Bachmann*
HIGH SCHOOL ORCHESTRA

"THE CHARACTER OF GOUVERNEUR MORRIS" - Lucie Ada Dolan

LARGHETTO - - - - - - - - - *Beethoven*
CHORUS

"THE DEMAND FOR PATRIOTIC VIGILANCE" Alexander Edward Crowley

ROMANCE SANS PAROLES - - - - - - - *L. Gregh*
HIGH SCHOOL ORCHESTRA

"THE STRENGTH OF THE PUBLIC SCHOOL" - - Sidonia Scheyer

SERENADE - - - - - - - - *DeKoven*
HIGH SCHOOL QUARTETTE

"A PLEA FOR ORGANIZED LABOR" - - - Charles Louis Klein

LOVE SONG—BEN JONSON - - - - - *Cauffman*
CHORUS

"THE TEACHER'S OPPORTUNITY" - - Frederick William Roder

MARCHE MILITAIRE - - - - - - *Schubert*
HIGH SCHOOL ORCHESTRA

ADDRESS - - - - - - - - -
THE HONORABLE LOUIS F. HAFFEN
President of the Borough of The Bronx

JUNE - - - - - - - - - *Schnecker*
CHORUS

ADDRESS TO THE GRADUATES - PRESENTATION OF DIPLOMAS
DR. ALBERT P. MARBLE
Associate City Superintendent
Chairman of Committee on High Schools and Training Schools

AMERICA - - - - - - - - -
CHORUS AND ORCHESTRA

Graduates

LILLIAN GLADYS AIKEN
MARY ATKINSON ANDERSON
VICTOR WILLIAM ANDERSON
LOI ACKERMAN BANKS
PAUL JONES BAUMGARTEN
MARGARETHA BECKER
RUDOLPH CHARLES BERGMANN
FLORENCE EDITH BLACKMAN
LENA BOCKER
ELLEN XAVERINE BORDEN
LEAH HELEN BRAUER
GRACE CLAIRE BRIGGS
LESTER GUSTAVE BRUGGEMANN
HARRY LANCASTER BURGESS
MARY GERTRUDE CABLE
LOUISA CERRUTI
BERNADET CLAIRE CONNOLLY
LILLIAN TERESA COONEY
ESTHER THERESA CROHN
IRENE GERTRUDE CROLEY
ALEXANDER EDWARD CROWLEY
UMBERTO ANTONIO DENOVELLIS
JENNIE ESTELLE DESDET
ELSIE PAULINE DIETZ
ETHELWYN DITHRIDGE
LUCIE ADA DOLAN
MAY DOTTENHEIM
MARY AGNES DRISCOLL
MARJORIE MCCLINTOCK EASTMAN
KATHARINE LORRAINE EDGERLY
MILLICENT EDWARDS
HELEN FRANCES EUSTIS
MARY EUSTIS
ETHEL GRACE EVERETT
JULIA VERONICA EVERS
HERMINA FARIAN
ELSWORTH WILLIAM FERDON
GEORGE CHARLES FEUERRIEGEL
JENNIE FREED
HENRY FRIEDRICH
KATHERINE IRENE GAFFNEY
KATHRYN CECIL GALVIN
FLORENCE GOLD
MORRIS GOODKIND
LOTTIE PAULINE GREMPLE
RAY EDNA HAMBURGER
VINCENT SUMNER HAYWARD
PAULINE HEILENDAY
WILHELMINE GESINE HEINS
HARRY ARCHER HEYMAN
MARIE LOUISE HILBERT
GRACE GERTRUDE HOWE
MARGARET LOUISE IWANOWIUS
WILLIAM JANSEN
CLARABEL KADE
EVELYN KAEMPF
AMY EMILY KAUFMANN
CHARLES LOUIS KLEIN
MARY KLEIN
RAYMOND KNOEPPEL
JOSEPHINE KOLB
RITA KOHN

EDITH LEE
FRITZ ADOLPH HERMAN LEUCHS
NELLIE MURRAY LINDSAY
JULIA TYROLER LIPPE
JOSEPH LOWENSTEIN
MARY ROSE LYONS
LETITIA VERONICA MCCONNELL
MARY CECILIA MCCORMICK
KATHARINE ROSE MCNULTY
MARGUERITE VERONICA M'GRATH
AUGUSTA SOPHIA STASIA MARTINI
ISABEL SHAW MARTIN
FRANK LOUIS MASON
AMELIA JULIA MASSOPUST
ELIZABETH MONICA MAXWELL
BELLA MEYER
JANET MILLER
ROSE MINDLIN
NANA LOUISE MOORE
HOWARD WALWORTH MOTT
WILLIAM MUIRHEAD, JR.
JANET EVELYN MULCH
ADA HERMINIE MULLER
LOTTIE KATHERINE MÜLLER
HENRIETTA NORTHSHIELD
MABEL LOUISE PETERSON
FLORENCE MARGUERITE POWERS
MAY KATHARINE QUINN
ROBERT CLAYTON REEVE
CHESTER LEONARD REIZENSTEIN
WALLINGFORD CONSTANTIN RIEGGER
BESSIE ROBINSON
FREDERICK WILLIAM RODER
LYDIA ELEONORA ROOD
CATHERINE REGINA ROSS
FLORENCE SAMMET
DONA SARUYA
AMY SCHAUFELBERGER
SIDONIA SCHEYER
MARION SCHONBERGER
MARY CAROLINE SCHWABENHAUSEN
EDNA WOLFSOHN SEELIGMAN
EUPHEMIA SHEARER
MIRIAM SICHEL
WILLIAM POSTLEY LITTLE SINCLAIR
MARIE LOUISE SOICH
ISIDOR AARON STEINER
JOHN WALTER STOCK
ROSE STRAUSS
JEAN WILSON TERRY
FLORENCE ADELE THOMPSON
TOMLINSON CARLILE ULBRICHT
MARION ELISE ULBRICHT
WALTER HAVILAND UNDERHILL
JESSE VAN DERHOVEN
HELEN IDA VEITH
ELZA VON HARTMANN
RUDOLPH CHARLES WAHLIG
GUSTAVE WERNER, JR.
ESTHER JANE WILLIAMSON
SARA WOLFF
JEROME ZUCKERMAN

The Program
for the
Fifth Annual
Graduating Exercises,
held on
June 27, 1904
at the new
school building.

Morris High School Collection.
The Bronx County Historical
Society Research Library.

HENRY A. ROGERS

PRESIDENT OF THE BOARD OF EDUCATION

FRANK L. BABBOTT

VICE-PRESIDENT

COMMITTEE ON HIGH SCHOOLS AND TRAINING SCHOOLS

FRANK L. BABBOTT, CHAIRMAN

M. DWIGHT COLLIER
JOHN GREENE
WILLIAM HARKNESS
CHARLES H. INGALLS

FREDERIC W. JACKSON
JACOB W. MACK
EDWARD D. O'BRIEN
HENRY N. TIFFT

BOARD OF SUPERINTENDENTS

WILLIAM H. MAXWELL

City Superintendent of Schools

GEORGE S. DAVIS
ANDREW W. EDSON
ALGERNON S. HIGGINS
ALBERT P. MARBLE

CLARENCE E. MELENEY
THOMAS S. O'BRIEN
EDWARD L. STEVENS
JOHN H. WALSH

The Program for the Fifth Annual Graduating Exercises,
held on June 27, 1904 at the new school building.

Morris High School Collection.
The Bronx County Historical Society Research Library.

Looking north on Trinity Avenue to front of Morris High School, c. 1910.

The Bronx County Historical Society Research Library.

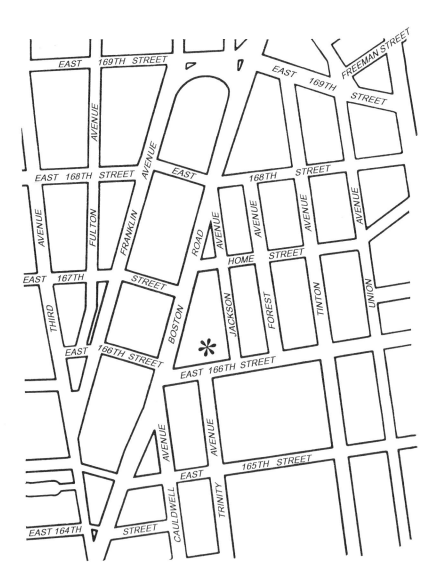

Modern street map of Morris High School neighborhood.
The asterisk (∗) is on the site of Morris High School.

The Bronx County Historical Society Research Library.

Conclusion

THIS STUDY of Morris High School in its formative years, from 1896 through 1904, provides background into the educational ferment that stirred New York City. It was the first coeducational high school in the city and the first high school in the booming Bronx. Dr. Goodwin, its influential principal, helped develop the city-wide curriculum and trained a next generation of principals.

The creation and early development of Morris High School were quite in keeping with the expansion that marked the metropolis at the time. This expansion was not only physical, but also spiritual. It was led by idealistic reformers who sought to "Americanize" the new immigrants who were arriving in increasing numbers each year. As historian David Tyack notes: ". . . the great majority of administrators and teachers were probably ethnocentric, proud of American middle-class standards, and confident that schooling could change the many into one people, *e pluribus unum*."[1]

The new public high schools, it was hoped, would be a great force in this effort. As the "people's college," the high school would make good citizens of many people who would otherwise be uneducated and unassimilated into the general culture. By its example and standards, the public high schools would strengthen the public elementary schools which were the limit of education for most of the people in the country.

In order to establish the public high schools, it was first necessary to centralize and professionalize the schools in the city of New York. The School Reform Law, passed in 1896, provided just such an opportunity. One of its major achievements was that it made New York ". . . the only city in the world, perhaps (certainly one of the very few), in which a child can pass successively through all grades of instruction – kindergarten, elementary, secondary and collegiate – at public expense."[2]

207

In conclusion, it is only fitting to return one last time to Nicholas Murray Butler, who, in February of 1900, in an address before the National Educational Association, made the following comment:

> In light of the nineteenth century no man dare prophesy what the twentieth century will bring forth. We only know that a democracy shielded by insight into the past and armed with trained minds, disciplined skills, and a scientific method, is as ready as man's imperfect wisdom can make it for whatever may come in the future.[3]

Today, the New York City public school system faces new challenges, but the dream of an educated populace remains. The twenty-first century looms ahead and public education must meet this new day as it did before, with strength of purpose and caring hearts.

NOTES

[1] David B. Tyack, *The One Best System: A History of American Urban Education* (Cambridge: Harvard University Press, 1974), p. 232.

[2] Editorial, *Educational Review* 15 (January, 1898): 96.

[3] Nicholas Murray Butler, "Status of Education at the Close of the Nineteenth Century," Address before the Department of Superintendence of the National Educational Association, February 17, 1900, *Meaning of Education: Contributions to a Philosophy of Education* (New York: Charles Scribner's Sons, 1915), p. 318.

The First Public High Schools of New York City

The Wadleigh High School building was opened September 17, 1902.
It was located at 114th-115th Streets between 7th and 8th Avenues.

The Bronx County Historical Society Research Library.

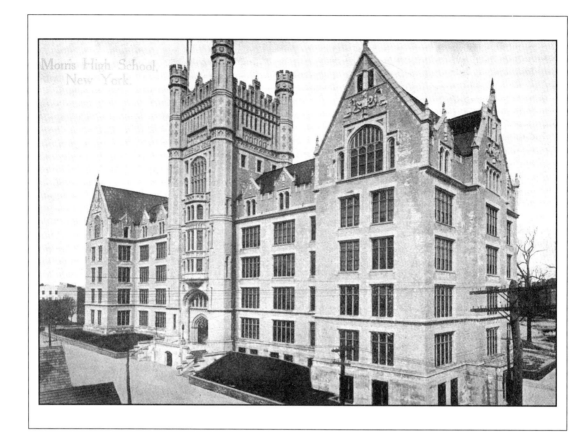

Postcard view of Morris High School, c. 1914.
Dedicated on June 10, 1904, the building was located on 166th Street
between Boston Road and Jackson Avenue.

The Bronx County Historical Society Research Library.

DeWitt Clinton High School on May 28, 1920, was located on
the west side of 10th Avenue between 58th and 59th Streets.
The building was occupied on February 19, 1906.
Today it is the home of John Jay College.

*Special Collections, Milbank Memorial Library,
Teachers College, Columbia University.*

Morris High School from Boston Road in the winter of 1907.

The Bronx Old Timers Collection,
The Bronx County Historical Society Research Library.

Bibliography

THE CHIEF resources for this work are primary materials ranging from Morris High School's scrapbook, registers, records, yearbooks, brochures, booklets, and correspondence, to the original minutes, journals and reports of the New York City Board of Education, its committees and the borough boards.

Late nineteenth and early twentieth century educational periodicals such as *School Review* and *Educational Review* and newspapers were used for contemporary reactions to the issues and events surrounding the formation of New York's first public high schools. Interviews with urban historians and individuals who attended Morris High School early in this century enhance the printed data.

Columbia University Teachers College Special Collections is the administrator of the New York City Board of Education records. The amount of Board of Education material is staggering. Thankfully, the staff has made enormous progress in a fifty-year project to organize this collection so that it can be utilized by researchers.

The early scrapbook and Volume I: 1897-1898 of the pupil register for Morris High School humanized the enormous amount of statistics and allowed the period to become more understandable. The Board of Education *Journals* are very factual, but have very little discussion of the nuances surrounding events or activities. The opening of Morris High School received only minimal attention. In fact, no mention of the June 10, 1904, building dedication ceremonies was found. Clearly the board steered away from anything that they felt might sully their mission. Another example of this attitude occurred at the November 24, 1902, meeting of the Board's Committee on High Schools and Training Schools. A letter from O.G. Angle, Secretary of the North Side Board of Trade, requested that a suitable plaque be placed on Morris High School honoring the effort made by the Board of Trade to change the name to Morris High School. The idea was turned down as inappropriate.[1]

The discovery of the 1901 teachers' educational credentials list was a great source of information, which allowed a further rounding out of the Board of Education *Journal* material. Describing a faculty that was nearly 90 percent college educated at a time when the United States norm was under 50 percent was further proof of Morris High School's pre-eminence in the field.

All the material examined was found and saved over the years by dedicated people, many unknown. In Morris High School, off the main corridor, there was a small room filled with boxes and the dust of decades that held many of these glorious records. To the keepers of such rooms and to all those who made a contribution to Morris High School and the creation of the New York City public high school system, my sincerest appreciation.

NOTES

[1]New York City, Board of Education, Minutes of the Committee on High Schools and Training Schools, November 24, 1902, Special Collections, Milbank Memorial Library, Teachers College, Columbia University, New York.

General Colin L. Powell, then Chairman of the Joint Chiefs of Staff,
visiting Morris High School on April 16, 1991. General Powell
graduated from Morris in 1954.

Chester Higgins, Jr. photographer/The New York Times.

SELECTED BIBLIOGRAPHY

Primary Sources

New York City, *Annual Report of the President of the Borough of The Bronx for the Year Ending December 31, 1902.* New York: Mail and Express Co., 1903.

Bates College Bulletin. Lewiston, Maine: Bates College, May 15, 1905.

Bates College General Catalogue. 1864-1930. Lewiston, Maine: Bates College, 1931.

Bates Student. Lewiston Maine: Bates College, April, 1891, 19:4; December 1896, 24:10.

Haffen, Louis F. *Borough of The Bronx: A Record of Unparalleled Progress and Development.* c. 1909. The Bronx County Historical Society Research Library, Bronx, New York.

High School Teachers Association of New York City. *Yearbook* 1906-07. New York: Ed. J. Smith Co., 1907.

The Morris Annual. 1905-1927. The Bronx County Historical Society Research Library, Bronx, New York.

Morris High School. Accounting of Costs of Building and Furnishing. 1904. Building History, Board of Education Archives, Special Collections, Milbank Memorial Library, Teachers College, Columbia University, New York.

Morris High School (Peter Cooper High School). List of teachers with qualifications and schools attended. June 9, 1901. Morris High School Collection, The Bronx County Historical Society Research Library, Bronx, New York.

Morris High School (Mixed High School). Register. 1897-98. Morris High School Collection. The Bronx County Historical Society Research Library, Bronx, New York.

Morris High School Scrapbook: 1897-1914. The Morris High School Collection, The Bronx County Historical Society Research Library, Bronx, New York.

New York City Board of Education. *A History of The Bronx Public Schools.* By Mark Price, confidential secretary to the Board of Education. March, 1945. The Bronx County Historical Society Research Library, Bronx, New York.

New York City Board of Education. Building Records cards. Special Collections, Milbank Memorial Library, Teachers College, Columbia University, New York, Series IV, H3f.

New York City Board of Education, Bureau of Reference, Research and Statistics. "Brief Historical Sketch of the High Schools of New York City." September, 1926. Special Collections, Milbank Memorial Library, Teachers College, Columbia University, New York.

New York City Board of Education, Bureau of Reference, Research and Statistics. "Year of organization of high schools." 1948. Special collections, Milbank Memorial Library, Teachers College, Columbia University, New York.

New York City Board of Education, Committee on Research. *Materials Suggested for Use in High Schools in Observance of the 100th Anniversary of the Board of Education.* 1942. Duane Library, Fordham University, Bronx, New York.

New York City Board of Education. *Fifty-fifth Annual Report.* Year Ending December 31, 1896. Special Collections, Milbank Memorial Library, Teachers College, Columbia University, New York.

New York City Board of Education. *Journal of the Board of Education.* 1894-1904. Special Collections, Milbank Memorial Library, Teachers College, Columbia University, New York.

New York City Board of Education. *Journal of the School Board for the Boroughs of Manhattan and The Bronx.* 1898-1901. Special Collections, Milbank Memorial Library, Teachers College, Columbia University, New York.

New York City Board of Education. Minutes of the Committee on High Schools and Training Schools. October 20, 1902, November 24, 1902. Special Collections, Milbank Memorial Library, Teachers College, Columbia University, New York.

New York City Board of Education. *New York City School Buildings: 1805-1956.* 1956. The Bronx County Historical Society Research Library, Bronx, New York.

New York City Board of Education, Office of the Borough Superintendent for Manhattan and The Bronx. Letter to the principals of schools concerning teacher qualifications. June 13, 1901. The Bronx County Historical Society Research Library, Bronx, New York.

New York City Department of Education. *Annual Reports.* 1898-1904. Special Collections, Milbank Memorial Library, Teachers College, Columbia University, New York.

New York City Department of Education. *Annual Reports of the City Superintendent of Schools.* 1899-1905. Special Collections, Milbank Memorial Library, Teachers College, Columbia University, New York.

New York City Department of Education. Committee on Sites and Buildings, Boroughs of Manhattan and The Bronx. *Minutes of Meetings.* 1898-1900. Special Collections, Milbank Memorial Library, Teachers College, Columbia University, New York.

New York City Department of Education. Course of Study for All High Schools: 1898, 1901 & 1902. *Morris High School Scrapbook: 1897-1914.* Morris High School Collection, The Bronx County Historical Society Research Library, Bronx, New York.

New York City Department of Education. Courses of Study for the High Schools of the Boroughs of Manhattan and The Bronx, 1898, 1901. *Morris High School Scrapbook: 1897-1914.* Morris High School Collection, The Bronx County Historical Society Research Library, Bronx, New York.

New York City Landmarks Preservation Commission *P.S. 31 Report,* July 15, 1986; LP-1435, *Morris High School Historic District Designation Report* December 21, 1982, LP-1258, *Morris High School (Interior) District Designation Report,* December 21, 1982, LP-1271.

New York City Department of Health death certificate of Edward J. Goodwin #3244, April 30, 1931.

New York State, Department of Public Instruction. *Fiftieth Annual Report of the State Superintendent.* Year ending July 31, 1903. Transmitted to the Legislature, April 15, 1904. Albany: Oliver A. Quayle, 1904. Milbank Memorial Library, Teachers College, Columbia University, New York.

New York State Legislature. *An act in relation to the common schools and public schools in the City of New York.* Chapter 387 laws of 1896.

New York State Legislature. *Compulsory Education Law.* Chapter 671 laws of 1894, as amended by Chapter 988 laws of 1895, Chapter 606 laws of 1896, and Chapter 459 laws of 1903.

New York State Legislature. *Newsboy Law.* Chapter 151 laws of 1903.

New York State, University of the State of New York. *Proceedings of the 17th Annual Convention of the Association of Colleges and Preparatory Schools of the Middle States and Maryland.* Columbia University, New York. November 17-18, 1903. Bulletin 310-317. Milbank Memorial Library, Teachers College, Columbia University, New York, pp. 3-149.

The Official Directory of the City of New York: The 1992-93 Green Book. New York City: City Publishing Center, 1992.

United States Bureau of Education. *Report of the Committee on Secondary School Studies Appointed at the Meeting of the National Educational Association, July 9, 1892.* Washington, D.C.: U.S. Government Printing Office, 1893. Special Collections, Milbank Memorial Library, Teachers College, Columbia University, New York.

United States Commissioner of Education. *Annual Reports.* 1897-98, 1904-05. Washington, D.C.: U.S. Government Printing Office. Milbank Memorial Library, Teachers College, Columbia University, New York.

Vertical file on Schools, The Bronx County Historical Society Research Library, Bronx, New York.

BOOKS

Abelow, Samuel P. *Dr. William H. Maxwell: Superintendent of Schools in the City of New York.* New York: Sheba Publishing, 1934.

American Historical Association. *The Study of History in Schools.* New York: Macmillan Co., 1899.

Barlow, Elizabeth. *The Forests and Wetlands of New York City.* Boston: Little, Brown & Co., 1969.

Berelson, Bernard. *Graduate Education in the United States.* New York: McGraw-Hill, 1960.

Boese, Thomas. *Public Education in the City of New York: Its History, Condition, and Statistics.* New York: Harper & Bros., 1869.

Bourne, William O. *History of The Public School Society of the City of New York.* New York: G.P. Putnam's Sons, 1873.

Brown, John Franklin. *The American High School.* New York: Macmillan Co., 1909.

Brown, John Franklin. *The Training of Teachers for Secondary Schools in Germany and the United States.* New York: Macmillan Co., 1911.

Brumberg, Stephan F. *Going to America, Going to School: The Immigrant-Public School Encounter In Turn-Of-The-Century New York City.* Washington, D.C.: U.S. Department of Education, 1982.

Butler, Nicholas Murray. *Across the Busy Years: Recollections and Reflections.* Volume I. New York: Charles Scribner's Sons, 1935.

Butler, Nicholas Murray, editor, *Education in the United States.* Albany: J.B. Lyon Co., 1900. Reprint edition. New York: Arno Press and the New York Times, 1969.

Butler, Nicholas Murray. *The Meaning of Education: Contributions to a Philosophy of Education.* New York: Charles Scribner's Sons, 1915.

Butler, Nicholas Murray. *The Meaning of Education and Other Essays and Addresses.* New York: Charles Scribner's Sons, 1905.

Chester, Lenore, et al. *Borough Representation: The Continuing Debate.* New York Citizens Union Foundation, 1989.

Clay, Felix. *Modern School Buildings.* New York: Charles Scribner's Sons, 1903.

Cohen, Sol. *Progressives and Urban School Reform: The Pubic Education Association of New York, 1895-1954.* New York: Teachers College, Columbia University, 1964.

Cremin, Lawrence A. *The Transformation of the School.* New York: Alfred A. Knopf, 1969.

Dain, Phyllis. *The New York Public Library.* New York: New York Public Library, 1972.

The Election of William H. Maxwell as City Superintendent of High Schools Emeritus. New York: Boy's Vocational High School, 1918.

Ellis, David M., et al. *The History of New York State.* Ithaca: Cornell University Press, 1967.

Garrison, Lisa. *The South Bronx and the Founding of America: An Activity Book for Teachers and Students.* The Bronx, New York: The Bronx County Historical Society, 1987.

Glazer, Nathan, and Moynihan, Daniel Patrick. *Beyond the Melting Pot: The Negroes, Puerto Ricans, Jews, Italians, and Irish of New York City.* Cambridge: MIT Press, 1963.

Hamlin, A.D.F., Snyder, C.B.J., et al. *Modern School Houses.* New York: Swetland Publishing Co., 1910.

Hammack, David, C., *Power and Society: Greater New York at the Turn of the Century.* New York: Columbia University Press, 1987.

Hartmann, Edward George. *The Movement to Americanize the Immigrant.* New York: Columbia University Press, 1948.

Hermalyn, Gary, and Kornfeld, Robert. *Landmarks of The Bronx.* The Bronx, New York: The Bronx County Historical Society, 1990.

Hertzberg, Hazel Whitman. *Social Studies Reform: 1880-1980.* Boulder: Social Science Education Consortium, 1981.

Hoffman, Mark. *The World Almanac.* New York: Pharos Books, 1993.

Horner, Harlan Hoyt, compiler and editor. *Education in New York State 1784-1954*. Albany: University of the State of New York, 1954.

Jenkins, Stephen. *The Story of The Bronx*. New York: G.P. Putnam's Sons, 1912.

Kaestle, Carl F. *The Evolution of an Urban School System: New York City 1750-1850*. Cambridge: Harvard University Press, 1973.

Johnston, Margaret R. *Memoirs of Herman Weiss Johnston: 1889-1969*. Published by author, 1977.

Kelley, Frank Bergen, compiler. *Historical Guide to the City of New York*. New York: City History Club of New York, 1912.

Kessner, Thomas. *The Golden Door: Italian and Jewish Mobility in New York City 1880-1915*. New York: Oxford University Press, 1977.

Krug, Edward A. *The Shaping of the American High School, 1880-1920*. Madison: University of Wisconsin Press, 1969.

Krug, Edward A. *The Secondary School Curriculum*. New York: Harper & Bros., 1960.

Laidlaw, Walter, compiler and editor. *Population of the City of New York 1890-1930*. New York: Cities Census Committee, 1932.

Loperfido, Francis J. *A Medical Chronicle of The Bronx*. Bronx, New York: Bronx County Medical Society, 1964.

Lyman, Susan. *The Story of New York*. New York: Crown Publishers, 1975.

Maxwell, William H. *A Quarter Century of Public School Development*. New York: American Book Company, 1912.

McNamara, John. *History in Asphalt. The Origin of Bronx Street and Place Names*. The Bronx, New York: The Bronx County Historical Society; 1984, revised edition.

Mintz, Max. *Gouverneur Morris and The American Revolution*. Norman, Oklahoma: University of Oklahoma Press, 1970.

Mullaly, John. *The New Parks Beyond the Harlem*. New York: Record and Guide, 1887.

National Educational Association, *Report of the Committee on College Entrance Requirements*. Washington, D.C.: NEA, 1899.

Nickerson, Marjorie L. *A Long Way Forward: The First Hundred Years of the Packer Collegiate Institute*. Brooklyn: Packer Collegiate Institute, 1945.

North Side Board of Trade. *The Great North Side or Borough of The Bronx*. New York: Knickerbocker Press, 1897.

Palmer, A. Emerson. *The New York Public School: Being a History of Free Education in the City of New York*. New York: Macmillan Co., 1905.

Plant, Irving. *Population Growth of New York City by Districts*. New York: Con Edison, 1948.

Quinn, Bro. Edward, editor. *Bicentennial of the United States Constitution Commemorative Issue, The Bronx County Historical Society Journal*. The Bronx, New York: The Bronx County Historical Society, 1987.

Quinn, Bro. Edward. *The Signers of the United States Constitution*. The Bronx, New York: The Bronx County Historical Society, 1987.

Ravitch, Diane. *The Great School Wars: New York City, 1805-1973: A History of the Public Schools as Battlefield of Social Change*. New York: Basic Books, 1974.

Roosevelt, Theodore. *Gouverneur Morris*. Cambridge: Houghton, Mifflin, 1888; reprint edition, Oyster Bay: Theodore Roosevelt Association, 1975.

Safire, William. *Lend Me Your Ears: Great Speeches in History*. New York: W.W. Norton and Company, 1992.

Shonnard, Frederic and Spooner, W. W. *History of Westchester County New York*. New York: New York History Co., 1900; reprint edition, Harrison, New York: Harbor Hill Books, 1974.

Strachan, Grace C. *Equal Pay for Equal Work: The Story of the Struggle for Justice Being Made by the Women Teachers of the City of New York*. New York: B.F. Buck, 1910.

Tyack, David B. *The One Best System: A History of American Urban Education*. Cambridge: Harvard University Press, 1974.

Ulmann, Albert. *New Yorkers from Stuyvesant to Roosevelt.* New York: Chaucer Head Book Shop, 1928.

Ultan, Lloyd, and Hermalyn, Gary. *The Bronx in the Innocent Years.* New York: Harper & Row, 1985. Second edition, The Bronx, New York: The Bronx County Historical Society, 1990.

Walker, James Blaine. *Fifty Years of Rapid Transit 1864-1917.* New York: Law Printing Co., 1918; reprint edition, New York: Arno Press, 1970.

Waterbury, Jean Parker. *A History of the Collegiate School: 1638-1963.* New York: Clarkson Potter, Inc., 1965.

Wheelwright, Edmund March. *School Architecture: A General Treatise for the Use of Architects and Others.* Boston: Rogers & Manson, 1901.

Whittemore, Richard. *Nicholas Murray Butler and Public Education 1862-1911.* New York: Teachers College Press, 1970.

Who Was Who, 1897-1942. Vol. 1. Chicago: Marquis Co., 1943.

Wynn, Richard and Joanne. *American Education.* Ninth Edition. New York: Harper & Row, 1988.

DISSERTATIONS AND THESES

Bain, Archibald Watson. "Co-Education in the Secondary Schools of the United States." Masters Thesis, Columbia University, 1908.

Becker, C.F. "A History of the Development of the Course of Study of Geography in the New York City High Schools 1898-1953." Ed.D. Dissertation, New York University, 1954.

Berrol, Selma C. "Immigrants at School: New York City 1898-1914." Ph.D. Dissertation, City University of New York, 1967.

Blan, Louis B. "The Elective System in Secondary Education with Special Reference to the New York City Public High Schools." Masters Thesis, Columbia University, 1908.

Carey, John Joseph. "Progressives and the Immigrant 1885-1915." Ph.D. Dissertation, University of Connecticut, 1968.

Carr, George Alvah. "Relationships between the Political and Educational Progressives." Ed.D. Dissertation, Cornell University, 1972.

Cerillo, Augustus, Jr. "Reform in New York City: A Study of Urban Progressivism." Ph.D. Dissertation, Northwestern University, 1969.

Derrick, Peter. "The Dual System of Rapid Transit: The Role of Politics and City Planning in the Second Stage of Subway Construction in New York City, 1902 to 1913." Ph.D. Dissertation, New York University, 1979.

Foley, Virginia Marie. "The Establishment of the City Superintendency of Public Schools in Five Nineteenth Century American Cities." Ed.D. Dissertation, State University of New York at Buffalo, 1972.

Gorelick, Sherry. "Social Control, Social Mobility, and the Eastern European Jews: An Analysis of Public Education in New York City 1880-1924." Ph.D. Dissertation, Columbia University, 1975.

Hammack, David Conrad. "Participation in Major Decisions in New York City, 1890-1900: The Creation of Greater New York and the Centralization of the Public School System." Ph.D. Dissertation, Columbia University, 1973.

Harris, Alice Kessler. "The Lower Class as a Factor in Reform: New York, the Jews, and the 1890's." Ph.D. Dissertation, Rutgers University, 1968.

Healey, O.S.F., Sister Mary Angelina. "The Educational Philosophy of Nicholas Murray Butler and Its Relevance for Contemporary Problems in Education." Ph.D. Dissertation, Catholic University of America, 1967.

Knerr, George Francis. "The Mayoral Administration of William L. Strong, New York City: 1895-1897." Ph.D. Dissertation, New York University, 1957.

Kransdorf, Martha. "Julia Richman's Years in the New York City Public Schools: 1872-1912." Ph.D. Dissertation University of Michigan, 1979.

Matthews, S.C.H., Sister Mary Fabian. "The Role of the Public School in the Assimilation of the Italian Immigrant Child in New York City, 1900-1914." Ph.D. Dissertation, Fordham University, 1966.

Mazaraki, George. "The Public Career of Andrew Haswell Green." Ph.D. Dissertation New York University, 1966.

Mooney, John Vincent, Jr., "William H. Maxwell and the Public Schools of New York City." Ed.D. Dissertation, Fordham University, 1981.

Neumann, Florence Margaret. "Access to Free Public Higher Education in New York City," Ph.D. Dissertation, City University of New York, 1984.

Rollins, Frank. "School Administration in Municipal Government." Ph.D. Dissertation, Columbia University, 1902.

Schick, Evan. "Neighborhood Changes in The Bronx, 1905-1960." Ph.D. Dissertation, Harvard University, 1982.

Shapiro, Herbert. "Reorganization of the New York City Public School System, 1890-1910." Ph.D. Dissertation, Yeshiva University, 1967.

Skolnik, Richard Stephen. "The Crystallization of Reform in New York City, 1890-1917." Ph.D. Dissertation, Yale University, 1964.

Spatz, Marshall C. "New York City Public Schools and the Emergence of Bureaucracy, 1868-1917." Ph.D. Dissertation, University of Chicago, 1975.

Stambler, Moses L. "The Democratic Revolution in the Public High Schools of New York City, 1898-1917." Ph.D. Dissertation, New York University, 1964.

Walsh, John V. "Social and Economic Backgrounds of Morris High School Students, A Study of the Social and Economic Backgrounds of 4,256 Students in Morris High School, New York, N.Y." Ph.D. Dissertation, New York University, 1937.

Weisz, Howard Ralph. "Irish-American and Italian Educational Views and Activities, 1897-1900: A Comparison." Ph.D. Dissertation, Columbia University, 1968.

ARTICLES

Berrol, Selma C. "William Henry Maxwell and A New Educational New York." *History of Education Quarterly* (Summer, 1968): 215-228.

Bolton, Frederick E. "Preparation of High-School Teachers: What They Do Secure and What They Should Secure." *School Review* 15 (February, 1907): 97-122.

Breeden, Adrienne, et al. "A History of the Black People in The Bronx." *The Bronx County Historical Society Journal* XIII (Fall, 1976): 80-88.

Butler, Nicholas Murray. "The Function of the Secondary School." Address before the Schoolmasters' Association of New York and Vicinity, March 8, 1890. *Meaning of Education and Other Essays and Addresses.* New York: Charles Scribner's Sons, 1905, pp. 151-183.

Butler, Nicholas Murray. "The Reform of High-School Education." *Harper's Weekly* 38 (January 13, 1894): 42-43.

Butler, Nicholas Murray. "Reform of Secondary Education in the United States. *Atlantic Monthly,* 1894, reprint, *Meaning of Education and Other Essays and Addresses.* New York: Charles Scribner's Sons, 1905, pp. 187-226.

Butler, Nicholas Murray. "The Scope and Function of Secondary Education." Address before the University High School Conference at Champaign, Illinois, May 19, 1898. *Meaning of Education Contributions to a Philosophy of Education.* New York: Charles Scribner's Sons, 1915, pp. 203-225.

Butler, Nicholas Murray. "Some Fundamental Principles of American Education." Address before the Convocation of The University of The State of New York, Albany, June 30, 1902. *Meaning of Education Contributions to a Philosophy of Education.* New York: Charles Scribner's Sons, 1915, pp. 321-342.

Butler, Nicholas Murray. "Status of Education at the Close of the Nineteenth Century." Address before the Department of Superintendence of the National Educational Association, February 17, 1900. *Meaning of Education Contributions to a Philosophy of Education.* New York: Charles Scribner's Sons, 1915, pp. 299-318.

Butler, Nicholas Murray. "What Knowledge is of Most Worth?" Presidential Address before the National Educational Association in Denver, Colorado, July 9, 1895. *Meaning of Education and Other Essays and Addresses.* New York: Charles Scribner's Sons, 1905, pp. 37-66.

Coy, E.W. "What is A Secondary School?" *Journal of Proceedings and Addresses of the Thirty-Fifth Annual Meeting of the National Educational Association, July 3-10, 1896.* Chicago: University of Chicago Press, 1896, pp. 613-618.

Curran, S.J., Francis X. "Fordham University." *The Bronx County Historical Society Journal* XVI (Spring, 1979): 7-14.

Dawson, Edgar. "The History Inquiry." *Historical Outlook* 15 (June, 1924): 239-250.

Doherty, Robert E. "Tempest on the Hudson: The Struggle for Equal Pay for Equal Work in the New York City Public Schools, 1907-1911." *History of Education Quarterly* (Winter, 1979): 413-434.

Draper, Andrew S. "The New York Secondary School System." *Addresses by the Commissioner of Education.* Albany: New York State Education Department. 1904, pp. 54-85.

Editorial. "City Superintendent Maxwell of New York." *Educational Review* 27 (January, 1904): 1-18.

Editorial. *Educational Review* 5 (May, 1893): 513-514.

Editorial. *Educational Review* 6 (June, 1893): 97-98.

Editorial. *Educational Review* 11 (May, 1896): 512-515.

Editorial. *Educational Review* 13 (May, 1897): 513-515.

Editorial. *Educational Review* 15 (January, 1898): 94-97.

Editorial. *Educational Review* 15 April, 1898): 414-415.

Editorial. *Educational Review* 27 (January, 1904): 21.

Editorial. "Public School Reform in New York and Brooklyn." *Harper's Weekly* 29 (February 9, 1895): 123.

Editorial. *School Review* 13 (March, 1903): 265-267.

Editorial. *School Review* 11 (May, 1903): 418.

Eliot, Charles W. "The Board of Education and the Professional Staff." *Public Education Association of the City of New York,* No. 22 (February, 1914): 1-15.

Elliott, Edward C. "The New York School System of General Supervision and Board of Examiners." *Public Education Association of the City of New York,* No. 18 (October, 1913): 1-16.

Goodwin, Edward J. "A Comparison of College Entrance Requirements." *Educational Review* 26 (December, 1903): 440-456.

Goodwin, Edward J. "Electives in Elementary School." *Educational Review* 8 (June, 1894): 12-21.

Goodwin, Edward J. "Electives in the High School: An Experiment." *Educational Review* 5 (February, 1893): 142-152.

Goodwin, Edward J. "The Objections to a Shorter College Course." *Educational Review* 25 (January, 1903): 21-27.

Goodwin, Edward J. "The School and The Home." *School Review* 16 (May, 1908): 320-329.

Goodwin, Edward J. "Some Characteristics of New York City High Schools." *Educational Review* 28 (October, 1904): 255-264.

Goodwin, Edward J. "Some Characteristics of Prussian Schools." *Educational Review* 12 (December, 1896): 453-465.

Hall, G. Stanley. "Adolescents and The High School, English, Latin and Algebra." *Pedagogical Seminary* 9 (March, 1902): 92-105.

Hanus, Paul H. "What Should the Modern Secondary School Accomplish?" *School Review* 5 (June, 1897): 387-400; 7 (September, 1897): 433-444.

Hartwell, S.O. "The Equipment of the High School Principal." *School Review* 9 (March, 1902): 160-166.

Hatch, William E. "The Modern High School Building." *School Review* 2 (June, 1903): 509-520.

Hermalyn, Gary. "The Bronx At The Turn of The Century." *The Bronx County Historical Society Journal* XXVI (Fall, 1989): 92-112.

Hermalyn, Gary. "The Harlem River Ship Canal." *The Bronx Country Historical Society Journal* XX (Spring, 1983): 1-23.

Hermalyn, Gary. "A History of The Bronx River." *The Bronx County Historical Society Journal* XIX (Spring, 1982): 1-22.

Hill, Frank A. "How Far the Public High School Is a Just Charge upon the Public Treasury." *School Review* 6 (December, 1898): 746-787.

Hollister, H.A. "The Programme of Studies for High Schools." *School Review* 16 (April, 1908): 252-257.

Locke, George Herbert. "Editorial Notes." *School Review* 11 (May, 1903): 418.

Maxwell, William H. "The American Teacher." *Educational Review* 25 (February, 1903): 146-167.

Maxwell, William H. "The Elective System in Secondary Schools." *Proceedings of the 17th Annual Convention of the Association of Colleges and Preparatory Schools of the Middle States and Maryland.* Columbia University, New York. November 17-18, 1903. University of the State of New York, Bulletin 310-317. Milbank Memorial Library, Teachers College, Columbia University, New York pp. 7-39.

Maxwell, William H. "My Ideals As Superintendent." *Educational Review* 44 (December, 1912): 451-459.

Maxwell, William H. "The Teacher's Compensations." *Educational Review* 27 (May, 1904): 468-477.

Murphy, Sister Miriam Ellen. "College of Mount Saint Vincent." *The Bronx County Historical Society Journal* XVI (Fall, 1979): 79-84.

Robinson, John Beverly. "The School Buildings of New York." *Architectural Record* 7 (January-March, 1894): 359-384.

Stambler, Moses. "The Effect of Compulsory Education and Child Labor Laws on High School Attendance in New York City: 1898-1917." *History of Education Quarterly,* (Summer, 1968): 189-213.

Stuart, George. "The Raison D'Etre of the Public High School." *Education* 8 (January, 1888): 283-295.

Syrkin, Marie. "Morris High School, Class of '16." *New Republic* Issue 3,590, (November, 1983): 22-27.

Van Rensselaer, M.G. "The Public Education Association of New York." *Educational Review* 16 (October, 1898): 209-219.

Wharton, G.W. "High School Architecture in the City of New York." *School Review* 2 (June, 1903): 456-485.

Williams, Alida S. "New York's School Problem." *Educational Review* 27 (April, 1904): 325-337.

Winger, Otho. "Practical Applications of Aristotle's Principle, Catharsis." *Education* 28 (March, 1908): 401-410.

Zoebelein, George. "Boundaries of The Bronx and Its Communities," *The Bronx County Historical Journal* III (July 1966): 51-75.

NEWSPAPER ARTICLES

"Another High School Head Chosen by the Board of Education." *New York Daily Tribune*, 20 May 1897, p. 5.

"City Club Aids Maxwell." *New York Times*, 24 January 1899, p. 6.

"The Cost of High Schools." *New York Times*, 30 March 1901, p. 9.

"Commencement Day at Amherst," *Springfield Republican*, 28 June 1905, p. 1. "Commencement Collection (Box 3, Folder 63), Amherst College Archives.

"Elastic Courses of Study." *New York Daily Tribune*, 20 June 1897, p. 1.

"Expert Calls School Courses Too Complex." *New York Times*, 13 June 1904, p. 6.

"For School Reform." *New York Daily Tribune*, 7 February 1896, p. 3.

"Greater New-York." *New York Tribune*, 8 June, 1895, p. 6.

"Grout Men Condemn City School Course." *New York Times*, 26 January 1904, p. 3.

"Half-Million Dollar High School Dedicated. *New York Times*, 11 June 1904, p. 6.

"How They Oppose the Bill." *New York Daily Tribune*, 9 April 1896, p. 1.

"Renovating a 1902 Novelty." *New York Times*, 19 September 1993, C/WR p. 7.

"In Memory of Miss Wadleigh." *New York Times*, 4 November 1888, p. 16.

"Jasper After Maxwell." *New York Times*, 30 January 1901, p. 7.

"A Model High School Building." *New York Daily Tribune*, 4 December 1898, p. 4.

"Morris High School Dedicated." *New York Daily Tribune*, 11 June 1904, p. 9.

"New Educational Ideas." *New York Daily Tribune*, 23 May 1897, p. 3.

"New York Bills on Trial." *New York Times*, 13 February 1895, p. 1.

"North Side High School." *Dickson's Uptown Weekly*, 6 March 1897, p. 5.

Obituary, Edward Goodwin. *New York Times*, 30 May 1931, p. 8.

Obituary, Frank Rollins, *New York Times*, 12 May 1920, p. 5.

"Possibilities of New Educational Charter." *New York Times*, 23 November 1901, p. 1.

"I Remember, Powell Says on Bronx Visit." *New York Times*, 16 April 1991, p. 1.

Stark, Irwin. "Miss Twamley Would Have Liked This Article." *New York Times*, 7 January 1978.

"Superintendent Jasper Answers Mr. Maxwell." *New York Times*, 18 April 1901, p. 1.

"The Teachers Protest." *New York Daily Tribune*, 27 March 1896, p. 6.

"Teachers Under Orders." *New York Times*, 24 April 1895, p. 6.

"To Enlarge The City." *New York Times*, 18 May 1895, p. 1.

UNPUBLISHED ARTICLES

Danyluk, Nestor. "The Last Years of Westchester Township and the Village of Williamsbridge." c. 1980. The Bronx County Historical Society Research Library, The Bronx, New York.

Hall, Robert A. "New York City Rapid Transit Chronology." 1945. The Bronx County Historical Society Research Library, The Bronx, New York.

"History of Morris High School: Establishment and Buildings." c. 1960. The Bronx County Historical Society Research Library, The Bronx, New York.

INTERVIEWS AND LETTERS

Becker, Murvin. Graduate of Morris High School, Class of 1910. Telephone interview with author, May 24, 1993.

Brock (Jurs), Irene C. Graduate of Morris High School, Class of 1914. Taped interview with James Musto, III, December 20, 1991.

Derrick, Peter. Manager of Long Range Planning for Metropolitan Transportation Authority. Interview with author, Bronx, New York, November 23, 1984.

Doherty, May. Graduate of Morris High School, Class of 1913. Telephone interview with author, January 22, 1985.

Eisenstein, Roslyn (Wax). Graduate of Morris High School, Class of 1929. Telephone interview with author, December 21, 1984, confirmed in letter to author, January 10, 1985.

Hammer, Armand. Graduate of Morris High School, Class of 1916. Letter to author March 6, 1986.

Lovinger, Monroe. Graduate of Morris Night High School in the 1920s. Interview with author, Bronx, New York, April 18, 1991.

Ultan, Lloyd. Professor of History, Fairleigh Dickinson University and Director, History of The Bronx Project. Interview with author, Bronx, New York, October 19, 1984, and November 16, 1984.

Ramos-Weir, Julie. Circulation Librarian, Oberlin College. Telephone interview with author, September 12, 1988.

PLAQUES

John Jay College of Criminal Justice. Located in the entryway to the auditorium. The college is located in the original building of DeWitt Clinton High School. Viewed by author on January 17, 1992.

THE MORRIS HIGH SCHOOL (SONG)

Marion Osgood Skeele

There's a song that fills the air,
        "Morris High School!"
You can hear it everywhere,
        "Morris High School!"
From the Battery to the Park,
In the day or in the dark,
You can hear the echo! hark!
        "Morris High School!"

CHORUS.

Then we'll sing to the praise of our school,
        Yes, we'll sing;
And we'll up with a cheer for our school,
        Make it ring!
And never for a minute
Will we forget we're in it;
So hurrah! three hearty cheers
        For Morris High School!

Oh, it's hard to put us down,
        Morris High School!
And we're known all over town,
        Morris High School!
For our colors clear and bright,
Rich maroon and purest white,
We defend with all our might,
        Morris High School!

On the field or at our books
Morris High School!
It is plain to him who looks,
        Morris High School!
There we're studious and fleet,
That we never brook defeat,
That we're pretty had to beat,
        Morris High School!

When we graduate at last
        From Morris High School,
And the work and play are past
        At Morris High School,
We'll come back and shout again,
Till the hills repeat the strain,
For the school without a stain,
        Morris High School!

Morris High School Annual, 1905.
The Bronx County Historical Society Research Library.

INDEX

ABOUT THE AUTHOR

GARY HERMALYN is the executive director of The Bronx County Historical Society, president of the History of New York City Project, Inc., and the chairman of The Greater New York Centennial Commission, Inc. Historian, educator and publisher, he earned a doctorate from Columbia University and is a graduate of the Bronx High School of Science. Dr. Hermalyn is the project director of *The United States Supreme Court* ten volume series, co-author of *The Bronx in The Innocent Years* and *The Bronx It Was Only Yesterday,* editor of the *Bicentennial of the United States Constitution* book series, and is an associate editor of the *Encyclopedia of New York City.*

THE BRONX COUNTY
HISTORICAL SOCIETY

THE BRONX COUNTY HISTORICAL SOCIETY was founded in 1955 for the purpose of promoting knowledge, interest and research in The Bronx. The Society administers The Museum of Bronx History, Edgar Allan Poe Cottage, a Research Library, and The Bronx County Archives; publishes books, journals and newsletters; conducts school programs, historical tours, lectures, conferences, archaeological digs and commemorations; designs exhibitions, sponsors various expeditions, and produces the *Out Of The Past* radio show and cable television programs; and proudly honors The Bronx High School Valedictorians at an annual ceremony. The Society is active in furthering the arts, in preserving the natural resources of The Bronx, and in creating a sense of pride in the Bronx community.

PUBLICATIONS OF
THE BRONX COUNTY HISTORICAL SOCIETY

The Beautiful Bronx, 1920-1950
  by Lloyd Ultan

The Bronx County Historical Society Journal
  published twice a year since 1964

The Bronx in The Frontier Era
  by Lloyd Ultan

The Bronx In The Innocent Years, 1890-1925
  by Lloyd Ultan and Gary Hermalyn

The Bronx in Print: An Annotated Catalogue of Books and Pamphlets About The Bronx
  edited by Candace Khuta and Narcisco Rodriquez

The Bronx It Was Only Yesterday, 1935-1965
  by Lloyd Ultan and Gary Hermalyn

The Bronx Triangle: A Portrait of Norwood
  by Edna Mead

Genealogy of The Bronx: An Annotated Guide to Sources of Information
  by Gary Hermalyn and Laura Tosi

History in Asphalt: The Origin of Bronx Street and Place Names
  by John McNamara

History of the Morris Park Racecourse and the Morris Family
  by Nicholas DiBrino

Legacy of The Revolution: The Valentine-Varian House
  by Lloyd Ultan

McNamara's Old Bronx
  by John McNamara

Morris High School and the Creation of the New York City Public High School System
  by Gary Hermalyn

The South Bronx and the Founding of America: An Activity Book for Teachers and Students
  by Lisa Garrison

Edgar Allan Poe: A Short Biography
  by Kathleen A. McAuley

Poems of Edgar Allan Poe at Fordham
  edited by Elizabeth Beirne

Edgar Allan Poe at Fordham Teachers Guide and Workbook
  by Kathleen A. McAuley

The Signers of the Constitution of the United States
  by Brother C. Edward Quinn

The Signers of the Declaration of Independence
  by Brother C. Edward Quinn

Bicentennial of the United States Constitution Commemorative Issue
  The Bronx County Historical Society Journal

Presidents of the United States
  by Lloyd Ultan

Elected Public Officials of The Bronx Since 1898
  by Laura Tosi and Gary Hermalyn

Landmarks of The Bronx
  by Gary Hermalyn and Robert Kornfeld

350th Anniversary of The Bronx Commemorative Issue
  The Bronx County Historical Society Journal

The First Senate of The United States
  by Richard Streb